A Life
in the
ARTS

A Life
in the
ARTS

*Practical Guidance and Inspiration for
Creative and Performing Artists*

ERIC MAISEL, PH.D.

An expanded workbook edition of
Staying Sane in the Arts

A Jeremy P. Tarcher/Putnam Book
published by
G. P. Putnam's Sons
New York

Most Tarcher/Putnam books are available at special quantity
discounts for bulk purchases for sales promotions, premiums,
fund-raising, and educational needs. Special books or book
excerpts also can be created to fit specific needs.
For details, write or telephone Special Markets, The Putnam
Publishing Group, 200 Madison Avenue, New York, NY 10016;
(212) 951-8891.

A Jeremy P. Tarcher/ Putnam Book
Published by
G. P. Putnam's Sons
Publishers since 1838
200 Madison Avenue
New York, NY 10016
http://www.putnam.com/putnam

Library of Congress Cataloging-in-Publication Data

Maisel, Eric, date.
    A life in the arts : practical guidance and inspiration for
creative and performing artists / Eric Maisel.
        p. cm.
    Rev. and expanded ed. of: Staying sane in the arts. © 1992.
    "A Jeremy P. Tarcher/Putnam book."
    Includes bibliographical references and index.
    ISBN 0-87477-766-6
    1. Arts—Psychological aspects.   2. Arts—Marketing.   I. Maisel,
Eric. Staying sane in the arts.   II. Title.
NX 165.M35   1994
700'.1'9—dc20   93-21257   CIP

Design by Lee Fukui

Printed in the United States of America
            6   7   8   9   10

This book is printed on acid-free paper.

For Ann

Acknowledgments

FIRST, I WOULD LIKE to thank my clients in the creative and performing arts for the privilege of working with them and learning from them.

Thank you, also, to readers of early versions of the manuscript and to the many others who in conversation or correspondence helped clarify my thinking on the issues raised in the book: Metece Riccio, Gary Camp, Peggy Salkind, Reneé Hayes, Evelyn and Bernard Virshup, Richard Lippin, Peter Ostwald, Susan Harper, Sally Moor, Aleka Chase, Summer Perry, Susan Forthman, Ed Hooks, Velina Brown, Julie Nagel, Geneen Mathesius, Susan Stauter, Laurie Gurman, Dorothy Haman, Trevor Southey, Jean Schiffman, Ralph Cardenas, Anne Russell, John Hensolt, Alan Rinzler, Aaron Manganiello, Mary Ann Leff, and Deborah Daly. My apologies to those I ought to have included here.

I would like to thank the book's editors, Jan Johnson and Rick Benzel, for the careful consideration they've given the manuscript and for their many important suggestions; my literary agent, Linda Allen, for her availability, wisdom, and counseling skills; and Jeremy Tarcher, for championing the book.

My greatest thanks I reserve for my family: for my mother, Esther Maisel; my aunt, Rose Luber; my son, David, living the musician's life; my daughters, Natalya and Kira; and my wife, Ann Mathesius Maisel. Their help and support have been of incalculable value to me, and they deserve stronger praise than words can manage.

Contents

Introduction:
The Guided Writing Program

I AM A PSYCHOTHERAPIST, novelist, and artists' advocate. As a psychotherapist I work virtually exclusively with creative and performing artists. Every week I meet with painters, singers, dancers, stand-up comics, playwrights, filmmakers, musicians—artists of all kinds. I meet with them individually, in groups, and in all-day workshops.

In working with artists I realized that the psychological and practical challenges I have personally faced in my own career as a fiction writer were identical to the ones with which my clients were wrestling. The more I thought, studied, and read, the more I saw how these same challenges operated in the lives of nearly all famous artists—the Beethovens, Picassos, Virginia Woolfs, Nijinskys, Jackson Pollocks—and no less dramatically in the lives of contemporary artists whose names are not household words.

I therefore conceived of this book as a way to make more explicit and understandable these special challenges and to provide strategies for meeting them. Each chapter examines an issue related to the artist's personality or life-style, quotes the thoughts of various artists on the issue, and provides suggestions for coping with or managing these pressing challenges.

My goal is to help the real artist in the real world. That artist is often uncertain about his own talent, wants to do art his own way but must also do business, is hard-pressed to make a living, possesses a personality that sometimes serves him well and sometimes does not, frequently has bouts of depression, and in general faces the toughest uphill battle one can imagine.

There's no such thing beneath the heavens as conditions favorable to art. Art must crash through or perish.
SYLVIA ASHTON-WARNER

In this context, I define the successful artist as the self-aware, resourceful artist who understands her personality, her chosen life, and the world so well that she can maintain her spirits, her relationships, and her creativity even as she wrestles with the day-to-day challenges that confront her. While she is not without anxieties and even eccentricities, black spells, periods of inactivity, and crises of faith, she weathers these and returns to champion her art.

I believe that the artist in contemporary Western society is guaranteed a life of grave difficulty because of his personality, because of the inevitable challenges he encounters, and because of the nature of the world in which he lives, which tends to neglect, devalue, and misunderstand art. It is unreasonable for a book that looks at the realities of the artist's life to skirt these hard truths.

But I did not write this book as a dirge of the artist's life. Rather, it is a celebration of the artist's heroism. A participant in one of the workshops I conduct, a poet and small-press editor, felt reminded by day's end of the importance of honoring the hard and courageous work she did as an artist. She said, "I leave here feeling stronger and more joyous about the choices I've made, the work I've done, and more confident about the work I'll continue to do."

As society's visionaries or rebels, artists often remain unthanked and unheard. I hope that as you read this book you will feel recognized and, in some small measure, rewarded for committing to the artist's life. I also firmly believe that you'll have greater success as an artist and will simply feel better if you take the time to carefully process the material presented here. There are many ways to do this—by discussing the issues with friends, by bringing them up in personal therapy, by using your art medium as a tool of exploration. In particular, I also recommend that you begin a practice of journaling or guided writing (described in detail below). I have found that guided writing aids in clearer thinking and more informed decision making.

This book is for creative and performing artists in all disciplines, for students and mature artists alike. Since the challenges confronting the artist persist throughout his or her lifetime, the need for self-guidance starts young and never ends.

It is also intended for the parents, children, siblings, and mates of artists, for art teachers, for career counselors, for agents and others who do business with artists, and for mental-health professionals who have occasion to work with artists. Other people who can benefit from the material in this book are those who work at an art discipline part-time, those who consider themselves amateur painters, actors, musicians, or writers, and those who have an abiding love of an art medium but who never ventured onto a career path in art.

FIGURING IT OUT FOR YOURSELF: A GUIDED WRITING PROGRAM

Only rarely in our lives do we determine to actively and consciously assess our current situation and guide ourselves down new pathways. Even if it dawns on us that it might be possible to systematically consult ourselves, we have little idea how to begin. How, after all, does a person consult himself? Isn't the idea something of a paradox? If we know what changes to make, why not simply make them? If we don't know what changes to make, how can we guide ourselves in the right direction?

A young man, a blocked writer, came to me for an initial counseling session. He wore a wry smile, which grew more rueful as the session progressed. Finally I commented on the smile. The writer replied, "Well, I feel like I'm getting exactly what I expected to get. I'm getting good advice. But I'm convinced that coming here was a mistake. I don't know what I need to do to start writing, but I know that *I* have to figure it out. The answer is figuring it out *for myself.*"

Even though he knew that he was his only true guide, he remained baffled. How was he to proceed?

By using focused and intentional writing, writing that engages the self, it's possible to pinpoint the challenges that confront you—challenges in your personality, challenges with your art (whatever your particular discipline), and challenges in the world—and guide yourself down new paths of your own choosing. At the same time, the maintenance of a regular and systematic writing practice

Teach yourself by your own mistakes.

WILLIAM FAULKNER

encourages you to be more disciplined, creative, and energetic, qualities that serve you as an artist even if your art is other than writing.

What is guided writing? Guided writing makes use of, as Alan Watts said in *The Way of Zen,* "the very genius of the human mind that it can, as it were, stand aside from life and reflect upon it, that it can be aware of its own existence, and that it can criticize its own processes." Engaged in a long-term process of discovery, you inquire of yourself about your past, present, and future. You ask questions of yourself and answer them. You make use of writing exercises of your own devising that probe your experiences. You create new exercises to probe further. You examine pertinent aspects of your personality, relationships, and life circumstances.

The regular practice of guided writing affords you the opportunity to help shape your personal journey. First, of course, the practice must be learned, just as the principles of meditation must be learned. But once learned, it becomes your own.

Writing is a way of coming to terms with the world and with oneself.

R. V. CASSILL

Without discipline, there's no life at all.

KATHARINE HEPBURN

A Fifteen-Point Guided Writing Plan of Action

1. Create a writing environment.

2. Begin to silence negative self-talk.

3. Use guided imagery.

4. Create a writing bubble.

5. Raise your level of tolerance for frustration.

6. Uncover problems and challenges by writing.

7. Narrow your focus.

8. Ask creative questions.

9. Write responses.

10. Read creatively.

11. Uncover tactics and solutions.

12. Make a plan.

13. Add contingencies to the plan.

14. Evaluate the results.

15. Create new plans of action.

Create a Writing Environment

The environment you're looking for in which to begin your daily guided writing is one in which you can actually write. It need not be a quiet place, unless you require a quiet place to write. It need not be an organized space, unless you require an organized space to write. It should, however, be a place where you can canalize energy and direct it from your deepest self to the paper or computer screen. You should be able to experience the sensation of being utterly lost in the present, absorbed, connected to your thoughts and feelings. That is the test. If you happen to choose an unlikely spot—an airport lounge, a hospital cafeteria, the corner of your yard next to the prickly pear cactus—and find you can write there, then that is a sacred spot, one of your writing haunts.

Still, in the beginning at any rate, such odd spots may fail to serve you. One will be too windy, another too noisy, another too public. In each, something will manage to distract you. Of course the problem will be only partly environmental. The greater part may involve your newness at writing and your desire to avoid writing. In a way you can't know yet what your ideal writing environment will look like. So, in lieu of knowing, it's sensible to construct an environment that gives you the best chance of succeeding. Such an environment should provide sufficient quiet and privacy. You bring the time and courage.

Begin to Silence Negative Self-Talk

Even before you begin your guided writing program, thoughts may occur to you that have the effect of draining meaning from the enterprise. Why, you wonder, are you trying out this writing program anyway? Where will you find the time for it? Can it possibly amount to anything? Our negative self-talk tends to severely limit us and derail our efforts. These self-denigrating thoughts are terribly familiar swimmers in our stream of consciousness, doubly hard to combat because we rarely take any real notice of them.

Negative, self-deprecating statements may arise from anxiety, guilt, or self-rejection. These demon self-statements can bring on depression and disease. Each is demoralizing and needs to be silenced. Your first job is to notice what self-limiting, self-rejecting

You are your own friend and you are your own enemy.

BHAGAVAD GITA

thoughts are present in your consciousness. Here are ten of the most common ones.

1. I'm so far behind, I can't catch up.

2. I write too poorly. My sentences stink.

3. I have so little time, I might as well not start.

4. I've always censored myself. I need to censor myself now.

5. If I put down the truth, it will be an indictment of myself.

6. Criticism hurts and I don't want to criticize myself.

7. Even though I'm the subject, I still don't know what to write, and that's humiliating.

8. I feel defeated.

9. My writing never satisfies me.

10. Why write? Nobody gives a damn about my struggles, myself included.

Some of these demon self-statements may be true. It may be true, for instance, that you censor yourself or that your grammar is shoddy. It may be true that self-criticism will hurt. Still, you must find ways of defusing these negative thoughts and labels. Practice dismissing these negative self-statements using the following techniques.

- Learn not to overgeneralize. Don't translate 10 minutes of weak writing into "I'll never be able to write."

- Learn not to catastrophize. Don't magnify your discomfort as you sit with pen poised by saying, "I've never felt this bad in my whole life."

- Don't predict that you'll fail to write. Don't say, "That sausage sandwich I ate for lunch is bound to prevent me from writing this afternoon."

Use Guided Imagery

Guided imagery (also called guided visualization) is a technique that uses verbal cues to encourage you to create a particular imagined, interior landscape.

For example, you might imagine yourself in the office of an esteemed director or the waiting room of your dentist. Guided imagery is used here to help you practice new assertive behaviors with the director or new stress-reduction techniques while awaiting a root canal. Or you might be led back into childhood in order to re-experience some painful or joyful moment—in the first case to grieve or to rage, in the second case to bring to the present moment a talisman of that past happiness. A cancer patient might use guided imagery to picture an interior battle being waged between healthy cells and cancerous cells, leading to defeat of the cancer. You might be encouraged to picture yourself in a beautiful, tranquil spot; encouraged then to select an object from that spot—say, a seashell; and helped to practice returning to that state of tranquility at will by retrieving that seashell from memory.

Your work is to discover your work and then with all your heart to give yourself to it.

BUDDHA

The following visualization is designed to help you commit to your decision to begin and continue the practice of guided writing.

Visualization: Commitment to Guided Writing

Relax now. Seat yourself comfortably. Close your eyes and go deep inside yourself. Breathe easily and deeply—in and out, in and out. Maintain the sort of awareness you might keep on a journey.

When you feel ready, go back, far back, thousands of years back, back to the dawn of humankind.

Notice that every generation had to rear children in order for you to be here today. See those generations, those parents and children, in all parts of the world, speaking their different languages.

Feel life in the caves, in the deserts, on the plains. See all that human spirit, that human activity, in all its richness and all its poverty—the pettiness along with the splendor; the hatreds, the fears, the superstitions; and the love, that which has always been luminous and profound.

Now move toward the present, into this century, into the line of your own family, your own times. Begin to feel your own personal history, visions from your childhood.

Come closer to the present. Put no labels on who you are. You are not man, woman, wife, husband, actor, painter, but a human being on a journey. Connect your journey to the journeys of all men and women, and approach the present moment.

Imagine the journey continuing in ways that excite and exhilarate you—in ways as rich as your grandest dreams, in ways that make use of your being, that support your sense of aliveness, that challenge and invigorate you.

Feel the journey continuing. Commit to it continuing. Commit to your mission.

Every stroke of my brush is the overflow of my inmost heart.

SENGAI

When you feel the reality of this commitment in your body—in your heart, in your stomach—open your eyes and proceed with your guided writing work.

Create a Writing Bubble

The next visualization is designed to help you create a writing bubble to help you remain with the thoughts and feelings that the practice of guided writing stir up in you. A writing bubble is a self-created private space. It's a translucent and semipermeable bubble that encircles you and isolates you from distractions. Because it is translucent and semipermeable you can see the pot boiling over on the stove, but only indistinctly; you can hear your baby crying, but only in a muffled way. In the bubble, your sense of time is altered. Time passes without being noticed. You are utterly lost in the present. When your writing bubble is in place you are more distanced than usual. Rather than being at the world's beck and call, jumping at every outer command, and rather than being a slave to inner turmoil, jumping at every inner command, you and your writing are together armored.

You can will your writing bubble into existence at your bidding. It takes only seconds to construct it. In bidding it to return you are making manifest your resolve: you are saying to yourself, "I am working."

This visualization will help you create your writing bubble. Record it and play it for yourself as needed at the beginning of a writing session.

Visualization: Developing a Writing Bubble

Relax now. Close your eyes and go inside yourself. Seat yourself comfortably and breathe easily, deeply—in and out, in and out. Feel your feet firmly planted beneath you, feel the regularity of your breathing. Attune to your breathing. Let go of all that has no place at this moment. Let go of your worries, let go of your doubts.

Begin to feel the presence of your own writing. Feel the words. See the words. Feel their presence within your own sphere of being.

You and your words are together. Build a bubble around you and them. Create a rich, protecive sphere, a private universe. Let in what you want, keep out what you want. You and your words are together.

Feel the feeling of being inside your writing bubble. Make it spacious and comfortable. Here you can write. The world will keep its distance. The bubble allows in light, allows in whatever you need. Inside it you and your words are together.

When you are ready, open your eyes. Continue to hold the feeling that you are present in your own writing world, protected and engaged. You and your words are together.

Nothing determines who we will become so much as those things we choose to ignore.

SANDOR MCNAB

Raise Your Level of Tolerance for Frustration

For most people the knot of resolve and the sense of missionary zeal needed to engage in hard self-examination come regularly but last only fleetingly. After an involving workshop or a charismatic lecture you feel ready to tackle the tasks you've set for yourself, but by the time you reach home that resolve has dissipated.

The ability to tolerate an uncomfortable state for minutes, hours, and days on end, to tolerate that discomfort again and again, week in and week out, is the key to maintaining resolve. An inability to tolerate uncomfortable feeling states will bring the enterprise of guided writing to a grinding halt.

If you're frustrated and stop writing, acknowledge that you feel frustrated. Walk around your chair and ask yourself, "Even though I'm frustrated, can I go on?" If the answer is a resounding no, shake off the feelings of guilt or failure that may begin to well up in you and go on with the business of your life with an easy heart. But in a corner of your mind make a deal with yourself that you'll return to your important work as soon as you're able.

Each time the feelings of frustration and discomfort return, acknowledge them. Say to yourself, "I am not going on with this piece about my mother because it makes me feel uncomfortable and I don't like feeling uncomfortable!"

Slowly you may learn to better tolerate frustration. You may begin to feel more comfortable, or at least easier with discomfort. You may leave your work less often or return to it more quickly. One day you may complete a rich, eye-opening piece of self-examination without once moving from your chair and exclaim, "That was easy!" Such ease is the fruit of a practiced ability to tolerate frustration.

I would like to learn, or remember, how to live.

ANNIE DILLARD

Uncover Problems and Challenges by Writing

You are ready and willing to write. How do you begin? The first (enormous) question you want answered is: "What is really going on in my life?" If the issues that have prompted you to begin this writing practice are very disturbing, you may want to push them away rather than look at them closely. This is therefore a time for courage and deep breathing. Write at length, over as many sessions as it takes, addressing your most important questions until you begin to uncover the problem areas that are presently troubling you. Ask big questions, such as: How do I see myself? How do others see me? What in my own personality is preventing me from feeling happy? What relationship has wounded me most? About what am I most self-critical?

At this time, I can't think of anything more meaningful than taking meaning apart.

MEYER VAISMAN

Narrow Your Focus

The problem areas you uncover may be large ones. They may be hard to grab on to or badly out of focus. They may involve important aspects of your personality or the way the world is constructed. The next challenge is to find methods for dissecting such large problems into a series of workable subproblems. One way to begin to narrow the focus is to ask yourself questions based on the challenges outlined in this book. Examples of such questions are offered in the Strategies section of each chapter.

As each new area of concern or interest comes into focus, you'll be adding a new ball to the ones you're already juggling. Be prepared to become a master juggler.

Ask Creative Questions

The issues, problems, and challenges that come into focus require creative exploration. Sometimes our thoughts are so stale on these matters, matters that perhaps we've brooded about for a long time, that only fresh, innovative questioning will allow us to get a new perspective on them. For example, when the issue is self-esteem, you might ask yourself the following sorts of questions:

1. What would it take for me to feel really proud of myself?

2. How would it feel to step into a powerful person's shoes?

3. What is it that I most fear hearing about myself?

4. When do I give away my personal power?

5. Why do I feel so ashamed of myself?

The inexpressible is the only thing that is worth expressing.
FREDERICK FRANCK

Or if the issue is work identity, you might ask yourself the following questions:

1. What impact does my work identity have on the rest of my life?

2. Am I equivalent to my art products or performances?

3. How many work identities do I have and how do they coexist?

4. How would I define what an artist does?

5. What is my job description?

Write Responses

Once you've chosen the questions you mean to address, work in absorbed and committed fashion to write responses that do the questions justice. Spend time at it. Lose yourself in the writing. Many fears, blocks, and distractions may prevent you from engaging yourself. You are, after all, asking yourself the hardest questions imaginable. You may fear that such poking and probing will do some unalterable damage in your life. But have faith that you will survive your revelations. Remember the three maxims of Zen Buddhism: great faith, great courage, great question. Continue faithfully and courageously with your great questioning of yourself.

Try not to reread as you go. Try not to censor the writing. When you feel the urge to stop, continue. Write for 40 minutes, 60 minutes, 90 minutes. Fill up pages with your writing. Shake away your writer's cramp. Feel drained if the experience is draining. Feel frightened if the experience frightens you. Then, when you feel you have finished, congratulate yourself: you have been working in a way that few people dare work.

Read Creatively

While looking for the light, you may suddenly be devoured by the darkness and find the true light.
JACK KEROUAC

Read your responses as creatively and courageously as you wrote them. Look to gain understanding and insight. Try to avoid the following pitfalls: feeling self-conscious about your writing mechanics or style; feeling unduly disappointed or impressed by your own words; or wondering whether the writing ought to be turned into a story or a poem. (We are always looking to make creative products out of our experiences!)

Take care of yourself as you read. You may be opening up wounds. You may be looking into dark corners that you've avoided looking into all your life. Your realizations may depress or enrage you. Remind yourself that your painful realizations are part of a process meant to serve you, not defeat you. Search out support if you need it.

Uncover Tactics and Solutions

You've begun to understand which challenges are presently the most troublesome in your life. You may have a clearer idea of the ways in which several different challenges interconnect or constellate. Have tactics for meeting these challenges also suggested themselves to you?

Possible solutions to the problems you've pinpointed are embedded in the writing you've just completed. If, for example, in the course of writing about the issue of self-doubt, you say in many different ways that you don't know whether you can complete the art project you've set yourself, a place to look for a solution is in the area of knowing. Do you need to learn a new skill, enlist the aid of a collaborator, or fathom how to persevere in the face of insufficient knowledge? Think about each possibility and experiment to determine which is the appropriate solution.

See how you've hinted between the lines at courses of action. Look for sparks of meaning to fly off the page and help you frame a plan of action. Constructing a plan of action is a crucial part of the process.

Make a Plan

Create as specific and detailed a plan of action as you can. What will you do and when will you do it?

Let's say you've determined that you're not happy with specific parts of your life as a dancer. First, you understand that something goes profoundly wrong in your intimate relationships, although you can't articulate what it is. Second, you have the sense that dancing is much less fun for you now than it once was, even though you have just been accepted into a prestigious dance company as a soloist. Lastly, you feel yourself plagued by a variety of anxieties, including severe performance anxiety, to the extent that you have begun to think of yourself as a real neurotic.

To have gotten this much clarity about your present situation is a real triumph. Each of these concerns is a serious challenge, and requires a specific (and different) plan of action. Certain strategies may have already suggested themselves to you in your writing; but in any case you need to construct concrete plans of action.

A plan of action designed to meet your first challenge (your putative failure at maintaining intimate relationships) might begin with a thorough self-examination of your personality. Are you unable to trust because of certain childhood or adult experiences? Is dance your first love, and do human beings run a poor second? Are you so critical of yourself and others that no one, yourself included, can stand up to the scrutiny?

A second element of the plan to meet this challenge might be to ask certain of your friends for their insights into your relational difficulties. The plan would also include your willingness to listen to their comments. Does a theme emerge? Do they see you as too intense, too overbearing, or too critical to maintain intimate relationships?

A third element of the plan to meet this challenge might involve researching the subject of dancers in intimate relationships. What have other dancers said about their ability or inability to maintain intimate relationships? For instance, John Gruen's interviews with Alexandra Danilova, Rudolf Nureyev, Rosella Hightower, Alvin Ailey, and 70 other dancers in his book *The Private World of Ballet* might prove informative and revealing.

A plan designed to meet the second challenge (to discover why

I haven't yet succeeded in understanding what has happened to me. I have very little time left to understand what I have not yet understood.

EUGÈNE IONESCO

The best way out is always through.

ROBERT FROST

dancing feels like a less rewarding pursuit to you these days) might include some or all of the following elements: an analysis of whether dancing injured has sapped your strength and enthusiasm; an analysis of the developmental rhythms of dancers' careers, to see if there are predictable valleys in a dancer's life and if you are in one of them; an existential analysis focusing on whether your values have shifted so that dancing is less meaningful to you now; an analysis of your definition of success to see if, now that you have achieved solo status, you perhaps need a new goal and a new dream.

Your treasure house is in yourself. It contains all you'll ever need.

HUI HAI

A plan designed to meet the third challenge (your many anxieties) might center around learning about the pros and cons of anxiety medications, and might include a trial visit to your local university-affiliated health program for performing artists.

Add Contingencies to the Plan

Your plan, which has the goal of effecting real change in your life, is likely to be hard to implement. You may balk somewhere along the line. You may backslide into habits you had hoped you'd eliminated. You may fail the first, second, or tenth time at doing your business more assertively or relating with your fellow actors more positively.

What will you do if you have trouble following your own plan of action? One answer is to make use of a behavioral contract, one of the tools of the behaviorally oriented psychotherapist. The psychologist Philip Zimbardo summarizes the behaviorist's point of view as follows: "Find the contingency that will maintain a desired response, apply it, evaluate its effectiveness."

You can enter into any number of behavioral contracts with yourself. Each such contract should contain, according to Zimbardo, the following seven elements:

1. Explicit benefits and privileges gained through specific performance, for example, a hot bath with light reading.

2. Specified consequences for failure to meet the terms of the contract, which could be a promise to flush $20 down the toilet for each day missed.

3. Bonuses for compliance with contract terms.

4. Monitoring of contracted activities, which simply means keeping track of your promise and noting your compliance.

5. Record-keeping of benefits earned.

6. Voluntary participation.

7. Right to outside arbitration in instances of alleged contract violation, which task should fall to a close friend.

Evaluate the Results

Periodically evaluate the results of your self-shaping work. How far have you come? What benefits have you reaped? What still needs to be done? At what sorts of things do you need more practice? What feelings remain troublesome? Are there new steps to be added to your plans? Have new tactics occurred to you? Do you need to set new goals for yourself?

The process outlined here is like a subtle feedback loop, where you feed yourself information and make changes based on the data you receive from yourself.

Learning is such a painful business. It requires humility from people at an age when the natural habit is arrogance.

MAY SARTON

Create New Plans of Action

You will be led down many tributaries as you effect change in your life. One tributary will lead to another. The plan you made in May to handle a certain challenge may not be an appropriate plan of action in December. By then the challenge may be to find effective ways of handling your extraordinary newfound success!

You will benefit in many ways if you manage to maintain this program. You'll become more disciplined and will overcome some of your natural resistance to self-exploration. You'll begin to identify problem areas in your life and begin to plan more effectively for change, effect real change, and monitor the changes you make.

Note to the reader. In places throughout the book, I write about the artist as *he,* and less often as *she.* The nature of this book does not allow for the alternation of gender pronouns chapter by chapter, and the present insufficiencies of language make finding a perfect solution impossible. I've tried to ameliorate the problem by addressing artists as *they* and by speaking directly to *you* as often as possible. I hope this seems a fair solution to a real problem.

The Challenges of the Artistic Personality | P A R T   O N E

Creativity *and* Talent

Songs are all written as part of a symphony.
BOB DYLAN

YOU ARE A CREATIVE or performing artist. You love to sing, dance, make images. You cherish the written word. Acting thrills you. Your pulse races when you drum. Your darkroom is a magical laboratory.

But will you be able to spend the rest of your life pursuing your passion, in the face of the many significant challenges that confront you? Can you carve out a career in art, achieve the level of success you dream of, secure a measure of comfort, and find time for both art-making and living? Can you survive the artist's life?

It is nothing less than survival we are talking about here, for few creative and performing artists in contemporary Western society can even earn a living from their art. A quarter of all working visual artists earn no money from their art, and another quarter earn less than $1,000 a year. Almost 90 percent earn less than $5,000 a year. Similarly disturbing figures can be quoted for poets, short-story writers, playwrights, novelists, independent filmmakers, pop singers, potters, jazz musicians, rock musicians, classical composers, art photographers—for all groups of creative and performing artists.

According to a Rockefeller Panel report commissioned to take an in-depth look at the financial realities of the performer's life:

> The miserable income of the majority of performing artists reflects both a shortage of jobs and the brief duration of employment that is

The first problem that an artist has is how to survive.
PHILIP GLASS

3

available. In all except the small handful of our major and metropolitan orchestras, musicians earn an average of only a few hundred dollars a year from their professional labors. During an average week in the winter season, only about one-fifth of the active members of Actors' Equity Association, the theatrical performers union, are employed in the profession. Of the actors who do find jobs, well over half are employed for only ten weeks—less than one-fifth of the year. For most opera companies the season lasts only a few weeks. The livelihood of the dancer is perhaps the most meager of all.

This is not a pretty picture. Why would a smart, ambitious, talented person choose to live such a life? Why have you chosen to struggle with cattle-call auditions, rejected fiction, indifferent gallery owners, a lack of recognition, and the other challenges that artists face?

The answers are severalfold. First, your need to express yourself and to manifest your creativity spring from very deep sources. Like a devout believer, you are moved by art in profound ways. Your connection to art is a reverent one, spiritually rich, intellectually lively, viscerally deep. You experience *rasa,* the Sanskrit word for the mood or sentiment that is evoked by a work of art. In you, what Alfred North Whitehead called "the impulse to originate" is stirred. You want to present to the world what the Navajo call *hozh'q:* the beauty of life, as seen and created by a person.

You value art and are confident of the contributions you can make in art. These needs and values translate into a sense of mission, a religious fervor. You consider the task sacred and the calling a noble one, and you are willing to make sacrifices and even martyr yourself for art. Emily Carr, the Canadian painter, said:

> Once I heard it stated and now I believe it to be true that there is no true art without religion. The artist himself may not think he is religious but if he is sincere his sincerity in itself is religion.

Stephen Spender, the British poet, wrote:

> It is evident that a faith in their vocation, mystical in intensity, sustains poets. From my experience I can clarify the nature of this faith. When I was nine we went to the Lake District, and there my parents

What shall I sing? What shall I paint? What shall I perform? I sing, I perform, I paint the real situation, to make people aware of what is going on and what are the deepest roots of our illness.

THICH NHAT HANH

read me some of the poems of Wordsworth. My sense of the sacredness of the task of poetry began then, and I have always felt that the poet's was a sacred vocation, like a saint's.

You feel that you have a special, vital role to play in society. From a considered vantage point outside of society, you observe, witness, and judge. As the German Expressionist painter Georg Baselitz put it, "The artist is not responsible to anyone. His social role is asocial."

You also feel the simple joy of doing art, of making music, of playing a part with other actors. You discover that you are good at it—good with words, good on your feet, good with your voice or your fingers, good at images. Art makes you feel alive. You find that the process of art-making—be it the quietly absorbed practicing, the rollicking rehearsing, the intense poetry writing, or the tempestuous encounter with a blank canvas—buffers you against the ordinariness of the world. "Painting is a way of forgetting oneself," the visual artist Joan Mitchell said. The sculptor Louise Nevelson confided, "In my studio I'm as happy as a cow in her stall."

You may also choose the artist's life because you are using art as a tool to help heal childhood wounds or as a means of expressing the pain in your life. The painter Barbara Smith said, "The intent of my work is to break out of a dark place." The painter Nancy Spero offered the following self-description: "I am the angry person sticking out her tongue." The painter Harmony Hammond said, "I want my work to demand your attention because I can get it in no other way."

Beyond all purist preconceptions, fantastic, aesthetic, or theoretical, is the imperious necessity to shout, to express oneself as one is.

ANTONIO SAURA

Certainly you may also perceive a career in art as a way to gain recognition, to stand out, to become known as a special and talented person. No doubt you feel you have valuable, innovative, beautiful work to do. Quite possibly you're hoping for fame and fortune. You may harbor the hope that people will one day applaud your achievements and call you great.

Lastly, you pursue the artist's life because you believe you could be the exception who proves the rule when it comes to money and success. Perhaps like the French painter Chaim Soutine you'll be discovered by a passing dentist, or like Jean Harlow you'll be discovered sipping soda in a drugstore. You see your novel making a mark and being hailed as a work of genius. You imagine yourself becoming a star and going from rags to riches overnight. The possibility that success may strike quickly, out of the blue, sustains and nourishes you.

You begin your journey as an artist from sacred motives, with dreams and high hopes, and also, perhaps, from a place of painful turmoil or other inner necessity. From these powerful drives comes your conscious decision to pursue a life in art, your resolve to call yourself an artist whatever the consequences. You are the one nodding in agreement when the painter John Baldessari says, "Art is about bloody-mindedness. It's not about living the good life. In the end, it's just you and the art."

You identify yourself as an artist. But just how good an artist are you, or how good can you become? Do you feel confident that you have the necessary skills and abilities to master your medium? Do your paintings manage to capture your passion and your ideas? Are you a virtuoso actor or pianist? Can you create characters and handle plot to your liking? Are you creative enough and talented enough to accomplish the artistic tasks you've set yourself?

Indeed, creativity and talent are the first challenges we might examine. In order to feel good about yourself as an artist, you need to manifest your creativity and make appropriate use of your talents. These are hard tasks to accomplish in their own right, made even harder by the fact that both *creativity* and *talent* are such puzzling terms.

I consider myself responsible, not to society, which dictates fashion and taste suited to its environment and its period, but to youth, to the coming generations, which are left stranded in a blitzed world.

OSKAR KOKOSCHKA

CREATIVITY AND THE ARTIST

It would be vain to try to put into words that immeasurable sense of bliss which comes over me directly {when} a new idea awakens in me and begins to assume a definite form. I forget everything and behave like a madman.

PETER ILICH TCHAIKOVSKY

Over the centuries, artistic creativity has been related variously to divine inspiration, madness, sheer genius, unnameable life forces, and cosmic powers. In modern times it has been linked to unconscious processes, the working out and sublimating of sexual instincts, attempts at wish fulfillment, and incipient neurosis. It has also been linked to the natural associational tendencies of a special mind; to the self-realizing and self-actualizing efforts of some individuals; and to the accidental presence of a certain collection of personality traits.

The psychiatrist Lawrence Hatterer, for instance, described in *The Artist and Society* the Freudian view as follows:

> The dominant theory of the creative person and act stems from Freud's concept of sublimation. Freud hypothesized that the creative act is rooted in transformed sexual energy, in the diversion of these energies to higher, more socially acceptable aims. Creativity, he felt, arose out of the artist's unconscious need to rid himself of mental tension.

The Freudian view is provocative, but so are the humanistic positions regarding self-realization and self-actualization championed by Carl Rogers and Abraham Maslow. Trait theory, as we'll see in chapter 2, also has something important to tell us about creativity, as do the existential theories of Rollo May, Victor Frankl, and others.

In my view, however, the most useful definition of creativity is the following one: people are artistically creative when they love what they are doing, know what they are doing, and actively engage in the tasks we call art-making. The three elements of creativity are thus *loving, knowing,* and *doing;* or heart, mind, and hands; or, as Buddhist teaching has it, great faith, great question, and great courage.

Creativity is no more mysterious than this. That hardly means, however, that manifesting one's creativity is easy. Artists, in order to be creative, are challenged to love enough, to know enough, and to do enough, and these tasks are as real and challenging as any human endeavor can be.

If we climb from that region of technique to the more spiritual sphere of interpretation, what anguish we experience in trying to find the soul of a composition behind the inert notation.

ANDRES SEGOVIA

Since you usually can expect no earthly reward, if you write poetry, you have to do it for the love.

ROGER BERGMAN

Loving

Love is the spirit that motivates the artist's journey. The love may be sublime, raw, obsessive, passionate, awful, or thrilling, but whatever its quality, it's a powerful motive in the artist's life. The actor Derek Jacobi distinguished this special deeply rooted drive from mere desire in the following way:

You have to have an absolute obsession and compulsion to act, not just desire; it's just not enough to have talent and want to express it; it's not enough. It's got to be more deeply rooted, more abrasive. The fire in the belly has got to be there. If there's no fire, you can't do it.

Art, even the angriest, darkest variety, is created out of love.
MEREDITH MONK

What is it that the artist loves? It is first and foremost the sheer power of whichever medium has attracted him. This is why he is an artist and not a botanist or an archaeologist: an art form has gotten under his skin. It may be the power of the book that gripped him, the power of dance, the power of music, the power of the image, or the power of the play.

Artists' expressions of this deep love and passion could be repeated here endlessly. Diane Burko, the visual artist, said, "I love putting paint on canvas, I love pouring it and watching new colors happen in my margarine containers." The painter Hans Hofmann claimed that "as an artist, you love everything of quality that came before you." Jorge Bolet, the pianist, said, "My gods were Hofman and Rachmaninoff. Every time I heard Rachmaninoff play, I said to myself, '*That* is what *I* want to sound like.'" François Gauzi wrote of Van Gogh:

> When discussing "art," if one disagreed with him and pushed him to the limit, he would flare up in a disturbing way. Color drove him mad. Delacroix was god, and when he spoke of this painter, his lips would quiver with emotion.

Your love is equally a love of the great masters of your medium, a love of the human being who had it in her to write the novel that transfixed you or who flew across the stage to the sounds of music. It is a love of Mozart's music and a love of the man, too—not a love of his personality, necessarily, but of his ability to express human potential.

The artist who does not love ardently may fall far short of his creative potentialities. He may not have enough "lubricating juice," as Virginia Woolf called it. He may move from piano lessons and small recitals to a good conservatory to a concert tour, mastering his technique and honing his skills along the way, but if he remains all the while out of love with music, his is a career, not a love affair.

We see again and again in the lives of special artists a profound youthful infatuation with their medium, with everything and anything connected with it—the good, the bad, and the indifferent. If books have mesmerized them, they will read everything; if painting, they will frequent every gallery, running to every visiting show. They may have no idea that they are about to devote their life to that medium; they simply feel in love. The actor Len Cariou said:

> *The love you liberate in your work is the only love you keep.*
> MAURICE PRENDERGAST

> I didn't have any thoughts about being an actor. I always *was* an actor. I'd go to films every Saturday. I had an insatiable appetite for films. You could see four films and a serial for half a buck. In 1959 when I read an ad in the local paper, "Young actors wanted for summer stock," all of a sudden I knew; there was a crunch in my head.

In the beginning, the artist may love indiscriminately, in a regular wash of infatuation. Many critics have observed, for instance, that Van Gogh as a youth consistently admired and respected the work of a host of minor artists; he praised better and worse artists together in the same breath. When Van Gogh was twenty, for example, he wrote to his younger brother Theo from London:

> There are clever painters here, among others Millais, who has painted the "Huguenot." His things are beautiful. Then there is Boughton, and among the old painters, Constable, a landscape painter who lived about thirty years ago; he is splendid, his work reminds me of Diaz and Daubigny; and there are Reynolds and Gainsborough, who have especially painted very beautiful ladies' portraits; and Turner. I see that you have a great love of art; that is a good thing, lad. Admire as much as you can; most people do not admire enough.

Critics have felt that such passages point to a noncritical streak in Van Gogh's nature. But to call this a lack of critical ability is to misunderstand the early infatuation of the artist. If we recognize that the artist is embarking on a love affair, into which one day he will throw his whole being, then these moments become not only understandable but also absolutely predictable. They have about them the feeling of puppy love, as the young person suspends his discriminating abilities in the pursuit of passion.

The artist therefore inflates the painting, the book, the piece of music in question because it has moved him. He calls it great because it has struck a great chord in him. If we remember the books or paintings or pieces of music that we loved as children and young adults, if we remember how we were moved in the moment of experiencing them, we may feel loathe to look back and recognize that a certain book was poorly written, that a particular painting was sentimental. In the moment we experienced that book or that painting, we were surely in love.

Chopin, experiencing Paris for the first time at 21, wrote to a friend:

I am in love with Mozart like a young girl. Immortal Mozart! I owe you everything. I have you to thank that I did not die without having loved.

SØREN KIERKEGAARD

> I doubt whether anything so magnificent as *Robert le Diable*, the new five-act opera by Meyerbeer, has ever before been done in the theater. It is the masterpiece of the modern school. There are devils, immense choruses singing through tubes, and souls rising from the tomb. The most extraordinary thing of all is the organ, the sound of which, coming from the stage, delights and astonishes one and almost drowns the orchestra.

The artist is transported by his medium, is delighted and astonished. That his medium is able to speak to him in this way is almost a proof of the existence of a god, or at least a special affirmation in the realm of the spirit.

Knowing

The young artist gobbles up everything he can in his medium because he has a need to know. Much of his knowing comes from this early period in life. The young singer listens to all of Billie Holliday's records and begins to learn the blues. The young writer reads all the works of Shakespeare and learns how language and drama operate. Throughout his life as well, the artist is driven to know enough, to take in all that is necessary for him to take in, even if, in the language of Zen, he must forget much of what he knows in order to work.

Knowing is both intuitive and rational, tonal and factual, conscious and unconscious. Actors as well as playwrights and directors, soloists and ensemble players as well as composers and conductors, carry inside them the work they are doing and operate in this multilevel way. They create the version of the piece they will play even as they peel potatoes for dinner. This ongoing inner learning and

knowing are no different for the creative artist or the recreative artist. Jorge Bolet, for instance, described his process of learning new
piano pieces:

> I never solved a major mechanical or interpretive problem *at* the key-
> board, only *away* from it. Even when I sometimes become so com-
> pletely baffled that I am utterly stuck for a direction in which to go,
> I return to the *music* and piece it out. I don't know about others, but I
> do know that *I* have never solved a major mechanical or interpretive
> problem at the keyboard. I have always solved it in my mind.

This is a knowing based on immersion. If you're an actor you
immerse yourself in a role, living and breathing the character. If
you're a dancer you become the deer or the swan. If you're a writer
you inhabit the scene of your novel. If you're a pianist you live inside
the sonata.

All artists are immersed in different waters, to be sure, and their
art reflects these differences. One is immersed in abstraction, another in realism. One is immersed in jazz, another in traditional
Andean flute music. But each, insofar as he or she is deeply creative,
is deeply immersed. As the psychologist E. W. Sinnott put it, "Inspiration, it is well recognized, rarely comes unless an individual has
immersed himself in a subject. He must have a rich background of
knowledge and experience in it."

Of course, what you know as an artist shifts and changes. You
learn more, forget, change your mind. What you do today informs
and alters what you knew yesterday; or, as the visual artist Frederick
Franck put it, "I have learned that what I have not drawn I have
never really seen." These shifts in knowing can produce frustrations.
You're happy with a poem you've just written; when you reread it you
note its flaws. You're happy with a morning's painting; in the afternoon the work looks dull. As the sculptor Stephen De Staebler recol-
lected:

> Giacometti once visited a friend and saw one of his plaster heads that
> he'd given the friend as a gift. He immediately pulled out a pen knife
> and began carving away at the head. It would never be right.
>
> The quest for the unattainable drives all artists. It has nothing
> to do with what others say about your work. Sometimes you get a

glimmer, you feel you've really touched something. Then the next day you look at it and wonder what it was you saw.

Knowing is not a cold and mechanical holding of a universe of facts, a strictly left-brain enterprise. It involves intuitions as well as ideas, feelings as well as beliefs. One artist may stress the importance of ideas in his work, and that may be a true self-appraisal. Another may stress intuition. The painter David Ligare, for instance, wrote, "Making paintings is a passion for me, but it is a passion of ideas rather than just pigment." The painter Jane Freilicher, on the other hand, said, "I believe I rely rather heavily on intuition and depend on an intuitive response from my audience."

While you may belong to one camp or the other, and assert that the idea is higher than the intuition or vice versa, on the sidelines we may speculate that there are more than a few ways of knowing.

If you approach an opera as though it were something that always went a certain way, that's what you get. I approach an opera as though I didn't know it.

SARAH CALDWELL

A man will turn over half a library to make one book.

SAMUEL JOHNSON

Doing

Loving is the heart of creativity, knowing is its brain, and doing is its musculature. Doing is effort of the sort described by Tchaikovsky in a letter to a friend:

> We must *always* work, and a self-respecting artist must not fold his hands on the pretext that he is not in the mood. If we wait for the mood, without endeavoring to meet it halfway, we easily become indolent and apathetic. We must be patient, and believe that inspiration will come to those who can master their *disinclination*. A few days ago I told you I was working every day without any real inspiration. Had I given way to my disinclination, undoubtedly I should have drifted into a long period of idleness. But my patience and faith did not fail me, and today I felt that inexplicable glow of inspiration of which I told you; thanks to which I know beforehand that whatever I write today will have power to make an impression, and to touch the hearts of those who hear it.

Doing is also execution, of the sort described by the Spanish painter Francisco Goya: "An artist, seeing a man fall from a third-story window, should be able to complete a drawing of him by the time he hits the ground."

A person is not an artist until he works at his art, no matter how eloquently he speaks during the cocktail hour or how fine are the images that come to his mind. As David Salle, the visual artist, put it, "It's easy to be an artist in your head." We, as artists, know this. We realize that often we are not able to translate our vision into splendid art. Even the finest artists write books that are not great, paint pictures that are not great, compose pieces that are not great, give performances that are not great, involve themselves in projects that are not great. But the artist can only try—and must try.

When you love what you are doing, know what you are doing, and do it, a confidence is bred in you that is the best stretcher of limits. Then you can say, as the visual artist June Wayne said, "Now, when I start something, I expect to carry it off."

You approach both a new work and a revival with the same amount of integrity and hard work.

PAMELA REED

TALENT AND THE ARTIST

Creativity is human potential made manifest. But what is talent? The dictionary (in this case Webster's *New World Dictionary*) informs us that *talent* is any natural ability, power, or endowment, and especially a superior, apparently natural ability in the arts or sciences or in the learning or doing of anything.

This definition is revealing on several counts. First of all, it defines talent in terms of abilities and powers. It suggests that an artist can answer the question "Am I talented?" in the affirmative if he can point to certain endowments that he possesses.

But which ones should he point to? What are the important ones in his art discipline? How many of them does he need in order to do good work? Do they all matter equally? Which, if any, are absolutely necessary? How much of a desired ability does he need—how great a vocal range, how long a leap, how fine a hand as a draftsman?

If we look at just a few art disciplines we see how difficult it is for artists to begin to answer these questions. Is it more important, for instance, for a pianist to possess virtuosity and be able to race her fingers up and down the keyboard, or to possess the ability to interpret music and express emotion through her playing? Is the talented actor the one who has the ability to be himself (and who perhaps can't be anyone else) or the one with the widest range? Is it more important for a painter to be able to render a likeness, compose a painting and balance its parts, possess a fine color sense, have a knack for new images or new ideas, or is the only talent that counts the ability to paint something that evokes a powerful response in the observer?

I'm not a natural singer, it's just sheer, slogging hard work for me. It takes six weeks of solid practicing before I'm ready to even let a soul hear me.

JULIE ANDREWS

As difficult as these questions are, an artist must grapple with them and attempt to answer them. In making the attempt he will gain a greater awareness of the demands and requirements of his field, of the skills and powers he presently brings to the task and of those he may still need. Only then will he be able to determine what talent means in the context of his particular art discipline. If he does not possess the requisite talent to achieve his goals, recognizing this will put him in a better position to make a strategic career decision.

For example, after such an assessment an artist may say to himself, "Well, I understand better what's needed in my art and what I have to offer. I think I'm talented—except in one, unfortunately important, area: I can't draw a straight line. Should I lie to myself and ignore the problem? Should I get out of art? If talent is innate, and I haven't a drawing talent, what am I supposed to do?"

Fortunately, the dictionary definition of talent points to a possible way out of this dilemma. That definition begins by asserting that talent is one or another innate ability of the individual, but goes on to call talent in the arts only an *apparently* innate ability. This is of crucial significance, because it allows the artist to put the following question on the table: "Is there a chance that I can learn to develop more talent?"

For example, consider Van Gogh. Van Gogh's drawings show a truly remarkable improvement over the course of the two years he set aside to intensely practice drawing. At the start of that period his sketches look clumsy and amateurish. With great ardor, thoughtfulness, and effort—by manifesting his creativity, in short—at the end of those two years Van Gogh was producing drawings that showed not only that he had mastered elements of technique but also that he had educated himself in ways that moved him far ahead of his classically trained peers.

Van Gogh's progress excites the artist. It seems to hold the clear implication that by acting creatively the artist may significantly increase his talent or make manifest significant talent he didn't know he possessed. Maybe a brilliant novel *is* within his grasp. Maybe he *can* achieve a breakthrough in the visual arts. Maybe he *can* play his instrument like a god.

The artist is comforted. But his good mood is interrupted by a new thought. He realizes that when he questions whether he is talented, as often as not he is comparing himself to the greatest or most talented artists of all time, or even comparing his talent to a level that no one has yet achieved—to some Platonic ideal of perfection. In doing that, he suddenly wonders, isn't he setting himself up for disappointment and failure? Won't he end up thinking of himself as a marginal talent or a minor artist, even if he realizes a sizable portion of his potential?

He sees the fruits of such unfortunate comparing in the words of the late novelist Jerzy Kozinski:

> There's no greater punishment than an insufficient talent. I have always been a very marginal novelist. A lesser talent. Yes, there's nothing wrong with that. Ninety-nine percent of mankind is, even in this I am typical. Would I like more talent? Yes. But you cannot get more talent. But I'm no different than most lesser talents. We're all lesser talents.

Rather than priding himself on novels like *The Painted Bird* and *Being There,* Kozinski put himself down. Perhaps his ironic self-indictment is more a piece of misanthropy than a statement about talent. It may even be a kind of convenient shorthand to describe a bankrupt artistic life. But it's just as likely that Kozinski spent his adult life comparing himself to the giants of literature and feeling himself a failure by comparison.

The artist, thinking about this issue, has to mutter to himself, "Wonderful. I want to increase my talent and manifest my creativity—in short, I want to do great work. But I mustn't set up the immortals in my field as a yardstick against which to compare my work, because if I do, I risk growing profoundly dissatisfied with my own accomplishments. I'll end up back at a place of not really feeling talented. And—worse yet!—when I make a mistake or produce a bad book or a bad painting, flub my lines or drop notes, I'll feel really terrible, having fallen so very far short of the ideal!"

Taking some time to consider this issue, the artist realizes how easy it is to disparage his own talent and to lower his self-esteem in

I read the play as many times as I can. I also sleep on it: I literally put it under my pillow.
ELIZABETH FRANZ

the process. He realizes also that when he calls another artist a marginal talent, he invariably means it as a criticism. Yet he knows in his heart that art is hard to do and that we should each be forgiven our very human limitations. Miracles of art do occur, but limits can only be stretched, not transcended. Even though he feels extraordinary when he senses brilliant music or a brilliant poem coursing through him as if God-given, he is nevertheless all too aware of his own great ignorance and insufficiencies.

I just hear a sound coming into my head and hope to catch it with my hands.

ERROLL GARNER

What should he do? Should he set his sights lower and not judge himself and others against the very highest standards? Should he regularly confess to frailty and ordinariness and act generously when he sees the frail and ordinary works of other artists? Or should he set his sights extremely high and risk almost certain disappointment?

The artist, puzzling over this matter, arrives at an answer. He determines that he means to shoot for the sky and to judge himself and others by the highest standards, come what may. He recommits himself to manifesting his creativity and his talent. But just like that, in the next split second, he's struck by another troubling question. "What," he wonders, "if being talented doesn't matter at all? What if it isn't the issue? What if it's even a hindrance?"

I occasionally play works by contemporary composers, and for two reasons. First, to discourage the composer from writing any more, and secondly to remind myself how much I appreciate Beethoven.

JASCHA HEIFETZ

This is a question that has troubled him before, one that regularly plagues artists. The screenwriter, the pop singer, the painter, the songwriter, the television writer look around them and everywhere see mediocrity rewarded, even demanded. The artist, already in turmoil as he tries to address the many sides of the talent issue, now thinks, "Here I am, doing everything I can to manifest my creativity and make use of my talents—and the public really only wants comedy that comes with a laugh track, fiction to take to the beach, and music driven by the beat of a drum machine! Why should I challenge myself if the public wants cat art and homilies?"

The artist now feels furious. He wonders if there is a way he can get even with the audience. He is reminded of a certain kind of modern artist, a John Cage or an Andy Warhol, who, perhaps also infuriated by this demand for mediocrity, throws the matter back in the face of his audience and mocks them with visions of ordinariness. Such an artist will try anything, for who's to say what's good or bad, and isn't he likely to garner applause even for his most ridiculous efforts?

Like Warhol, such an artist paints soup cans and pastel-colored prints of Marilyn Monroe and ironically demands of the world, as Warhol demanded, "I want everybody to think alike. I think everybody should be a machine." Like Yoko Ono, the artist gives a "silent concert," demanding that the audience supply the music. No matter what he does—whether he plays radio static as his concert piece or crafts clay turds as his museum piece—the artist can't shock or wake up the public or succeed at irony. The audience simply doesn't get it. As the French Dadaist artist Marcel Duchamp put it, "I threw the bottle-rack and the urinal in people's faces as a challenge, and now they admire them for their aesthetic beauty."

The artist now finds himself in a fine stew. But suddenly a new question intrudes: "Isn't all this brooding about my talent really pretty disgusting? Am I really so ego-driven and narcissistic?" Feeling much too self-involved, he announces to himself, "No, I won't allow talent to be the issue any longer! I'm going to stop massaging my ego and acting prideful. In fact, there's so much important social and political work to be done in the world, I'm going to make use of the talents I possess, just as they are, in the service of a good cause."

He determines that he will no longer hold individual expression in higher esteem than community or global welfare. He nods in vigorous agreement when he comes upon the writer and painter Suzi Gablik's call for a more socially minded art:

> Today, there is still a pervasive sense that only by divorcing themselves from any social role can artists establish their own individual identity. But it strikes me that, as the dangers to planetary survival escalate, the practical consequences of such an attitude are becoming increasingly apparent. Our modernist notions of freedom and autonomy, of art answering only to its own laws, the pure aesthetic without a function, begin to seem a touch ingenuous. We simply cannot remain committed to our disembodied ideals of individualism, freedom, and self-expression while everything else in the world unravels.

For reasons flowing from the same sort of argument, the artist may determine to use her art to make a political statement. She may decide, for instance, to give up painting and devote herself to what was previously denigrated as "craft" work, as a protest against male privilege and gender-based inequities. As Elaine Reichek, the

It took me fifteen years to discover I had no talent for writing, but I couldn't give it up because by that time I was too famous.

ROBERT BENCHLEY

A talent somewhat above mediocrity, shrewd and not too sensitive, is more likely to rise in the world than genius, which is apt to be perturbable and wear itself out before fruition.

CHARLES HORTON COOLEY

American visual artist, put it, "It's political to choose a form that is a craft—not painting, not sculpture, not in the tradition of high white art."

The artist may or may not arrive at this or a similar place, and may or may not long remain there. What is certain, however, is that throughout his career he will question himself about the issue of talent, perhaps out of conscious awareness if the issue is too dangerous or painful, but no less closely for that. He will question himself, doubt himself, and brood about the sufficiency of his talent, no matter how talented he happens to be. He may be gifted with Placido Domingo's voice, but still doubt his ability to hit the high notes in a Wagner opera. He may have the command of language of a Virginia Woolf, the drawing skills of a Picasso, or the melodic touch of a Mozart, but, falling short with a given book, painting, or sonata, label himself a failure.

He will question himself throughout his career, but as likely as not in a haphazard, self-critical, and confused way. Almost certainly he'll avoid interrogating himself systematically about the matter, especially if he's unhappy about the way his art is going or fears that he's untalented. But in fact such a systematic examination is the most profitable way for an artist to deal with the question of talent.

The matter needs to be put squarely on the table and given conscious attention. For you do need to know what abilities are required in your art discipline, in what measure they are required, and in what measure you possess them. You may learn that drawing isn't what matters, but expressive power. You may learn that your "talent to amuse" is more valuable than you'd ever imagined. You may finally understand the real nature of your strengths and discover how to make yourself into an even stronger artist.

Once you've accomplished this assessment, however (and unless it turns out that you're lacking such an important endowment that you really must alter your sights or even change your career plans), it becomes far more profitable for you to focus on creativity than on talent. For it is within your power to become more creative, no matter what the upper limits of your talent might be. And by being creative you make the most of your talents.

Make every effort you can to bring your passion, knowledge, and will to bear on your art-making. Challenge yourself to love

I am for an art that is political-erotical-mystical, that does something more than sit on its ass in a museum.

CLAES OLDENBURG

enough, to know enough, and to draw on that knowledge, to work at your art and to master your disinclination to work. Continue to dream and continue to believe yourself special, for if you stop dreaming you lose some of your motivational energy, love less, and grow less creative. Continue to learn, practice, and explore. Give your work your best effort. Ultimately the very question of the sufficiency or insufficiency of your talent may melt away as you manifest your creative nature.

It is better to make a piece of music than to perform one, better to perform one than to listen to one, better to listen to one than to misuse it as a means of distraction, entertainment, or acquisition of "culture."

JOHN CAGE

STRATEGIES

At the end of each chapter in this book, you'll be presented with an array of strategies designed to help you reflect upon the issues outlined in the chapter. Both my students and psychotherapy clients have found these strategies helpful. However, the best strategies for *you* do not necessarily appear in these prescriptive sections. Ultimately, the best strategies are the ones you create for yourself and test by trial-and-error experimentation, since those are the ones custom-tailored to fit your personality and circumstances.

As you remember from the guided writing program, step 7 asks you to narrow your focus so that you present yourself with manageable questions to write about. The following are questions you might ask about the issues raised in this chapter. On creativity:

1. What do I mean by creativity? How is it different from talent?

2. Do I believe that I can be more creative? In what ways? What must I do to become more creative?

3. Do I love my art enough? Do I feel passionate about art?

4. How can I test whether I love art enough? (Might I base one test on the poet Rilke's advice to a young friend: if I can imagine doing something other than write poetry, might I be better off not pursuing the poet's life?)

5. If I feel less ardent than I think I should, how can I increase my love for my art? How can I really and truly fall in love with my medium (or fall in love with it again)? (One

*Nothing is more odious than
music without hidden meanings.*
FRÉDÉRIC CHOPIN

approach might be to ascertain whether I ever really *chose* to be an artist, or if, instead, it was something that just happened. Consciously choosing, perhaps even in a ceremony I devise for the occasion, may liberate my passion and start my lubricating juices flowing.)

6. Do I know enough to work creatively? Is there any knowledge I feel I'm lacking? Am I insufficiently aware of traditions, technical aspects of my medium, or current trends and fashions? Given that it is impossible to know everything, is there *one* area of knowledge that would be really beneficial for me to increase?

7. Do I work hard enough at my art? Do I spend enough hours at it? Do I give it enough consideration?

8. Have I developed ways of mastering my disinclination to work? Do I have a repertoire of strategies? If not, will I put such a repertoire together?

On talent:

1. What do I mean by talent? How would I define it?

2. What does it mean to be talented in my particular field? What skills and abilities does someone in my field need? How many of them do I need in order to do good work? Do they all matter equally? Are any absolutely necessary?

3. How talented am I? What are my strengths and weaknesses? To what extent do I possess the skills and abilities I need?

4. Do I consider the skills or abilities I lack to be the kind that one either innately does or does not possess? Or do I believe that they can be acquired or enhanced through practice or learning?

5. Does the matter of talent in my case seem to revolve around one or a few certain abilities that I seem to possess in insufficient measure? Will I create a plan to test myself for those abilities? Will I work hard at manifesting them before deciding that I don't possess them?

6. Having assessed my talent as best I can, what do I see as the right fit between my talent and my career aspirations? Am I setting my sights too high or too low?

7. Against which great masters do I compare myself? Against what set of ideals do I compare my talent? Will I consider myself insufficiently talented if I fall short of matching the accomplishments of some great master or the requirements of some set of ideals?

8. Because I see that mediocrity sells in the marketplace, do I doubt that talent is really an issue in my field? Do I need to concern myself with matters other than talent in order to have a career?

9. Because of the path I've chosen to take as a community artist (or a collaborative artist, a craftsperson, a pop artist, a postmodernist, and so forth), how much or how little should the matter of talent concern me?

It is in the ability to deceive oneself that the greatest talent is shown.

ANATOLE FRANCE

There lives in the sculptor's soul something which compels him to imbue his intention with a heroic boldness and with a joy in achieving monumental effects.

ERNST BARLACH

Examine creative blockage. Perhaps what you perceive to be your insufficient talent may really be a matter of blockage. Are you prevented from manifesting your full talent because of anxiety, guilt, fear, or ignorance? If so, you can access your native talent by eliminating those blocks.

One client, a singer, added several notes to both ends of her vocal range by learning to quell her performance anxiety. Another client, previously censoring the contradictions in his nature, began to paint more powerfully when he allowed himself to "tell dark stories" as he painted self-portraits. These are but two of the myriad ways blockage and talent can interconnect. Chapter 4 focuses on blockage, and strategies for overcoming blocks are offered at the end of that chapter.

Work on a mighty theme. What's the biggest subject you'd like to tackle? The most important book? The most ambitious painting? The most complicated film? What's the most amazing piece of music to add to your repertoire? What existentially resonates for you?

You may doubt that you can realize your grandest ideas. But doubt is only a certain kind of thinking. If you work attentively on a mighty theme for just a short while, honoring the difficulties but courageously returning to the work, you will grow more creative. Attempt your *Crime and Punishment* or Ninth Symphony.

Affirm that you can create or perform. Affirm that you can pull off what you attempt. Don't give your fears a second thought. One client, a singer who doubted her ability to form her own band, learned to assert herself by affirming that she was competent to do whatever needed to be done. She auditioned musicians, put together a set, searched out gigs, and performed in the band named after her.

Your affirmations can be spoken or written, general or specific. "I can do it," and "No problem," said under your breath, are examples of powerful affirmations.

Carry your work differently. Much of the artist's work, including that of the performer, is done out of conscious awareness. Your fictional characters first speak to one another, then they speak to you. The emotional point of the concerto you're learning comes to you in a dream.

But for the work to get done that way, you need to have a spacious place in your unconscious where it can gestate and incubate. If you disown the work or treat it with indifference, it will have no life within you. If, however, you're enthusiastic about the work, curious about its outcome, and finally disturbed or obsessed by it, and if you're committed to birthing it, it will live within you even as you balance your checkbook.

Periodically surprise yourself with the question, "Where is my work?" Sense if it's nearby or far away. How quickly does it come back? In a split second? If you can't bring it back immediately, spring the question on yourself more often. Nag yourself. The nearer the work is, the more attention it is being given just out of conscious awareness.

If you are a performer, also create. If you're tired of auditioning for inferior roles, roles that you don't respect or that bear no resemblance to your inner reality, write your own performance piece. If you're tired of your band playing only cover tunes, compose. If you're an ensemble player, consider writing a quartet. If you act, consider directing. Don't restrict your creativity by labeling yourself a servant and not a master.

I became a photographer. That was the very first time that I wasn't being led around by the nose by someone else.

RODDY MCDOWALL

Change formats. Paint larger. Paint smaller. Work within the limits of the sonnet or concerto form. Work outside those limits. Write a novel in the first person. Write a short story in the second person. Put down your flute and pick up a piccolo. Each such change affords you a new piece of knowledge and forcibly shifts your perception of the limits of your medium and the limits of your talent.

Turn things on their ears. Do a painting in the Cubist style. Put new colors on your palette. Play one note and draw its sound; hear it as if for the first time. Play an emotion on your oboe—improvise. Write naked. Take your band to the beach and play by the water. Redesign your flute so that it fits your fingers. Write the shortest story you have ever attempted—one paragraph long.

Every artist should be allowed a few failures.
ELSA LANCHESTER

New Looks

Take a new look at the world and at the art you make or perform. If you break free of your habitual ways of thinking, seeing, hearing, and doing, you may be led to an artistic and personal revolution. Have you underestimated your talent? Are you disconnected from what you know and love? Turn everything on its head. You may turn over a rock and find your powerful painting style or fresh fictional character underneath.

For example, are you an accomplished musician but still have trouble sight-reading? You may simply have never gotten the idea of the logical relationship between written notes and the keys of your instrument.

Flip a grand staff and line it up with your piano keys. Are you seeing the relationship for the first time? This way of comprehending the relationship between instrument keys and musical notation is adapted from Eloise Ristad's *A Soprano on Her Head,* Real People Press, Box F, Moab, UT 84532.

Discover ways of working more deeply and effectively. Notice attention leaks. What distracts you? How do you handle distractions? How might you handle them more effectively? What thoughts disturb or derail you? Inoculate yourself against them. Fend them off. Dispose of them. Write them down, then drop them in an elegant little box you keep on the corner of your desk for that purpose.

Recognize how you work best. Are you flooded with images on

train trips? Grab a pad and ride the trolley out to the ocean. Is it important that you remember your past successes? Keep a framed copy of the cover of your last book where you can see it. Is it important to focus on an upcoming deadline or to purposely forget about it? Do you work best with Vivaldi on in the afternoon but in complete silence in the morning? Create the conditions that elicit your best work.

Track your creativity. Even the most persistently creative person can sink or meander into long, unpleasant, and dispiriting uncreative periods. Keep tabs on your creativity. Remember the three components of creativity: loving, knowing, and doing. You can propel yourself into a creative outburst by choosing any of the three as a starting point. Find your creative spark by working, by choosing a project and launching into it. Rekindle your creative spirit by learning something new—an unusual photographic technique or repertoire piece, the ins and outs of a new brand of oil pastels. Or rejuvenate yourself by falling in love with art again, by spending time with a masterwork.

Our greatest weakness lies in giving up. The most certain way to succeed is always to try just one more time.

THOMAS EDISON

CHAPTER 2

The Puzzle *of* Personality

I have inside me an unchanging, undying need to be somebody else.
That, however, is paradoxically coupled with the unchanging de-
sire to express myself.

LAWRENCE LUCKINBILL

THERE IS NO SINGLE right way to look at personality, an artist's or anyone else's. Personality is sui generis and larger than our attempts to describe it. To suppose that any theoretical orientation—psychoanalytic, behavioral, systems, or any other—can more than partly and poorly capture the essence of human personality is to make the logical mistake known as reductionism.

Every man carries in himself the germs of every human quality, and sometimes one manifests itself, sometimes another, and the man often becomes unlike himself, while still remaining the same man.

LEO TOLSTOY

Therefore the following examination of the artist's personality should be considered merely as one way to approach the question, How are artists different from nonartists? Here we'll think of the artist's personality as if it were constructed of certain building blocks, using an approach known as personality trait theory.

Trait theory was once a popular alternative to the type-and-drive personality theories of Sigmund Freud and other psychodynamic thinkers. To this day the majority of personality inventories and intelligence tests used by psychologists are based on the assumption that particular traits can be meaningfully named and reliably assessed. This approach to personality theory especially fascinated many of the researchers interested in understanding creativity and the makeup of the creative individual. A large literature grew up chronicling attempts to determine which traits, taken together, added up to creativity in the individual or distinguished creative people from less creative people.

This is a fruitful approach for several reasons. First, it helps us to understand the powerful dynamism present in the artist's personality. It seems contradictory to call an artist both shy and conceited, introverted and extroverted, empathic and self-centered, highly independent and hungry for community—until we realize that all of these qualities can be dynamically present in one and the same person.

Indeed, this dynamism regularly perplexes and buffets the artist. He may begin to consider himself crazy for longing to perform even though public performance frightens him, or neurotic for feeling competent at the piano but incompetent in the world. He may come to possess the vain hope that he can live quietly, like other people, his personality statically integrated in some fashion, and then feel like a failure when the contradictory forces at play within him prevent him from feeling relaxed even for a minute. Once he realizes, however, that this puzzling contradiction *is* his personality, he is better able to accept himself and to understand his motives and actions.

Second, this approach offers us an additional way to understand what it means to call an artist difficult. By that label we usually mean that an artist is narcissistic, high-strung, flamboyant, arrogant, or self-involved, but we can rightly also mean that the artist is difficult in the same sense that a complex novel or string quartet is difficult. The artist lives in a state of greater dynamic tension than the nonartist and so is likely to demand more, desire more, withdraw further into himself, witness better, laugh harder, and bellyache louder. This may not be easy for anyone to take—the artist included—but it is a reflection not of a single quality like selfishness but of a whole array of interactive qualities.

The 10 personality traits we'll examine here have been culled from the creativity literature, from the biographies and autobiographies of artists, from my conversations with artists, and from my work with artist clients. As you read about them, you might profitably ask yourself the following questions and apply them to the guided writing program:

I have made it appear as though my motives were wholly public-spirited. I don't want to leave that as my final impression. All writers are vain, selfish and lazy, and at the very bottom of their motives lies a mystery.

GEORGE ORWELL

- In what sense is it desirable that an artist possess this trait?

- Does an artist in my discipline particularly need this trait?

- What might be the repercussions of having too much of this trait?

- What might be the repercussions of having too little of this trait?

- Is this trait equally useful in my art life and my everyday life?

- If this trait is valuable to me as an artist but an impediment in my everyday life, how will I manage this contradiction?

The creative person is both more primitive and more cultivated than the average person.

FRANK BARRON

The following, then, are the traits we'll consider:

1. Intelligence

2. Introspective stance

3. Discipline

4. Honesty

5. Empathy

6. Self-centeredness

7. Self-direction

8. Assertiveness

9. Resiliency

10. Nonconformity

INTELLIGENCE

How mad should Hamlet be?   SIR JOHN GIELGUD

Intelligence and creativity are not directly correlated, but artists typically possess a keen intelligence. In experimental studies writers have been shown to score higher on a variety of measures of intelligence than do lawyers, doctors, or college professors.

Intelligence, of course, is not a single ability but a cluster of

I think that we are responsible for the universe, but this does not mean that we decide anything.
RENÉ MAGRITTE

abilities. Among them are cognitive flexibility, intellectual playfulness, an analytic capacity, a proficient memory, a rich imagination, and a penchant for originality. Each has its particular value for the artist and each its particular shadow side.

For example, cognitive flexibility, which is the ability to see two or more sides of an issue and especially the ability to tolerate ambiguity, is generally considered one of the hallmarks of the emotionally healthy person. The unpleasant vibration that attends to complexity—to complex international situations, moral situations, or interpersonal situations—causes the average person to seek refuge in slogans and rote positions. Artists, on the other hand, often possess the ability to see many sides of an issue and feel duty-bound to acknowledge and affirm ambiguity.

Artists whose nature or upbringing prevents them from maintaining a wide-ranging flexibility are in danger, in life and in their art, of adopting rigid and airless positions that let no light in. Such artists are less free to experiment, to let go of a genre, to allow ambiguity to enter into their work. Artists more able to tolerate complexity and ambiguity, on the other hand, are themselves confronted by a variety of risks, including the possibility that they will become passive as a result of their excellent understanding. The writer who sees into the heart of his villain as clearly as he sees into the heart of his hero may find his plot slipping away from him, his book coming not to a climax but to an ambiguous ending.

Intellectual playfulness is another aspect of intelligence that artists regularly exhibit. It is a quality apparent, for instance, in the paintings of a Paul Klee or a Joan Miro, the architecture of an Antonio Gaudi, the elegant humor of a Jane Austen, the ironic stance of Dostoevsky's Underground Man, and the music of Mozart. When the painter Chuck Close says, "In my work the blurred areas don't come into focus, but are too large to be ignored," we imagine him spending time focusing and unfocusing images in his mind's eye, just as a child might spend time focusing and unfocusing images in the viewfinder of his first camera.

The less playful artist is in danger of producing art that will be labeled heavy or dull. The more playful artist is in danger of producing art that will be labeled shallow or silly. All artists are destined to veer in one direction or the other, and consequently will have to deal with one label or the other the length of their careers.

If playfulness is a right-brain aspect of intelligence, then a capacity to analyze is the left-brain aspect. It's the capacity reflected in the jazz musician Ornette Coleman's observation, "If I play an F in a tune called Peace, I don't think it should sound the same as an F that is supposed to express sadness." The artist with a capacity to analyze is able to make use of logic, to compare and contrast two styles or two works of art, and to appraise the strengths and weaknesses of his own work.

Only exceptionally rational men can afford to be absurd.
ALLAN GOLDFEIN

Artists relatively lacking in these analytic qualities are like miners who are less able to distinguish among ores. They may happen upon gold and not know it, or they may be seduced by anything that glitters. Artists who are most able to analyze, on the other hand, may be challenged by their own high standards. They may be all too aware of the shallowness of the words their character in the play is forced to speak, too aware of their instrument's imperfections, too aware of their failure to handle green shades subtly. Their hyperawareness may turn into hypercriticality, so that their output dwindles badly. As Dorothy Parker put it, "I can't write five words but that I change seven."

Artists also possess a special sort of memory. For instance, they can hold in memory the essence of all the books they've ever written, without remembering the name of a single character in them. As the writer Molly Keane put it, "If you were to give me some old book of mine, I'd read it with great surprise as though I had no connection with it at all." Your memory is specialized and miraculous. Part of the miracle lies in your ability to let go of what you no longer need to remember, and part of it lies in your refusal to take in what has no value for your art.

Your memory is more selective than the nonartist's. While the nonartist collects facts, you collect glances, glimpses, nuances, images, and tonalities. You remember the essences of performances that stirred you. You have snapshot memories of Gothic churches seen from the train and of schoolgirls huddling in the rain and laughing in the piazza. These are not memories you can draw on to make conversation during the cocktail hour, but they have extraordinary value in your creative life, and this is why you retain them.

That your memory works this way can disable you, however, when it comes to doing business. The splendid image of that Gothic church, which you can bring up at will, is not the image to conjure with as you try to interest an editor in a new idea. For such tasks you must access other parts of your memory banks—parts in which you may have stored precious little information.

Imagination, like memory, is one of the miracles of human consciousness. Its essence is captured in the joyous words of the young Russian writer Natalya Baranskaya: "My imagination takes me so many places—it flies and I fly with it!" But the imaginative life is not available in equal measure to every human being, not even to otherwise intelligent people; nor is the possession of an intense and fiery imagination without its dangers.

If you are an artist with too little imagination, you may produce work that you realize is hackneyed and trite. Or you may pride yourself on your dexterity, fluency, and competency, playing music or writing with commendable technical skill, but you may balk at engaging your own imaginative faculty. The more your personal and cultural traditions demand that you act by the letter of the law, in constrained and safe ways, and insofar as you are not rebellious, the more your imaginative faculties may wither away and the more passive and conforming an artist you may become.

If, however, you have too vivid and untrammeled an imagination, you're in danger of being led about by your imaginings. Withdrawing into a world of fantasy, you may wall yourself off from the world. The artist who lives too deeply in his imagination is less able to find peace than is the artist whose imagination is united with real-world purposes. The painter Francisco Goya's dictum applies here: "Fantasy abandoned by reason produces impossible monsters; united with her, she is the mother of the arts and the origin of their marvels."

Artists, bringing their imagination, analytic ability, memory, and the rest of their intelligence to bear on an artistic question, arrive at original ideas and strive for originality in their work. As the painter Georges Braque put it, "The poet can say: the swallow knifes the sky. Thereby he makes a knife out of a swallow."

Performing artists, too, are eager to bring their personal stamp to a role or a piece, no matter how much they admire some past performer's interpretation. Whereas surgeons want to replicate their past operations and lawyers want to make use of their boilerplate documents and their previously successful arguments, artists typically prefer not to repeat themselves.

The artist in whom this impulse is weak may be satisfied with a

My talent as an artist is to walk across a moor, or place a stone on the ground.

RICHARD LONG

A bit of thread can set a world in motion. I start from something considered dead and arrive at a world. And when I put a title on it, it becomes even more alive.

JOAN MIRÓ

formulaic way of working, which limits his creativity but which may cement his success. The artist in whom this impulse is great will be troubled by his own doubts as to whether his reckless and exhilarating voyage into the unknown will lead him to success or to disaster.

While intelligence is generally valuable to artists and necessary for their success, it is also a risky possession. Artists who are able to look deeply into the mysteries of the universe may feel out of step with their culture and may recognize that their culture fails to prize intelligence. They may do original work that is not understood by anyone. They may experience their artworks as imperfect vehicles for communicating their thoughts.

Working on a character is like spilling a bunch of beads on the floor, and working to get them all on a string.

BARNARD HUGHES

This latter problem may be particularly vexing. The artist must do more than think: he must successfully manipulate his medium in order to convey in concrete fashion all that his intelligence has to offer. He must not only fathom the universe but also find the means of expressing that knowledge. This is a problem akin to the one Sir Isaac Newton confronted when, upon arriving at an intuitive understanding of the motion of the planets, he had to invent calculus in order to prove the correctness of his vision.

The less intelligent artist will perhaps be less bothered by the need to invent calculus, but will also have a less profound understanding of the universe. The highly intelligent artist, on the other hand, may be exactly so bothered and may brood about whether his art has successfully made manifest his ideas. Does his monochromatic painting, his epic poem, his meditative sonata, or his eccentric performance really capture what he had in mind? These are questions that, if long brooded upon, inevitably lead to depression.

INTROSPECTIVE STANCE

It's one thing to be intelligent and another thing to enjoy thinking, to relish the time spent alone with one's thoughts, to happily muse, imagine, and analyze. Artists, who are introspective by nature, typically enjoy spending time in this fashion and may even prefer solitude to the company of others. Able to work by themselves, artists are often lost in a state of dreamy thoughtfulness of the sort described by the painter Hans Hofmann when he wrote, "The first red spot on a white canvas may at once suggest to me the meaning of 'Morning redness,' and from there I dream further with my color." Artists are not introspective—meditative, thoughtful, lost in time and space—because they wish to ignore the world. They're introspective because out of that attitude artistic answers flow.

What I am seeking, in fact, is a motionless movement, something equivalent to what is called the eloquence of silence, or what St. John of the Cross meant, I believe, by dumb music.

JOAN MIRÓ

The artist who is made uncomfortable by this special silence will produce much that is superficial and unrealized. The challenge for the artist who loves this silence with all his heart, on the other hand, is that he must sometimes rejoin the world; the world, after all, also has much to offer.

Artists bring this state of dreamy thoughtfulness with them wherever they go. As the Russian composer Modest Mussorgsky put it, "Whatever speech I hear, no matter who is speaking nor what he says, my mind is already working to find the musical equivalent for such speech." When we liken the artist to a dreamer, we are referring to this aspect of personality.

The artist who has least permission from himself to dream in this fashion may find himself growing tired of art-making, for by not dreaming he is growing old. The thoughtful dreaming of the artist serves as a fountain of youth. The artist who most evidences this thoughtfulness may, however, be relatively lost to the world. Especially if his reveries have an obsessional edge to them, so that he can't escape them—so that he is *always* dreaming of the musical equivalent of speech or *always* calculating how to capture the image before him—then he is bound to find himself intensely distanced from other human beings.

The editor Burton Rascoe wrote, "What no wife of a writer can understand is that a writer is working when he is staring out the window." But of course wives and husbands of artists understand this perfectly well. What they find hard to countenance is the artist's bold delinquency in staring out the window so long and so often, while the needs of those around him go unmet.

DISCIPLINE

Artists have available to them two working states, absorption and concentration, and each feels qualitatively different. When artists are absorbed they are lost in time and space and oblivious to their surroundings. As the dancer Kay Mazzo described it, "You prepare and prepare for a role, but the minute you're onstage, you are lost, lost in what you are doing." This is a trance state in which the artist finds the hours slipping silently past as she writes, paints, practices, or performs.

That this state of absorption is valuable goes without saying. Inspiration flows from it. The choreographer Maurice Bejart wrote, "When I start to work, I have a total vision of the final work—this vision lasting but one second." The absorbed mind sees whole books, whole ballets, whole movies in a flash.

Concentration, on the other hand, is much more of an effortful state. Artists force themselves to concentrate when they feel no particular inspiration and have no real desire to work but nevertheless demand of themselves that they must act in a disciplined fashion. If the artist in a trance works with an unfurrowed brow, the concentrating artist's brow is furrowed and her jaw set. While absorption is the ideal creative state, an artist must also be able to concentrate, to work in the face of distractions, for often absorption will elude her.

Some artists never realize that they must sometimes demand this discipline of themselves. They may simply leave their work too quickly. The concentrating artist, who is too aware of her surroundings, of time passing, of the hardness of the work, and of the silence around her, may announce to herself that she is wasting her time and may leave her work, not realizing that the trance state she desires is only minutes or seconds away.

Every so often I lead all-day workshops for writers who consider themselves blocked. Most have struggled for months—sometimes years—producing little or no writing. In the workshop I present didactic material about creating an environment conducive to writing, and committing to a particular piece of writing, the day's "mission piece." Then, for the majority of the rest of the day, participants write. Invariably, they lose themselves in their writing. When the time for a promised break arrives, I call for another half-hour of writing, and then another—and everyone continues writing, stopping only to shake out a tired arm.

Why is this? How is it that they can easily, fully, and dramatically lose themselves in a workshop setting but not in their own environment?

Part of the answer is perhaps obvious. These writers are ready to

When you're in the theater, you must work incredibly hard. Your life is regimented and you must store up your energy for that one burst of light.

VERA ZORINA

I've found students shocked to learn that it can take me three years to finish a poem.

CAROLYN FORCHE

work; by committing to the workshop, by publicly acknowledging their blockage, by setting aside a Sunday, they've readied themselves to write. Perhaps the supportive group feeling also encourages them (although I do the same work in individual sessions, with similar results). It may be that by sitting with them for those hours, not writing and not daydreaming and doing *nothing* except holding the idea that the group will write, I make it possible for them to remain undistracted and absorbed.

But something of a mystery remains. If blocked artists are so close to working in absorbed fashion, so close that after an introductory hour they can work steadily all day long in a workshop setting, what prevents them from making that same leap to absorption in their own home? It is a mystery that a long discussion of blocks would still not answer. But it appears as if the gulf between the productive artist and the blocked or frustrated artist may in reality be a tiny one—while, at the same time, remaining enormously difficult to cross.

HONESTY

I still put romance in films when I can, but the realities of materialism, corruption, and injustice interfere. I try to reflect how I see things, not create a fantasy world.

RAINER WERNER FASSBINDER

You have the desire to honestly communicate the truth as you understand it. Frequently you're the only one in your neighborhood making such an effort. You're the one who must tell your grandmother's story, your father's story, or your own story as best you can. And since the truth is frequently painful and rarely profitable, few except you are interested in championing it.

In this regard you are society's primary holder of positive human values. You agree with the visual artist Ben Shahn, who said, "I hate injustice, and I hope to go on hating it all my life." Standing apart, holding your own counsel, attuned to both the beautiful and the moral, you are the one able and willing to point out the naked emperor, the stench coming from the closet, the starvation right around the corner, the colors of the far mountains as the eye really sees them.

In all of this you make judgments as an independent observer, not as the third vice-president of a corporation or an assistant deputy district attorney. Many dangers naturally attach to this position of independent observer, not the least of which is managing the pain and indignation that come with clear sight.

There are cynical artists who withhold the truth from their art in order to gain an audience and make money, just as there are cynical clergy who preach while neither loving nor believing. But the analogy reminds us that the cynical artist risks great pain when he acts faithlessly.

You never paint what you see or think you see. You paint with a thousand vibrations the blow that struck you.
NICHOLAS DE STAËL

Other artists will tell only a fraction of what they know to be true, or will alter or subvert the truth, because of self-censorship, a desire to be popular, or a desire not to offend. As the French writer Jean Cocteau put it, "After you have written a thing and you reread it, there is always the temptation to remove its poison, to blunt its sting." Elmore Leonard, the popular mystery writer, said, "I leave out the parts that people skip." These are both manifestations of the impulse to have and keep an audience, an impulse the righteous pastor in his pulpit also understands.

But as the visual artist Les Levine put it, "Artists are going to die like anyone else—do they want to leave behind a lot of work they don't believe in?" Every artist internally debates this issue. Should he sing the equivalent of a jingle or the equivalent of a hymn? Should he sing in harmony or protest injustice? Should he tell the dark truth about the alcoholism in his family or entertain his fans with his command of language?

As the visual artist Martha Rossler wrote, "The main effort of most of mass media is to get you to succumb to magic and lose your critical ability. I want the work to be more of an irritant." But if truth is an irritant, how is the truth-telling artist to survive? You may never frame the question to yourself in so many words, but you must nevertheless address it the length of your career.

The artist who most keenly feels the need to tell the truth will make the fewest concessions, will resist falsification the most, and may, like a scorned prophet, find himself vilified and misunderstood. The artist who is more accommodating, on the other hand, who more willingly embraces the commercial and the false, may himself be embraced but may wonder if he is squandering his precious time on earth.

EMPATHY

One actor does not cry on the stage, yet he makes the audience cry. Another actor is bathed in bitter tears, but the audience does not respond.

MICHAEL SHCHEPTKIN

I seem preoccupied with our collective past, and our individual pasts—things that happened to us at an earlier point of life which may have a bearing on what we do now.

DAVID HWANG

While the powerful artist is also the self-centered artist, it is not paradoxical to suggest that he is also more empathic than the next person. This is not to say that artists are necessarily compassionate or sympathetic. They may be; for the ability to empathize makes it easier to sympathize, but empathy is not compassion. It is rather a certain kind of insight, an ability to correctly identify the thoughts and feelings—even the whole inner reality—of another person.

The artist less able to empathize is perhaps better equipped to maintain a single-minded and self-serving stance with regard to his career. He may feel comfortable writing formulaic fiction, because the one-dimensionality required of his characters suits him perfectly. He may, in his business negotiations, take good care of his own interests, feeling content to remain in his own shoes. He may also recognize, however, that his art does not run deep.

An actor's a guy who, if you ain't talking about him, ain't listening.

MARLON BRANDO

The artist more able to empathize is at considerable risk, for he is likely to be severely buffeted by the plight of others—indeed, by the plight of the whole human race. As the artist recording images of starvation or the vanishing wilderness, as the writer of existential fiction, as the composer writing in a minor key, he may find personal happiness elusive as his attention is drawn to human misery.

While the artist who empathizes least is challenged to act decently, the artist who empathizes most is challenged to maintain sufficient boundaries between himself and others. Then he can dare to experience another's reality without drowning in that reality.

SELF-CENTEREDNESS

Of course, to start with, I love all my pupils. Then I find the talented ones. They are always the most arrogant.

ALEXANDRA DANILOVA

One of the more troubling paradoxes of the artist's personality is that artists, champions of human values and heroic in their journey, able to admire and to analyze, are nevertheless often arrogant creatures. Perhaps the simple explanation for this is that the self-trust and self-direction that artists require, amounting to a healthy respect for their own vision and values, equal a powerful self-centeredness. They demand of themselves that they remain firmly in their own shoes, even at the expense of the hurt feelings of others. As the writer Susan Braudy put it, "I'm basically a treacherous person with no sense of loyalty. I'd write openly about my sainted mother's sex life for art."

When one likes something passionately, the rest is excluded from consideration, naturally.
PIERRE SOULAGES

The artist not equipped with this necessary arrogance will be repeatedly sidetracked or subverted by the agendas of others. He will lack a sufficient sense of purpose, will frequently stall and block, and will bring a nagging passivity to his art career. His resolve to do great art may remain a potent idea only, a kind of unexpended force in his body. He is likely to accomplish much less than he otherwise might, support others rather than find support for himself, attempt the small rather than the large, and rebound less well from rejection.

The self-centered artist, on the other hand, is challenged to remember that he is neither god nor superman, but a human being with human limitations. He hasn't the time to turn every idea into a book, the ability to top each work with a greater one, the energy to toil ceaselessly at his art, nor the right to trample others as he pursues his goals. If he mistakes or oversteps these limits he will put himself in harm's way and may find himself struck down by his own obsessional energy, by burnout, by depression, by self-abuse, or by the angry complaints of those whose rights he has cavalierly trampled.

SELF-DIRECTION

Anybody who makes public art has to invent the territory as he or she walks through it.

MARY MISS

Just as the restless, committed, curious, and perhaps obsessed explorer follows the river from bend to bend, shooting rapids and pulling himself out of the water, so the self-directed artist launches himself on an exploratory art journey. He judges which fork in the river he will take, when he will rest and when he will push on, who he will take with him or whether he will travel alone. While he doesn't possess unlimited freedom as he journeys, bound as he is by the demands of his personality, by his time and place, and by circumstances beyond his control, he does possess unrestricted permission from himself to explore every available avenue.

The passionate act breaks free, through its very dynamism.

PAUL-EMILE BORDUAS

The contemporary artist must especially direct and trust himself, because he lives in a constantly changing art environment. The performance piece, the installation piece, the wrapped building, the computer artwork are all aspects of an art vocabulary that resembles no previous one. As Pablo Picasso put it, "Beginning with Van Gogh, we are all, in a measure, autodidacts. Painters no longer live within a tradition and so each of us must re-create an entire language."

The artist who insufficiently directs and trusts himself is likely to fail to find his own voice. This failure is particularly dangerous in an era lacking the safety net of tradition. The less self-directing artist is probably best characterized as ambivalent. He finds it hard to choose among his projects, finds it hard to settle on one medium or one style, finds it hard to choose between tackling commercial or personal art. He may easily block at every turn.

If he will not choose which fork in the river to take, who will? From where will the message come? Will it be found at a workshop? He may attend many workshops. Will it be found at the foot of a mentor? He may search for a teacher, a spiritual leader, a motivator. Will it be found in group wisdom? He may join a church or a movement in order to receive guidance.

The supremely self-directed artist, on the other hand, may find himself unable to countenance other people's opinions and feedback. This intolerance causes him to experience great loneliness and joylessness, the terrible fruits of this existential stance. He possesses tremendous passion for artmaking, and he understands his medium as well as anyone can, for he has really explored it. But he is likely to be haunted by what he has not explored, perhaps love and intimacy especially. As one composer exclaimed bitterly about himself: "Beethoven can write music, thank God—but he can do nothing else on earth."

ASSERTIVENESS

When a new man faces the orchestra—from the way he walks up the steps to the podium and opens his score—before he even picks up his baton—we know whether he is the master or we.

FRANZ STRAUSS

Some traits in the artist's personality appear to be passive, and others aggressive. The artist's introspective stance, for example, lends a passive quality to his life, but side by side with that passivity is an assertiveness that logically flows from his passion, self-centeredness, and self-direction. This assertiveness is part of the necessary arrogance of the artist.

We look for new sonorities, new intervals, new forms. Where it will lead, I don't know. I don't want to know. It would be like knowing the date of my death.

PIERRE BOULEZ

If asserting yourself makes you feel anxious, frightened, or guilty, you will hesitate to argue with the director who's cut your best monologue, to take to task the editor who's failed to deliver on his promise to champion your new book. You will be unable to aggressively forge new art.

If, on the other hand, you're especially eager to assert yourself, you may discover that your undeniable power is not a great gift to bring to relationships; it may make them feel as abrasive as sandpaper. You're likely to regularly alienate everyone around you.

Related to assertiveness is an ability to take risks. Every medium is risky, and a certain fearlessness, which may or may not be in evidence elsewhere in your life, is required as you leap across the stage, allow your watercolors to drip perilously down the expensive paper, or determine to spend the next three years working on a novel about whales.

The more fearful and conforming you are, the more you'll see danger as you approach your art-making. If, on the other hand, you're willing to take *any* risk, you're in danger of manifesting too great a heroism. To take one example, you may ignore the demands of the marketplace and produce mighty work that no one wants. Your epic poem, heroically created, may remain forever in a corner of your drawer. You will have asserted yourself, but to what end?

RESILIENCY

If your mind breaks because of the training, all is lost.

PAOLO BORTOLUZZI

I have always been driven by some distant music—a battle hymn, no doubt—for I have been at war from the beginning.

BETTE DAVIS

All art is a revolt against man's fate.

ANDRÉ MALRAUX

Artists must be survivors. They must earn a living or find enough support to stay alive. They must bounce back from their depressions and return to the fray after repeated rejections, after their shows close, after their novels are remaindered. To meet the challenges they face requires great resiliency.

Everyone must bounce back from disappointments, but not everyone chooses so adventurous and challenging a life. Checks for the civil servant and the tenured teacher arrive each month. The soldier and the shop clerk may spend months engaged in routine tasks. But the artist runs risks at every turn.

The writer James Dickey said, "We have always had a tradition in America of hounding our artists to death. The best poets of my generation are all suicides." Sinclair Lewis wrote, "Every compulsion is put on writers to become safe, polite, obedient, and sterile." Whether the challenges come from without, as Dickey and Lewis propose, or from within, the artist must pray that he is elastic enough to bounce back from each jarring drop to the pavement.

NONCONFORMITY

Good rock stars take drugs, molest policemen, and epitomize fun, freedom, and bullshit. Can the busiest anarchist on your block match that?

RICHARD NEVILLE

Nonconformity is best thought of as the sum total of the ways in which artists, resolved to manifest their individuality, revolt against prevailing customs and beliefs. Both the guitar-smashing rock star and the reclusive Emily Dickinson epitomize this quality.

Sometimes, for instance, artists may espouse the most conservative of values, as Dostoevsky did in arguing for a return to religious orthodoxy. Yet to call such an artist "conforming" is to make a fundamental mistake. Such artists are rebelling in their own principled ways against what Melville called the "colorless, all-color atheism" of the average man, just as the angry comic or the revolutionary painter is revolting against the status quo.

We have the sense that powerful artists are always nonconformists and rebels, even though one may pledge allegiance to God, another to humankind, and a third to the devil. Artists who rebel the least, who are architects of rather than opponents of the status quo, may fit neatly into their society but may not speak or know their own mind. Artists who are entirely rebellious and nonconforming, on the other hand, are bound to upset everyone—themselves especially, since they have so much of the whirlwind within them.

Art disturbs, science reassures.
GEORGES BRAQUE

STRATEGIES

Personality is a puzzle, made more puzzling by the fact that we're never able to investigate ourselves in completely objective fashion. But as limited as we are, we nevertheless can draw many inferences about ourselves by examining our thoughts and feelings, by noting and analyzing our behaviors, by studying how people interact with us, and by reflecting on past events. There are many paths to self-understanding, personal growth, and healing. Use the following strategies as first steps on your journey of self-exploration.

Use guided writing to isolate core personality issues. Some of the events and dynamics in our lives are so profoundly traumatic that if we fail to address them and fail to recover, as best we can, from their effects, we risk living severely impaired lives. The wounds left from having parents who were alcoholic, abusive emotionally, physically, or sexually, mentally disturbed, controlling, withdrawn, or unavailable rarely heal of their own accord. Use the following questions, and others that you create, to help you begin to address these core issues.

1. Who am I? What is my real identity (or what are my many identities)? Who or what am I describing when I talk about my "self"?

2. What are my most pressing personality issues?

3. What was the single most damaging aspect of growing up in my family?

4. Was I an abused child? How did that abuse affect and shape me? Do I now abuse myself? Am I self-destructive or dependent on alcohol or drugs?

Friends and pupils often have heard me say that in my ideal music school, psychoanalysis would be a mandatory part of the general curriculum.

CLAUDIO ARRAU

5. Am I in charge of my life? What prevents me from taking charge?

6. How would I describe the artist's personality? Do I see it as primarily a healthy or unhealthy one?

7. What makes me an artist? Do I possess the qualities I think an artist needs?

8. How does my artist's personality help or hinder me in the rest of my life?

9. What do I most need to change about myself?

10. How will I investigate my personality? Is it time to start personal psychotherapy, intensive journaling, or a 12-step program? Should I take a few psychology or counseling classes, begin a mindful meditation practice, or write an analytical autobiography? What specific efforts will I make in order to better understand myself?

Use your art medium as a tool for growth and healing. The following exercises, which are adapted from Evelyn Virshup's *Right Brain People in a Left Brain World,* employ visual media. Also create exercises for yourself that make use of the art medium you know best.

Visual Media Exercises

1. Close your eyes and fantasize a chasm. Design a way of crossing that chasm, considering that you have every means known (or even unknown as yet) at your disposal. Draw your solution.

   Observe your solution silently. Note the size of the chasm (problem) and the inventiveness, efficiency, and safeness of the solution. If it is a rope bridge, is it tied securely?

If it is a huge chasm, does that represent how you feel about the problem? Did you reach the solution with little thought, or give it a great deal of consideration?

Observe nonjudgmentally. See if you can reach new conclusions about crossing this chasm—if you can come up with new, more varied ways of coping with problems.

2. Fold a large piece of paper into quarters. Silently draw on the first quarter a symbolic representation of *"Where do I come from?"* After a few moments, draw on the second quarter, *"Where do I want to go?"* Next, draw symbolically *"What is in my way?"* Finally, draw a representation of *"How am I going to overcome my obstacles?"*

Grow aware of what you perceive as the obstacles confronting you and your own solutions to overcoming these obstacles.

3. Take a fantasy trip with closed eyes. Walking along a country road with a fishing pole over your shoulder, you come upon a stream. Cast a line into the water and, after a few moments, reel in what you have caught in your fantasy. With your eyes open, draw what you have caught. Now write a story about the object at the end of the line. In a sense you will be talking about yourself and how you feel about your life at the moment. How do you see yourself?

4. Create two animals on one piece of paper. They don't have to look like anything you've ever seen before. Take about 10 minutes for the drawing. Describe the animals you have drawn. Write down three adjectives about them. Note what expressions the animals have. Are you able to make up something the animals might want to say to each other? Can you write free verse or fantasy about what the animals say or do?

The second animal often has contrasting qualities from the first. This exercise generally reveals polarities, contrasts, or conflicts within a person; it will show different, sometimes opposing facets of personality. The absence of hands or feet may suggest helplessness; the absence of a mouth suggests difficulty in communicating. Observe and learn from the fantasy animals you've created.

An artist should never lose sight of the thing as a whole. He who puts too much into details will find that the thread which holds the whole thing together will break.

FRÉDÉRIC CHOPIN

*You must remain your own
witness, marking well
everything that happens in this
world, never shutting your eyes
to reality.*

ETTY HILLESUM

5. The use of clay, modeled in silence with eyes closed, is an effective way to become aware of one's self. As you feel the clay and squeeze, pound, jab, caress, or do what you wish to it, consider that this material is really you. Say to yourself, "This is me, this is how I am feeling now." Spend 10 to 15 minutes experiencing the power of clay with no coiled pots, ashtrays, or other goals in mind; just silently feel the clay with your eyes closed. Then study the form of the clay with open eyes, looking for new images to suggest themselves. If you intuitively become aware of a glimmer of an image, grasp it and develop it. This is your metaphoric mind speaking to you.

Examine each of the ten personality traits discussed in this chapter. Single out the one trait that you feel is most important for you to better understand. How does it operate in your life? Do you want more of it or less of it, or more of it at certain times and less of it at others? Look at two personality traits together. Would you like a slightly different balance between them? A radically different balance? In your present circumstances, for instance, is it important that you not empathize with the director, who perhaps has good reasons for taking away your solo song in the third act, and work instead on assertively retaining that solo? Or, conversely, is it more appropriate that you restrain your assertiveness and practice empathy?

Examine each of the 10 traits in turn. Define each for yourself. Use them as subject matter for a series of paintings, songs, or poems. Treat them as puzzle pieces and familiarize yourself with the ways they interrelate and interact in your personality makeup.

Examine the idea that there are human limits. Do you believe there are human limits or do you believe that everything is attainable? What are your personal limits? Which of them can be stretched? How might you stretch them? Which can't be stretched?

There is much that cannot be accomplished in life. Whole novels will not work. Whole years may go by with no offers of important acting work. Many challenges will confront you that you will not be able to adequately meet. This is your truth, and every other person's truth as well. Learn your limits and begin to accept them, even as you struggle to stretch them in order to manifest your greatness.

Of Moods *and* Madness

The funny part, the laughter, is given to the audience, but the come-dian is left with the bitter dregs.

JACK CARTER

Depression is a disorder of mood, so mysteriously painful and elu-sive in the way it becomes known to the self—to the mediating intellect—as to verge close to being beyond description. It thus re-mains nearly incomprehensible to those who have not experienced it in its extreme form, although the gloom, "the blues" which people go through occasionally and associate with the general hassle of everyday existence are of such prevalence that they do give many individuals a hint of the illness in its catastrophic form.

WILLIAM STYRON

THAT MANY CREATIVE AND performing artists are visited by severe depression remains much of a secret, even though the biographies of artists, anecdotal and clinical evidence, and recent psychological studies speak to that truth.

Artists are certainly not alone in this. A great many people suf-fer from bouts of depression. Studies indicate that from 4 to 10 per-cent of adult women and from 2 to 4 percent of adult men suffer from depression at any given time. Many more are confounded by the blues. But a far higher percentage of creative and performing artists suffer from debilitating depressions. Recent studies suggest figures of 30, 40, 50 percent, and higher.

One study by Dr. Samuel Janus of 55 successful comedians concluded that "the vast majority of funny men are sad men." Dr. Janus reported that most of the comedians he studied were severely depressed offstage. "There are numerous indications," he wrote, "that many of our top comedians, if one listens to their routines, are really crying out loud."

It seems to me, as an actress for all of my life, that actors as a race are prone to depression more consistently than most people. We are a race of depressives.

RITA GAM

Dr. Nancy Andreasen conducted a study that looked first at 15 writers associated with the University of Iowa Writers' Workshop and was later expanded to include 15 additional writers. Dr. Andreasen concluded that 43 percent of the writers evidenced some degree of manic-depressive illness; a full 80 percent sought treatment for mood disorders; and two of the 30 committed suicide.

Dr. Kay Jamison, in a study of 47 British artists and writers, found that 38 percent had sought treatment for mood disorders, compared to fewer than 2 percent in the general population. Half the poets in the group, and two-thirds of the playwrights, sought treatment.

These and similar studies suggest that creative and performing artists are more often challenged to deal with depression than are people who are not drawn to the arts. William Styron, in his memoir on his own incapacitating depression, names some of his famous fellow sufferers: Virginia Woolf, Randall Jarrell, Sylvia Plath, Jack London, Anne Sexton, Ernest Hemingway, Hart Crane. Among musicians we might list Rossini, Schumann, and Beethoven.

Fred Cutter points out the unambiguous suicidal imagery in the works of 500 well-known painters, among them Jackson Pollock (*Ten Ways of Killing Myself*), Andy Warhol (*The Suicide*), Edvard Munch (*The Suicide*), and Paul Klee (*Suicide on the Bridge*). It seems that the artist's mood is often a black one, black enough at times that he considers suicide.

Depressive episodes often begin early in the artist's life, sometimes in childhood, often in adolescence. Isolated, sensitive, feeling different from his peers, the artist is frequently the victim of depression as a teenager. The poet Maxine Kumin explained:

> I was a very lonely kid, very introspective. I felt very much at odds with my environment and my culture. I was just a real loner, taking my solace in books. I think I was terribly, terribly moody as an adolescent. I had very dark moods. I was very depressed.

Is there a single reason why artists are so likely to be visited by depression? Almost certainly not. There are, first of all, too many sorts of depressions. Some are called neurotic, others existential; some are associated with mania and as such are considered part of a special cyclical disorder (called manic-depressive illness or bipolar disorder). The depressions called major, like William Styron's, are sometimes accompanied by florid psychotic features.

Some forms of depression may have a significant biological or genetic link, as is suspected of the depression that occurs in manic-depressive illness. Some depressions seem more rooted in fury, some in self-hatred, some in loneliness, some in sadness. Others seem triggered by envy, boredom, or hopelessness. Some seem in a sense adaptive—the depressed person conserving psychic energy, withdrawing from the pressures of the world, and taking a break from attempting to master anxieties.

In the life of an artist, the incidents that can bring on depression are too numerous to catalog: the rejection of a latest poem, the good luck of a fellow poet, a loveless visit home, the rent coming due, the loss of a new love, roaches appearing in the refrigerator. As many different self-disparaging and despairing thoughts can bring on depression as there are stars in the sky. Indeed, the very look of the starry sky can bring on an existential depression.

We might identify a characteristic artist's personality and make the case that something in that personality is the key to this high incidence of depression—say, that artists are more introspective than the next person (which is usually the case), or more open to experience and therefore more sensitive, or that they typically experienced loss or abandonment in childhood. Still we would be left with too many important individual differences to draw any conclusions.

One artist might be the more ambitious, and so more depressed if her career foundered. Another artist might be more open to experience, and so more exposed to pain in the world. A third might be more intelligent, and so more prone to existential depressions. I harbor the suspicion that the many personality traits we reviewed in chapter 2, which appear so often and to such a marked degree in the makeup of the artist, open the artist up to the possibility of depression. Some combination of these traits may even, taken together, turn out to be a kind of blueprint for depression, although we don't know this for certain.

Suffering can not be paid for in the currency of a few pictorial "good deeds."

PIERRE ALECHINSKY

But whatever the sources of your moods, you're bound, when you're depressed, to suffer from some or many of the following: sadness; boredom; fatigue; insomnia or excessive sleep; significant weight loss or gain; loss of hope; indecisiveness; diminished interest and diminished pleasure in your usual activities, including artmaking; diminished sex drive; irritability; inertia; restlessness; diminished ability to concentrate; loss of self-esteem; morbidity; recurrent thoughts of death; and suicidal ideation.

During recent decades much of actor training has come close to psychotherapy because both have similar goals: getting emotions out into the open and getting in touch with self.

MARSH CASSADY

Each feature of the depressive episode challenges you. To overcome your insomnia you may begin taking sleeping pills and develop a habit. To combat your inertia you may opt for stimulant drugs. Artists often turn to drugs to combat their depression. James Taylor, the singer and songwriter, who described his bouts of severe depression as "unexplainable black moods," said, "There's a type of despair that I experience as being very deep. In the past my tendency was to crawl in a hole and poison myself, intoxicate myself."

The artist who becomes involved with drugs on a regular basis is likely to experience depressive episodes that are then related to his drug use. The singer-songwriter Paul Simon described such a period in his life, while he lived in London:

> It was very unsatisfying, the drug use, although I started out loving it. But at the end, it was bad. I couldn't write. It made me depressed. It made me antisocial. It brought out nastiness in me. When I'd deal with people while I was high, I'd listen to them and think "Boy, he's really stupid. That guy's really phony. Phony smile, phony everything." And the same thing with me. I'd say, "Oh, boy, you really are ridiculous. Absolutely ridiculous."

Artists are regularly troubled by depression and by the ineffective or self-abusing coping mechanisms they employ to fight their depression. But their lighter moods often prove troublesome as well, for the "up" artist is frequently manic and neither happy nor at ease in the universe.

THE MANIC ARTIST

For many artists manic episodes or manic-edged moods, like depressive episodes, begin early in life. The artist may experience clinical mania, a state with a potent pressurized feel to it, characterized by pseudoeuphoria, irritability, grandiosity, a decreased need for sleep, an increased activity level, a racing mind, and sometimes hallucinations and delusions. Or he may experience hypomania, a milder and less impairing version of the disorder, which less divorces the artist from reality. Most likely, he will experience an even milder mania, but one that will distinctly color his moods and give him the sense that he is racing along, perhaps in decent spirits but under real pressure.

I had this driving ambition— I was going to be a simply smashing actor.
LAURENCE OLIVIER

Your intense, driven, and sometimes enthusiastic way of being may have a manic feel to it. This restrained mania may become one of your most characteristic moods: your mind racing, hands moving, dreams vivid, art more alive to you. The visual artist Patricia Tavenner said, "My head and my hands never stop." The poet Richard Wilbur told of fellow poet Theodore Roethke, "He would arrive at the door bearing cases of champagne and silver dollars for the children, and when he felt himself getting too manic he would spend an hour or more under our shower, cooling down."

I attribute part of this manic edge to the fact that artists are gambling every day. You gamble that you will be spotted in your present small role and discovered, or that the right magazine will publish your story, or that you haven't made a foolish choice in pursuing poetry instead of medicine. You also gamble each time you start to do your art. Art-making is one of the greatest gambles of all. As Helen Frankenthaler, the visual artist, put it, "No matter how fine or meticulous or tortured a picture may be in execution, the risk or chance of its working or not working is always there, no matter what the method."

It is a high-stakes gamble, after all, to work with all of your being on something that has so great a chance of failing. Alberto Giacometti, the sculptor, wrote, "To my terror the sculptures became smaller and smaller. Then they became so minuscule that often with a final stroke of the knife they disappeared into dust."

To face such a life of risk-taking, you have to rev yourself up. In fact, a kind of mania is the predominant mood in many art communities. As the visual artist Sandy Walker said of the contemporary New York art scene, "Living in New York is like living with your finger in the socket."

Who can sustain such intensity in their work? Not to crash after a painting or writing jag or a brilliant performance seems almost more unnatural than crashing. As Georges Braque said upon seeing Picasso's *Les Demoiselles d'Avignon* for the first time, "It is as if someone had drunk kerosene so he could spit fire." After spitting fire, what is the artist to do? Sit and smile contentedly?

Passionate when you're really working, moved by the performances you see or the books you read, aroused by color, excited by the look of your city, stirred by the possibility of applause, anxious, your nerve ends exposed, you may live manically; and you may be, at your most energized and vital, a person ready to plummet.

The torpor of human impulses is a necessary background to the divine shaft of light, as silence is broken by a cry.

OSKAR KOKOSCHKA

This alternation of intense moods, from mania to depression, from enthusiastic encounter to discouraged retreat, may be the natural way of the artist, the creator, the inventor. Michael Kalil, the architect and artist, struggling to design a scale model of his habitation module, said, "First I got excited, then I got depressed. My background disintegrated: there was no up and down." The author J. D. Salinger, in an autobiographical note, described himself as "alternately cynical and Polyanna-like, happy and morose, affectionate and indifferent." The writer E. L. Doctorow offered up the following advertisement for manic depression: "The writer's life is a daily crisis. Very great ups and downs. I would like to qualify as a full-blown manic depressive, because any state that is really realized would be very productive for a writer."

Whether this alternation of mood is inevitable or not, whether it mimics manic-depressive illness or is just a distant cousin, you will be challenged to deal with it more often than you might wish—maybe even constantly.

THE ARTIST AND ANXIETY

As if your manic and depressive moods weren't burdensome enough, you're also likely to experience severe anxiety. All of us must wrestle with anxious feelings and the physical and emotional consequences of stress and anxiety. The problem of anxiety seems to be growing, prompting the psychiatrist Barry Blackwell to write, "We can predict that with the arrival of the millennium the whole of America will be taking tranquilizers."

In addition to the anxiety inherent in simply being human, as an artist you are also confronted by performance anxiety. The painter and the musician, the writer and the actor alike are performing. Your performances will be judged, and the specter of embarrassing failure haunts many an artist's life. In a 1987 survey of 2,212 professional classical musicians, for instance, 24 percent complained of experiencing severe performance anxiety. Twenty-seven percent used beta-blocker tranquilizers to help ease their anxiety.

Much anxiety also wells up in the artist when it comes to taking care of business. This is a form of anxiety I see hundreds of times in my clinical work with artists. Meetings with gallery owners, curators, literary agents, publishers, casting directors, and other representatives of the business end of art, because these meetings feel so momentous and fraught with possibility, frequently terrify artists.

Is it really necessary to encumber oneself with this anxiety to bring to life things that have no apparent reason for stirring?
POL BURY

On top of being human, a performer, and, of necessity, a businessperson, you also possess personality attributes that invite anxiety. You accept as your stock-in-trade a sensitivity to the doings of the world—and the world can be a fearful place. Fascinated by the human condition, alive to the historical moment, you are one of our culture's witnesses. One of your goals is to speak through your art about what you witness, and witnessing makes you more vulnerable to feelings of anxiety.

This is both your burden and your gift to society. As the Russian-American visual artists Vitaly Komar and Aleksandr Melamid put it, "It is our fate and our misfortune that we live in history. An artist who doesn't know history paints like a cow, because cows have no memory."

The artist wants to witness. If he desired that less, or if the world appreciated his witnessing more and criticized and rejected him less, he might feel less anxious. It may be, as the visual artist Louise Nevelson said, that "all great innovations are built on rejections." But that fact does nothing to help quiet the artist's nerves or raise his spirits. That you are striving, that you have dreams and ambitions, are sources of anxiety. As Paul Klee put it, "He who strives will never enjoy this life peacefully." Willem de Kooning made the same point with a different aphorism: "Art never seems to make me peaceful or pure."

ANGER

Artists often feel rageful. Anger, in fact, may be one of their dominant moods.

Part of my disease is anger.

JIM CODY

*When I paint, I liberate
monsters, my own monsters, and
for these I am responsible. One
does not choose the content, one
submits to it.*

PIERRE ALECHINSKY

What, exactly, do you rage against? That you are poor, unrecognized, and isolated? That art is hard to do and that you can't stop doing it? That your relationships frequently don't work; that you feel a part of no community; that you are visited by depression? You may be furious at the marketplace: furious that popular movies are homogenized fairy tales, that the audience for real work is so small, and that the audience for your own brand of art is an even smaller fraction of that already small number.

You may also be angered by your critics, by academics, by theorists. Auguste Renoir once exploded, "Don't ask me whether painting ought to be subjective or objective. I don't give a damn!" The visual artist David Smith said, "We've let anthropologists, philosophers, historians, connoisseurs, mercenaries, and everybody else tell us what art is or what it should be. I think we ought to very simply let it be what the artist says it is."

You may also rage at the same things that anger other human beings—that your grandparents died in the Holocaust, that your great-great-grandparents were kept in chains. Gender issues may infuriate you, a fury sarcastically expressed by the painters Larry Rivers and Frank O'Hara: "All we painters hate women; unless we hate men." As the novelist Marilyn French put it:

> I think women are very, very angry. I don't think people probably have any idea how angry women are, because women are trained to be nice. Women are extremely angry. And if my books have anger in them, it's because that anger is out there in the world.

EMOTIONAL DISTURBANCES AND MADNESS

As these affective and anxiety states grow more severe in a given artist, they may constellate into certain recognizable syndromes. One artist may manifest his anxiety by experiencing severe and prolonged pain that appears to have no organic cause; the clinical syndrome is known as psychogenic pain disorder. A second artist might manifest his anxiety by engaging in repetitive behaviors, such as washing his hands a hundred times a day; this clinical syndrome is known as obsessive-compulsive disorder. A third artist may manifest his anxiety by needing to avoid crowds and public places, a clinical syndrome known as agoraphobia.

These individuals, while impaired and in pain, do not as a rule break with reality, but some artists do. In our exploration of the emotional well-being of artists it's important that we consider the matter of madness and the artist's relationship to it.

The individual with the childhood history, personality, identity, aspirations, and inner makeup of the artist almost certainly is at greater risk to go mad than is the next person. Madness appears to run at the rate of about 1 percent in all cultures at all times. Even if the rate were no higher for creative and performing artists, at least tens of thousands of our artists would find themselves severely challenged to remain sane. But the rate of madness is almost certainly higher than 1 percent among artists.

While this is a controversial statement—indeed, nothing less than a mouthful, and not easily amenable to scientific proof—it is nevertheless a sensible assertion. For whatever else it may be, madness is in significant measure a special kind of intense acting-in, a departure from everyday reality to the insulated battlefield of a stormy inner reality. The artist, self-absorbed, intense, and thriving on his own inner life, regularly lives closer to such a departure than do his less introverted, less imaginative, and less agitated brothers and sisters.

Because the artist experiences such intensity in his inner life, he is at greater risk to go mad. The intensity that flows in a pattern of highs and lows—of creative effort and lassitude, enthusiasm and depression, fruitful hours and blocked hours, the birth of a project and its death, performances and the aftermath of performances—subjects the artist to disturbances and disorders of mood. When that intensity grows so great that it cannot be discharged in any usual way, then the artist begins to resemble a boiler about to explode.

This image from mechanics is not meant to seduce us into ignoring the psychology of the matter, for we are talking about human beings going mad, not boilers exploding. The image may remind us, though, of how tumultuous are the forces within the person we call mad. Even the person who descends slowly into madness, declining a little each year, growing a little more eccentric, less capable, and less communicative, began the descent with a roiling storm blowing through him, overpowering his limited human ability to prevent a descent into madness.

We were all a little nuts in the Dorsey band. Ziggy Elman, a great trumpet player. Joe Bushkin on piano, another nut. The Pied Pipers were all crazed, every one of them. Connie Haines was on the verge of becoming nuts.

BUDDY RICH

What Is Madness?

It would seem appropriate to continue this discussion of the artist's relationship to madness with a sensible definition of madness—or, in clinical language, of psychosis. But it's a bit of folly to define something we do not understand. We do not understand whether, and in what measure, the individual contributes by his thoughts and feelings to that state of deterioration, personality disorganization, disordered thinking, or regression we call psychosis. We do not know whether the psychotic is visited by madness, as one is unexpectedly visited by relatives; or whether he makes his own madness, as one contributes to one's own high blood pressure by failing to handle stress effectively; or whether he invites his own madness, as one invites a friend to dinner. We do not know what part of madness is hereditary, what part environmental. We do not know if brain irregularities cause schizophrenia or are the result of schizophrenia.

I am one individual, imprisoned in myself, hanged and condemned to solitary in my own ego for life.

               JEAN TUNGUELY

What we do know is that the insane person can sometimes maintain knowledgeable contact with the world, can make rational and subtle calculations with respect to that outside world, even while he appears to be manifestly insane. This fact, derived from retrospective reports of the formerly insane and from studies that conclude that madmen can act sane in order to get the institutional benefits and privileges they really want, suggests that the madman is more in contact with the world than he lets on or than we might think. His madness, terrible to behold, is perhaps more like a screen than a wall, or more like a wall with chinks in it. It may be that the psychotic has not so much disintegrated as retreated into his psychotic state; retreated, as the psychiatrist Malcolm Bowers put it, from sanity.

From that place of retreat he still observes the world. One may, for instance, burn a catatonic schizophrenic's fingers without him flinching. But at a later date, if he's so inclined, he can report on every nuance of every gesture made by the one who burned him. This hardly means that the madman is playing a wild charade. It means rather that we must wonder where he is and what he is doing, how he got there and if his wires are crossed or his soul disturbed.

We understand madness so little that clinicians define it by how it looks rather than by what it is. If you looked a certain way—if you laughed inappropriately, coined new words, complained of a dull thud in your chest, failed a mental-status exam, and hoarded food—you, too, would be called mad. If, especially, you demonstrated one of the hallmark signs of madness—delusions or hallucinations—and couldn't point to a drug trip or to specific brain damage to explain your communications with Mars, you could count on acquiring that label.

We know precious little about madness. With that enormous disclaimer, let us take a stab at one view of madness. If even partly true, this view would help explain why the artist and the madman face the similar grave danger of an unplanned departure into virulent acting-in.

All powerful language produces in us the idea of the void.
ANTONIN ARTAUD

A View of Madness

We said that a special inner intensity characterizes the everyday experience of the person who goes mad. In the child this intensity is as likely to manifest itself in restlessness, irritability, and an inability to concentrate as it is in any clear withdrawal from the world.

Whether this intensity and subsequent acting-in come from hereditary or environmental factors, or an interaction of the two, remains an open question. For the moment we will assume that madness has a psychological component and that it is not simply a defect in the brain's machinery. This point of view is reinforced by a pair of special cases of madness: battle fatigue and the brief reactive psychosis sometimes seen in newcomers to a foreign land. The incidence of psychosis is considerably higher both in the trenches and among refugees and new arrivals in foreign places than it is in the general population. These particularly stressful situations, in which the individual comes to feel profoundly powerless and extremely and abnormally isolated, are no doubt initially met by the individual's first line of ego defenses.

For example, psychically leaving the scene—dissociating—is a common temporary defense of children who are molested and abused. It is also implicated in the strange cases of psychogenic fugues and amnesias, where the individual disappears from his New York law partnership one day and resurfaces a year later as a short-order cook in a small town in Kansas, with no memory of and blissfully unconcerned about his past. In mild forms it is an every-day defense, a staple of the repertoire of ways we protect ourselves.

But for some significant number of soldiers experiencing weeks of constant bombardment, and for some significant number of refugees experiencing the wild disruption of fleeing their homelands, these everyday defenses prove inadequate. Hearing their own voices only, in an ever-stranger dialogue with themselves, they finally break; they go mad. They retreat from or are forced to flee sanity.

Even if they were predisposed to madness (the genetic link), we nevertheless intuitively understand that we, too, might break under such conditions. Anyone might. And in that case we are forced to admit that each of us is susceptible to the onslaughts of madness.

We may argue, then, that the person who will go mad experiences life as if he were a stranger in a strange land, or as if he were under constant bombardment. For him the normal range of ego defenses proves inadequate. He more and more disengages from the world and more and more retreats into his acting-in world. In the characteristic fashion of madness, these pressurized feelings and thoughts are transformed and embodied, and a war begins between the forces of good and evil in the madman's own mind.

If psychic intensity is one hallmark of the madman, and severe isolation a second, a special kind of internal splitting is a third. Something in the makeup and experiences of these individuals causes them to hold in warring opposition two extreme positions: one of power, omnipotence, and godlikeness, on the one hand, and one of loathesomeness, insignificance, and pained injury, on the other. These positions are extreme forms of positive and negative inflation. The individual, at once grandiose and abased, simultaneously maintains a subjective sense of godlikeness and a subjective sense of victimization. We might call this his *god-bug* sense of himself.

These extreme antithetical positions are regularly evidenced in madness. As Edward Edinger, a Jungian analyst, pointed out in *Ego and Archetype:*

> Taking on oneself too much of anything is indicative of inflation because it transcends human limits. Too much humility as well as too much arrogance, too much love and altruism as well as too much power striving and selfishness, are all symptoms of inflation.

I didn't know what was expected of me. I was a dummy. I thought perhaps I was on the wrong planet. My teachers could have been speaking Russian or Chinese as far as I was concerned. I would sit perplexed, drinking ink.

ANTHONY HOPKINS

As a child and a young adult, before he goes mad, the individual rarely splits off and embodies his thoughts and feelings in so radical a fashion. Yet the process of positive and negative inflation probably begins early on. The child, perhaps initially distanced from his parents and perhaps needing that distance to survive, grows to feel different. Understanding himself to be different, he's likely also to think of himself as special. He feels a little uncanny in his growing envelope of isolation; his language and jokes become private, his preoccupations obsessional, his connection with the world more tenuous. If the reasons for his growing isolation are rooted in the terrors and pressures around him, in the messages he receives or in the experiences he must endure, then he will also feel injured, abject, small, and hurt. In this view we might call Cinderella a likely candidate for madness.

I never liked the middle ground—the most boring place in the world.
LOUISE NEVELSON

Our candidate may become the hard-to-reach child, the impatient child, the agitated, preoccupied, moody, strange, or withdrawn child. If he is relatively less injured and relatively more competent, he may look healthy enough until he breaks suddenly in young adulthood. This is the path of the reactive psychotic. If, however, he is relatively more injured and less competent, his decline into strangeness may begin early on and may proceed undramatically toward complete disintegration. This is the path of the process psychotic.

Whichever the case, the young person, although already acting-in, doesn't yet build for himself an army of warring factions. He may begin to identify with Christ or Napoleon, but Napoleon isn't yet present within him as an active participant in a fomenting drama.

The troubled person doesn't, after all, really feel like a god—he feels less potent than that. And he doesn't really feel like a bug—he feels more significant than that. At the outset he possesses an existential understanding of his own humanness and at least a confused idea of the nature of human limits. But the disputes between his contradictory feelings, waged in the dream arena of his mind, percolate. They begin to erupt as bizarre behaviors and obsessional episodes—the compulsive hunt for a flawless nectarine or for positive proof of Shakespeare's identity. These are the opening salvos of the full-fledged war to come.

When will this inner war erupt? Most typically in late adolescence or early adulthood, when the young person attempts to enter

For the role I had to imagine Lucifer. I had to imagine the eternal agony of a lost soul. I've been through hell, and I thought, "Who better than I would know how the Devil feels?"

MERCEDES
MCCAMBRIDGE

into a first intimate relationship or to break away from home. Such moments bring the hurt and haughty youth's extreme and unregulated self-identifications into collision with one another and with the world. Is he a god to his first girlfriend—or a worm? Is he omnipotent in his college dormitory—or impotent? The strain of facing the special terrors of relationship sends the youth further inward. There the battle intensifies.

The first psychotic episode, perhaps following a painful rejection or a stressful altercation, likely commences with a prodromal period lasting hours, days, weeks, or months. During this time the youth appears to be growing stranger and deteriorating. He seems to become more eccentric, more absent, more self-referential, less able to take care of himself. He is likely to sleep little, to make phone calls at three in the morning, to begin to talk to himself on buses. He begins to preach the gospel or curse and rage in public. The world begins to see him as someone to avoid.

To the youth, however, this may seem like a time of great energy, great sensory awareness, and great import or moment. He may feel frightened or ecstatic; at any rate, everything is fraught with meaning, intensified. Everyone is speaking about him, looking at him. Nothing can be overlooked. He begins to see visions, to hear voices. Great, portentous events are on the horizon.

In his book *Retreat from Sanity,* the psychiatrist Malcolm Bowers reports on the experiences of a 20-year-old visual artist:

> He describes a mystic or "cryptic" state during which the solutions to various problems seem obvious. In these states he feels capable of bringing together the arts and sciences, his separated parents, and himself into harmonious "oscillation" with the world. Going without sleep heightens the mystic state and improves his "freedom and vision" in painting. In this state he cannot tell whether he is "thrilled, frightened, pained, or anxious—they are all the same."

One 38-year-old music teacher reported on his growing madness: "God actually touched my heart. The next day was horror and ecstasy. I began to feel that I might be the agent of some spiritual reawakening. The emotional experience became overpowering."

We may wonder, as many have wondered, if this prodromal period doesn't represent a valiant attempt on the person's part to make sense of his warring feelings by, in effect, inviting them to come forward and do battle openly and plainly. If it is indeed a kind of invitation, then it is easy to understand how feelings of ecstasy and expectation might accompany the invitation.

R. D. Laing, in the period when he believed (along with many other radical psychiatrists) that madness was a quest on the madman's part to break free and grow, quoted one patient's understanding of his psychosis in an article in *The Psychedelic Review:*

> I believe I caused the illness myself. In my attempt to penetrate the other world I met its natural guardians, the embodiment of my own weaknesses and faults. I had forced untimely access to the "source of life," and the curse of the "gods" descended on me. Then came illumination. A new life began for me and from then on I felt different from other people.

The growing consciousness is a danger and a disease.
FRIEDRICH NIETZSCHE

There is no genius without a mixture of madness.
ARISTOTLE

The central feature of this budding psychotic episode is that the individual cannot or will not turn off his obsessional intensity. Perhaps he can't help himself; or perhaps the battle is a last desperate attempt to bring peace through warfare, a violent attempt at synthesis or reorganization.

When Shakespeare said that "the lunatic, the lover, and the poet are of imagination all compact," he announced their common bond: their "seething brains." The madman is besieged by his own thoughts. If his language grows loose and autistic and if he coins new words, it is probably because his way of speaking begins to reflect the complex and conflictual inner dialogue in which he is participating. His language is certainly not meaningless. The psychiatrist Harry Stack Sullivan, for one, called the madman's linguistic efforts "very high order abstractions."

If we do not understand the madman, it is perhaps because we are not up to doing the work that would be required to understand him, just as we may not be up to doing the work required to understand *Finnegan's Wake,* James Joyce's protracted dialogue with his mad daughter, or the cantos of the sometimes mad poet Ezra Pound.

Madness as a Human Experience

The madman's experience appears to be a very human one. He believes that he is worth something, and this worth is magnified as his brain relentlessly seethes. He feels himself injured and misunderstood, and these feelings are intensified as his mind reels, until they produce a fantastic inner landscape.

We intuitively understand how Ivan, in Dostoevsky's *The Brothers Karamazov,* goes mad as he broods on the painful existential questions that torment him. We intuitively understand how someone whose eyes seem to bleed as he stares at the landscape with his brush poised—as Cézanne described his own sensations while painting—is harboring within him the possibility of madness.

If a writer's ego ever wilts, he is ruined. Every morning he has to persuade himself, all over again, that putting words on paper is the most important thing in the world.

JOHN FISCHER

Perhaps this process is adaptive for those who go mad. Perhaps anxiety or anger is dissipated in madness and perhaps madness brings release, as a loud, wild, and heartfelt scream can bring release. To breathe, perhaps, the madman must explode. And, tragically, by exploding he is sometimes destroyed.

To further underscore this humanness we may look in another direction. The Minnesota Multiphasic Personality Inventory, or MMPI, is one of the more widely used personality inventories. It is an empirically normed test, which means that, rather than being theory-driven, its questions were selected according to their ability to distinguish between two populations, one hospitalized in psychiatric instititions and the other not hospitalized. If, for instance, both groups answered yes the same number of times to a given question, that question was discarded, since it possessed no discriminating power. If, however, one group answered yes or no rather more often than the other group, that question was retained.

Several scales were developed in the course of analyzing the data. One scale was called the Schizophrenia Scale. If an individual managed a significantly high score on this scale, on the order of two standard deviations above the mean, and other scales had a certain characteristic look to them, the subject had responded in a manner closely resembling the responses of those hospitalized individuals labeled as schizophrenic.

We may well ponder for a moment the sorts of questions that distinguished between the two groups and the sorts of answers these schizophrenic patients typically gave. Asked if they preferred daydreaming to doing anything else, they tended to answer yes. Asked if they thought they were understood, they tended to answer no. Asked if they thought they'd often been unfairly punished, they tended to answer yes. Asked if they thought they got all the sympathy they ought to get, they tended to answer no. Asked if they'd ever been in love with anyone, they tended to answer no. Asked if almost every day something happened to frighten them, they tended to answer yes.

These are only a few of the items on the Schizophrenia Scale. Among the remaining questions are ones that probe for eccentricities, hallucinations, delusions, and the like. The madman seems, in this analysis, to be a hurt, lonely, fearful, misunderstood, and introspective individual who also demonstrates certain signs of madness. It does not surprise us to find that artists, according to the psychologist Frank Barron's MMPI studies, tend to show slight elevations on the Schizophrenia Scale. For the artist is intensely involved enough with his own thoughts, and misunderstood, injured, and isolated enough to begin to climb that scale.

It's the way to get over a deep inferiority complex, being onstage; you become another person and shed your own frightened personality.

SHIRLEY BOOTH

Treating Madness

Everything is a burden. Is there anything that does not weigh on me?

EUGÈNE IONESCO

How can madness be treated? Some would argue that medication is the treatment of choice, the only treatment really. Others argue that drugs simply quell the organism, that they are no more a treatment than is a tranquilizer dart fired at a raging rhino. But if the madman isn't to be tranquilized, how is he to be helped to turn off his intensity? How is he to allay his anxieties? How is the madman to find peace, rather than wage war?

The story of the Belgian colony of Gheel may give us a clue in this matter. Legend has it that an Irish king, after the death of his wife, was persuaded by the devil to propose marriage to his own daughter. The terrified and outraged girl fled to Belgium, where her father found her and killed her. L. J. Karnosh and E. M. Zucker wrote in the *Handbook of Psychiatry:*

> In the night the angels came, recapitated the body and concealed it in the forest near the village of Gheel. Years later five lunatics chained together spent the night with their keepers at a small wayside shrine near the Belgian village. Overnight all the victims recovered. In the 15th century pilgrimages to Gheel from every part of the civilized world were organized for the mentally sick. Many of the pilgrims remained in Gheel with the inhabitants of the locality, and in the passing years it became the natural thing to accept them

into the homes and thus the first "colony" was formed and for that matter the only one which had been consistently successful.

What is most real for me are the illusions I create with my paintings. Everything else is quicksand.

EUGENE DELACROIX

Our previous discussion suggests that the madman must persuade himself that he is neither a god nor a loathsome creature. If he can do that he may relieve himself of both burdensome self-identifications. He must also find safe ways of escaping his self-protective cocoon of isolation as he begins to engage and accept the world. He must also neutralize his intense self-consciousness and escape from his own brooding thoughts.

It may be the case, then, that the effectiveness of a milieu like the colony of Gheel is rooted in its ability to help the madman accomplish just these necessary goals, by accepting him and offering him a normalizing routine and simple work. This is not to say that one can't go mad or remain mad in the company of cows. But digging may be more therapeutic than electroshock or antipsychotic medication, especially if that digging is not a task in a hospital garden but a piece of natural work in a natural landscape.

We may end this brief discussion by asserting that madness, as the painter Jim Dine said about his own intensity, is not the least bit funny. But it may be as human a reaction to the perils of living as are the anxieties, depressions, and addictions that plague so many of us.

Few of us will find ourselves the Napoleon or the Virgin Mary of the locked ward. Few of us will need, as a consequence of our inner preoccupations, to lend our minds out to the visiting forces of good and evil. But if we are artists we perhaps understand that we have a certain affinity with madmen. It is not that we crave, worship, or respect madness. Nor do we take our eccentricities and obsessions to be tokens of our family resemblance to the madman. Rather we understand in what measure we share with our afflicted brothers and sisters an intensity that sometimes threatens to crack the walls of our living vessel.

This excursion into a theory of madness has value because it suggests that a life lived deep in an envelope of isolation is potentially a hazard to mental health. Artists who live in self-imposed isolation, bound up with their own thoughts and processes, must find ways to regularly break out into the sun and shadow of everyday reality in order to remain well.

The painter Paul Klee exclaimed in his diary, "Am I God? I have accumulated so many great things in me!" But we also remember these other words of Klee's, quoted earlier: "He who strives will never enjoy this life peacefully." The lucky artist may be the one who, while in human measure a god, has nevertheless found satisfactory ways of escaping the relentless firing of his synapses.

My vocabulary was chosen out of the intensity of my concern.
WILLIAM CARLOS WILLIAMS

STRATEGIES

The following section includes both self-help strategies and information about professional resources. Many of the challenges discussed in this chapter appropriately call for professional consultation, with respect both to diagnosis and to treatment. The following strategies focus on ameliorating depression and anxiety; for information on the diagnosis and treatment of psychosis, please consult the National Alliance for the Mentally Ill, 2102 Wilson Blvd., Suite 302, Arlington, VA 22201, 1-800-950-6264; or the National Mental Health Consumers Association, 311 South Juniper St., Suite 902, Philadelphia, PA 19107, (215) 735-2465.

Deciding If You Need Help

Answers to the following questions offer diagnostic clues in the assessment of depression. They are not offered to help you make a formal self-diagnosis, but rather to alert you to the signs of depression. A yes answer may be suggestive of depression; or, in context, it may be suggestive of some other condition. Please consult a licensed or certified mental-health professional if you suspect that you are presently affected by depression.

1. Have you experienced a depressed mood (dysphoria) for at least two weeks?

2. Have you experienced a diminished interest or diminished pleasure (anhedonia) in your usual activities for a period of at least two weeks?

3. Have you recently experienced a significant weight loss, weight gain, or other change in your appetite?

4. Are you sleeping more than usual (hypersomnia), do you have significant difficulty getting to sleep, or do you awake early in the morning and find it difficult or impossible to get back to sleep?

5. Do you experience a significant amount of fatigue or are you in a persistent state of low energy?

6. Are you experiencing a lessened sex drive or menstrual disturbances or irregularities?

7. Are you having severe trouble with memory lapses, concentration, or decision making?

8. Do you have thoughts about death and/or suicide? Do you have a plan to commit suicide?

9. Do you experience feelings of worthlessness, guilt, helplessness, and/or hopelessness?

10. Do you experience much tension or irritability or find yourself worrying a great deal about relatively minor matters?

Treating Depression

If you're regularly or presently depressed, muster your available energy and begin to treat your depression. A comprehensive treatment plan includes most or all of the following elements. You may also want to contact the National Depressive and Manic-Depressive Association, Merchandise Mart, P.O. Box 3395, Chicago, IL 60654, (312) 939-2442 for information and a national listing of self-help groups.

As a first step in the treatment of depression, seek a medical work-up. Obtain a diagnosis and treatment of any medical problems that may be implicated in your depression. If you have undiagnosed diabetes, for instance, which renders you impotent, the impotence may bring on a depression.

Examine the role prescription drugs may be playing in your depression. Stopping or changing medications may be indicated.

Stop the use of abused substances. These include alcohol, marijuana, and cocaine.

Consider the introduction of antidepressant medications. Some people benefit greatly from antidepressant medications such as MAO inhibitors and tricyclics; some benefit only minimally. For others, such drugs appear to have no effect at all. Similarly, some people more easily tolerate the side effects of antidepressants than do others. Opting to include antidepressant medications as part of your treatment program is a personal choice that you should make in an informed manner, in consultation with a physician. Educate yourself about the possible benefits and likely side effects.

Do family-of-origin work. Insight therapy can help you better understand how the dynamics of your childhood formed you and perhaps scarred you. Low self-esteem, a self-critical nature, undiluted rage at a parent, long-term reactions to childhood loss and abandonment, and other crucial residue of growing up can precipitate depressions. You can tackle this family-of-origin work by yourself, with the help of workbooks and self-help books, or in individual or group psychotherapy. Several books on the market can help orient you to the psychotherapy process and offer advice about selecting a psychotherapist. A few of these include:

> *How to Do Self-Analysis and Other Self-Therapies,* by Louis Gottschalk. Northvale, NJ: Aronson, 1989.
>
> *The Lavender Couch: A Consumer's Guide to Psychotherapy for Lesbians and Gay Men,* by Marny Hall. Boston: Alyson Publications, 1985.
>
> *Making Therapy Work,* by Barbara Gangi, Fredda Bruckner-Gordon, and Gerry Wallman. New York: Harper & Row, 1987.
>
> *When Talk Isn't Cheap: Or, How to Find the Right Therapist When You Don't Know Where to Begin,* by Mandy Aftel and Robin Lakoff. New York: Warner Books, 1986.

If you tackle this work by yourself, with the help of your guided writing practice, consider using the following questions to focus your thoughts.

- Did a depressed atmosphere pervade my childhood home?
- Did my parents seem defeated?

If the healing cannot be achieved within the person of the artist, then we should not hope for the healing to be practiced in the environment and in society.

THICH NHAT HANH

- Were my parents pessimists?

- What in the way I was brought up might be contributing to my depression?

- Is there some issue between my father and me that must be aired or cleared up before this depression will lift?

- Is there some issue between my mother and me that must be aired or cleared up before this depression will lift?

- Is my depression related (even after all these years) to my parents' divorce, the loss of one or both of my parents, or their emotional abandonment of me?

- Does depression seem to run in my family? If so, to what do I attribute that pattern?

The mind loves the unknown. It loves images whose meaning is unknown, since the meaning of the mind itself is unknown.
RENÉ MAGRITTE

Focus on the expression of feelings, insight into feelings, and acceptance of feelings. Much depression is rooted in unexpressed and unexamined feelings. For you, as an artist, it's important to ventilate feelings associated with the challenges outlined in this book. You may feel sorrowful that you're not sufficiently recognized, guilty about spending too little time at your art, rageful at a marketplace that is uninterested in or antagonistic to your art products, envious of your fellow artists. These feelings, as long as they remain unexpressed and unacknowledged, knot your depression in place.

Do cognitive work. How you habitually speak to yourself can depress you. If you glance at the list of 10 negative self-statements in the Introduction, you'll see what an arsenal of ways we have of devaluing and dismissing ourselves, of taking the starch out of our own sails. Examining your personal array of negative self-statements and beginning to alter what you say to yourself (the central processes of cognitive therapy) are important steps in your battle plan to fight depression.

Do existential work. Family-of-origin work, which takes place in the present, looks backward. Existential work takes place in the present and focuses on you as you are right this minute. Will you take responsibility for your own well-being? Will you commit to making the changes you deem necessary? Will you reinvest meaning in your art and write again or audition again? Will you rehearse and get ready for your concert or will you stay in bed? Will you do battle with your own excuses, your lassitude, your disinclination to work? Will you come up with your own reasons for living?

Examine your interpersonal dynamics and environment. Daily interactions with the other people in your life can make you anxious and depressed. Look at the different relationships that form your interpersonal life. We'll do more of this in chapter 8, but for now ask yourself: Is a particular peripheral relationship disturbing you? A particular central relationship? A lack of relationship? Actively address these issues, remembering that, while there are limits to what you can interpersonally accomplish, such limits can be stretched significantly.

Learn stress management. Stress-management techniques include meditation, yogic and other deep-breathing practices, regular exercise, biofeedback and autogenic training, and the use of visualizations and progressive relaxation. They also include taking time-outs for yourself, growing assertive, decreasing your sense of learned helplessness, and extinguishing inappropriate, habitual thoughts. Include in your program of stress management whatever soothes you and releases tension—a soak in the tub, a massage, browsing in a bookstore or museum. Treat yourself to something relaxing every day.

Treating Anxiety

Like depression, anxiety is typically treated with medication, talk therapy, or both. The program described above also serves as an anxiety-reduction program, with the same proviso that a medical work-up be included as a first step in managing your anxiety.

Other Personal Responsibility Strategies

Take charge of your energy. When the performance ends and you're too wound up to relax, it's up to you to find ways of draining your battery that don't harm you. You're the one in charge of accepting or refusing the speed, cocaine, heroin, marijuana, or alcohol. You're the one who says yes or no to joining the group after the show, the one too wired to go home, the one full of barely contained energy while waiting for your book to be published. How will you manage your

Your acting partner is not assigned to be a surrogate parent or a lover or to meet your emotional needs.

CATHERINE GAFFIGAN

Dance is of all things the most concentrated expression of happiness and everyone needs to find happiness, to search for an ideal escape.

VIOLETTE VERDY

energy? Find the active or meditative techniques that work for you, master them, and use them.

Accept that you are a live wire coursing with electricity. Your dramas, your lustiness, your fantastic irrationalities, your passions are liable to shock and dismay you. Sometimes you'll feel high-voltage despair and high-voltage disappointment. Sometimes you'll rage out of all proportion to events in your life. These outsized feelings are you with your insulation off, awash in a shower of emotional electrical sparks. Become your own personal master electrician to control that energy.

Take charge of your moods. If your mania or depression is so gripping that only medication will touch it, you are in charge of seeking out and accepting medication. It is up to you to manage the anxiety that prevents you from doing business effectively, that hinders your ability to perform or audition, that causes you to block.

Beer, speed, cocaine, heroin, or champagne are not the long-term answers. Cutting yourself with a razor so that the pain will bring you back to life is not a long-term answer. Compulsive eating is not a long-term answer. Sleeping around is not a long-term answer. Inside you know better. Look for better answers and commit yourself to the courageous effort required to put your new answers into practice.

Explore mental-health counseling. Treatment for depression and anxiety-related ailments is available in hospital and clinic settings and from psychiatrists, psychologists, and certified or licensed mental-health counselors (including family therapists and clinical social workers) in private practice. Psychiatrists, who are medical doctors, can dispense medications, including antidepressants, tranquilizers, and antipsychotic drugs, and may also employ talk therapy. Other mental-health practitioners engage in one form or another of talk therapy, supplemented sometimes by art therapy or psychodrama techniques.

Some hospital clinics or free-standing clinics specialize in the treatment of depression and/or anxiety-related conditions. Many use a behavioral or cognitive approach, others employ antidepressant or antianxiety medications as the basis of treatment. Some specialize in work with certain issues, like assertiveness, or with certain populations, like survivors of incest or abuse.

As actors, we must be strong enough to be vulnerable, and we must be prepared to reencounter our own deepest feelings.

ANN BREBNER

Usually the lowest-cost psychotherapy in a given community is available through college and university counselor-training programs, where clients are seen by interns and trainees. These interns are not necessarily too young or too inexperienced to help.

A number of books on the market discuss shopping for a therapist, as noted above. You may wonder, however, whether you should be looking for something in particular in your therapist. Should the therapist be an artist or be trained to use art media in the therapeutic process? Neither is necessarily a criterion. Such a therapist may not in fact be very clear-eyed about artists' issues; those issues may have perhaps remained unexamined and unresolved in his or her own life. On the other hand, the therapist who loves art may bring an extra measure of empathy to the counseling process.

He who plays the piano keeps sane.

ITALIAN PROVERB

You are well advised to ask yourself the following questions as you begin work with a new therapist. Does the therapist seem particularly ignorant about the realities of the artist's life? Does he or she want to glamorize or romanticize the artist's life, on the one hand, or dismiss or devalue art, on the other hand? Does the therapist seem to imply that you should grow up? Does he or she look up to you or down on you? Is he or she cold, smug, controlling, or abusive? If you find yourself answering any of these questions in the affirmative, you may want to consider whether that therapist is appropriate for you.

In some locales A.R.T.S. Anonymous groups, based on the 12-step model, offer artists emotional support. Further information can be obtained from A.R.T.S. Anonymous, P.O. Box 175, Ansonia Station, New York, NY 10023, (212) 969-0144. In your area you may find other support groups led by psychotherapists, artist-therapists, or career counselors interested in artists and artists' issues.

Mental-health and career-counseling services for artists may also be available through certain special programs. The Institute for the Performing Artist at the Postgraduate Center for Mental Health in New York, for instance, provides psychiatric help for artists. The Actors' Work Program at Actors Equity (see Appendix 2 for address) helps performers find long-term careers to supplement their acting income or to replace their acting careers. The Career Transition for Dancers program, a joint project sponsored by five performers' unions, helps dancers look to a future after dance.

With respect to chemical dependency issues, meetings of Alcoholics Anonymous, Narcotics Anonymous, and other 12-step programs are held regularly in thousands of locations across the country, and occasionally artists organize all-artist AA and NA groups.

Seek appropriate medical services. Creative and performing artists can often take advantage of health-care-plan group rates by joining their local professional arts organizations.

Artists frequently experience special medical problems associated with their art careers. The musician and the dancer, like the athlete, often play with pain. The glazes that potters use include hazardous chemicals, as do some of the materials used by printmakers, painters, and other visual artists.

In recent years, these special health needs have begun to be addressed. Several clinics now exist in different parts of the country whose primary purpose is treating performing artists, and a specialty known as arts medicine has begun to attract the interest of physicians, many of whom are themselves versed in one of the arts. Information on these programs can be found in the occasional newsletters of the International Arts-Medicine Association, 19 South 22nd St., Philadelphia, PA 19103. Books discussing the potential health hazards of art materials and safety issues in the artist's environment are available from the American Council for the Arts, 1285 Avenue of the Americas, New York, NY 10019.

Examples of the resources available include the following:

- The Northwestern School of Music presents a regular summer course entitled The Medical Problems of Musicians: An Introductory Survey for Performers and Teachers.

- A symposium on the medical problems of musicians and dancers is presented each summer in Aspen, Colorado, in conjunction with the Aspen Music Festival, and is cosponsored by the Aspen Music Festival and School, the Cleveland Clinic Foundation, and the Performing Arts Medicine Association.

- Other programs across the country include: the Boston Arts Medicine Center, the Musical Medicine Clinic at Massachusetts General Hospital, and the Musician's Clinic, Brigham and Women's Hospital, all in the Boston area; the Medical Program for the Performing Arts, Jewish Hospital, St. Louis; ArtsMed Medical Specialists for the Performing Artist, University of Michigan, Ann Arbor; the Performing Arts Medicine Program and Multipurpose Arthritis Center, Indiana University; Resources for Artists with Disabilities, New York City; the Performing Arts Medicine Clinic at the Glendale Adventist Medical Center, Glendale, California; Doctors for Artists, a nonprofit referral service in New York City, offering artists discounted medical services in 14 areas of medical specialization; Pacific Voice Care (for singers), San Francisco; and the Health Program for Performing Artists at the University of California at San Francisco Medical Center, offering specialized services for dancers, singers, actors, and musicians, including medical treatment for the special hand problems of musicians, performance anxiety, and depression.

PART ONE EXERCISES

The Artist's Personality

In the Introduction I defined the successful artist as the self-aware artist who understands herself, her life as an artist, and the world in which she lives. The exercises that follow and that appear at the end of each part help you gain that personal understanding and are meant to be used in conjunction with your guided writing program. If you haven't begun that program yet you might return to the Introduction now, refresh your memory about its purposes and steps, and begin.

Exercise 1. Self-doubt

Artists are regularly plagued by doubts. These doubts may be small and gnawing or large and pervasive; the artist may doubt herself as an artist or doubt herself as a person. These doubts can prevent artists from working and are surprisingly powerful obstacles, for who would think that a sudden, perhaps objectively baseless doubt could incapacitate a person? And yet just such doubts derail careers and disrupt lives.

How can these doubts affect artists? Monet scrutinized his last paintings and burnt a great many of them. Renoir, at the height of his career, suddenly doubted that he could draw and determined to travel to Italy to practice sketching. Camus, doubting his work, ironically disparaged his novels by calling them "slim." Hardy, worried that as a self-taught man he wasn't the equal of Oxford and Cambridge graduates, obsessed on that theme in one of his great last novels, *Jude the Obscure.*

But what exactly is a doubt? To define "doubt" personally and to gauge its importance in your life are the goals of this exercise. In Webster's *New World Dictionary,* "doubt" is defined in all of the following ways. Use your journal to record your reactions to these definitions and to the questions that follow.

If we travel around the country with a play, we know how different audiences can be. Ultimately we must rely upon our own judgment, our own taste, our own perception of what the play should be.

        MURRAY SCHISGAL

To doubt (the verb):

1. *"To be uncertain in opinion or belief."*

- Are you uncertain about the direction or quality of the artwork you're presently doing?

- Are you uncertain about the reception your work will receive?

- Are you uncertain about the goodness of your past work?

- Are you uncertain about how to meet or manage the marketplace?

2. *"To be inclined to disbelief."*

- Are you *inclined* to disbelieve that you have the ability, talent, creative resources, skills, or general wherewithal to do your artwork effectively?

- Are you *often* so inclined, *regularly* so inclined, or only *sometimes* so inclined?

3. *"To hesitate."*

- Just as you approach the canvas, computer screen, script, or instrument, do you hesitate?

- What doubt enters your mind then? Can you describe it?

4. *"To be skeptical of."*

- Are you skeptical about your chances of succeeding in the art marketplace because you aren't well connected or don't seem to possess a seller's personality?

- Are you skeptical of the public's taste?

- Does that skepticism sap your motivational juices?

A doubt (the noun):

    1. "A wavering of opinion or belief."

- When the idea for a story comes to you, do you waver in your opinion about its potential goodness, rather than embarking on the writing of it?

- When the desire comes over you to paint in a new idiom, do you waver in your opinion about the smartness of moving in a new direction, rather than determining to waste, at worst, a few feet of canvas?

- Do you make up your mind to audition for a part and then waver in your opinion that you're the right person for the role?

- Can you transform this wavering into true reflection?

    2. "A lack of conviction."

- Are you *convinced* that you're an artist?

    3. "A condition of uncertainty."

- As you travel your path are you regularly uncertain about which road to take?

- Are you more confronted by questions about choices than by stretches of continuous work?

    4. "A lack of trust or confidence."

- Do you trust yourself?

No doubt it is useful for an artist to know all the forms of art which have preceded or which accompany his. But he must be very careful not to look for models.

             PABLO PICASSO

Perhaps you can write better if you leave the mistakes.

          JORGE LUIS BORGES

Consider these many definitions, for much that prevents you from thriving as a person and as an artist may be located there. Then comment on the following.

1. Even if I'm uncertain about the work I'm doing, it's better to do the work, mistakes and all, than procrastinate and block.

2. It's better to obsess about the *work,* rather than about my *doubts* about the work.

3. When a doubt strikes, I know what I'll do to combat it (list your strategies for combating doubt).

Exercise 2. Compulsion

Productive artists, of the sort who appear almost incapable of *not* creating, frequently speak of being driven by an inner compulsion to work. What is this inner compulsion? Can you acquire it if you don't already have it? Would a person desiring some sort of "normal life" even want to acquire it? Comment on the following.

I have to work, because acting is a muscle. It must be exercised.

LEN CARIOU

1. You're either born with this inner compulsion to create or you're not.

2. This inner compulsion must flow from a conviction that you're special and have something important to contribute. I'm not sure I feel that special.

3. All people do things to help relieve themselves of their anxieties. The compulsion to create is one anxiety-reduction mechanism in human beings.

4. If I honor this inner compulsion, which indeed I feel, I would become a compulsive person.

5. I recognize this inner compulsion in myself, but I don't trust it and don't want to entertain it.

6. This inner compulsion is just another name for the life force. I mean to nurture it and manifest it, even if many internal and external blocks impede my way.

7. In order to manifest this vitality or life force, I think I must take more risks, show more courage, and be truer to myself.

8. I do not recognize this crying need in myself, and perhaps that means that I should make a good life for myself outside the arts.

Exercise 3. The Avant-Garde Artist

Often artists feel it imperative to create or perform work that is unfamiliar, idiosyncratic, and inaccessible. They do this in order to express themselves in ways that are unavailable through conventional means. The Kafkaesque in literature, post-modern deconstructive imagery in rock videos, and repetition in the music of Philip Glass are each rooted in this need. One variation of this idea is expressed in the Russian language by the word *ostranenie:* art as defamiliarization, art that makes familiar perceptions seem strange.

But do artists working in this fashion grow alienated from their time and place? Comment on the following questions.

1. Do you produce work that is difficult and inaccessible?

2. Do you engage in defamiliarization in your art?

3. Does this way of working help you or harm you as a person?

4. Does this way of working isolate you from others?

5. Does the act of creating difficult art further distance you from this time and place?

6. Can you move in your life (if not in your art) from deconstruction to reconstruction, from alienation to involvement? Do you think you might want to?

Exercise 4. Obstacles to Self-knowing

The notion that each of us possesses blind spots is at once a provocative and upsetting idea. Is it really true that we are prevented, or prevent ourselves, from knowing ourselves? Comment on any of the following that ring true for you.

1. I realize that in certain areas of my life I refuse to know myself very well.

2. Like everyone, I have my defenses.

3. I've had many troubling experiences about which I refuse to think.

4. I would not like the me I would see if I saw me too clearly.

5. I can defend myself from the attacks of others, but only if I consider them "bad" or "wrong" and me "good" or "right."

6. Who has the time to look for blind spots?

7. I am already too nearly my own worst enemy to dare poking around, looking for other blemishes and weaknesses in myself.

8. Criticism hurts, especially self-criticism.

9. Rejection hurts, especially self-rejection.

10. If I began to see in those areas where I am now blind, I would have to make radical, scary changes in my life.

How might you see what you are now blind to? Comment on each of the following.

1. I have certain recurrent troubling thoughts and feelings or engage in certain recurrent troubling behaviors which I *know* I avoid really thinking about.

2. I can learn about my blind spots by asking other people to report on the blind spots they observe in me.

3. I can learn about my blind spots by willing myself to remember what I already know about them.

4. I can interrogate myself (perhaps by using guided writing).

The century of airplanes deserves its own music. As there are no precedents, I must create anew.
CLAUDE DEBUSSY

Without resistance you can do nothing.
JEAN COCTEAU

Exercise 5. Group Associations

Every artist possesses important group associations and identifications. A given artist will also be, besides an artist, an African-American, a woman, a single mother, a middle-aged ex-wife with ancestors who came from Africa, Trinidad, and Baton Rouge, etc. Who is she first of all? Who is she second of all?

I saw only white women on television and I started to think, "Did I fall asleep and wake up in Scandinavia?"

DENISE NICHOLAS

She may experience herself as a woman first: that is, as a person alert to the ways in which she is addressed and treated as a woman and the ways in which she reacts as a woman. Or she may experience herself as an African-American first: that is, as a person alert to the ways that she is addressed and treated as an African-American and the ways in which she reacts as an African-American.

It matters with which group or groups an artist identifies. If she identifies herself as a writer first, she may sit comfortably around a table with other writers, half of whom are men: but if she identifies herself as a feminist writer, she may or may not want to keep such company. Each self-identification affects how a given artist will feel in a certain group, whether the group is made up of mothers at a playground or art collectors at a party. Beyond that, it will affect how she feels about all issues, and thereby will profoundly affect her work.

It's very important for me as a black writer to change how Western civilization—which includes black people—perceives black people. That's at the heart of what I do.

CHARLES FULLER

With which groups do you identify? Which are your primary identifications? How is the answer to the question "Who are you?" affected by your group identifications? Comment on those of the following statements that apply to you.

1. At this point in my life, I seem to be identifying with one group in particular.

2. I experience both positive and negative consequences of identifying so strongly with this group.

3. Because I identify with this group, I find myself at odds with other groups and even identify them as "the enemy."

4. Along with this primary identification, I also identify myself with several other groups, including . . .

5. Possessing several group identifications leads to certain challenges and conflicts.

6. To stop identifying myself with a certain group or groups may have positive consequences.

7. To stop identifying myself with a certain group or groups may have negative consequences.

8. Whether burdensome or not, it is natural and even inevitable that I possess many group identifications.

Exercise 6. Anxious Situations

The following exercise, which I use with students in the personal and professional assessment classes I teach, is an example of an elaborate technique to encourage self-questioning.

Invent a character to go where you wouldn't go. Think for a minute about the sorts of places that, because of your personality, principles, or upbringing, you would never venture into. Invent a character with the sort of personality traits, principles, or upbringing that would allow him or her to venture into one of those places. Follow that character there. Describe the setting in some detail and indicate why the character is successful or comfortable in that setting and why, by contrast, you are not.

Exercise 7. Metaphors for Transformation

The transpersonal psychologist Ralph Metzner describes "ten classical metaphors of self-transformation." He writes in *The Journal of Transpersonal Psychology*:

> In prior periods, in the mystical and religious literature of East and West, and in the secret oral traditions of esoteric, spiritual schools, the teachers have resorted to myths, parables, similes, symbols, and metaphors to allude to that strange process that changes *us, our selves.*

Metaphorically speaking, how would you like to change? Do any of the following ten metaphors pique your interest? What concrete steps must you take in order to implement the changes you want? (Use your guided writing program to map out those changes.)

1. The movement from dream-sleep to awakening.

2. The movement from illusion to realization.

3. The movement from darkness to enlightenment.

4. The movement from imprisonment to liberation.

5. The movement from fragmentation to wholeness.

6. The movement from separation to oneness.

7. The movement from being on a journey to arriving at the destination.

8. The movement from being in exile to coming home.

9. The movement from seed to flowering tree.

10. The movement from death to rebirth.

Tchaikovsky thought of committing suicide for fear of being discovered as a homosexual, but today, if you are a composer and not homosexual, you might as well put a bullet through your head.
SERGEI DIAGHILEV

It is in the process of making something which stands on its own integral structure that the creator contacts a concrete reality outside his subjective life and moves into the realm of the transcendent.
JOSEPH ZINKER

The Challenges of the Work | PART TWO

CHAPTER 4

Blocks

What can ruin a first-rate writer? Booze, pot, too much sex, too much failure in one's private life, too much attrition, too much recognition, too little recognition, frustration. Nearly everything in the scheme of things works to dull a first-rate talent. But the worst probably is cowardice.

NORMAN MAILER

BLOCKING IS ONLY in part about producing. Creative blocks also provide information about your moods, the messages you received in childhood, the environment in which you live, your vitality or lack of vitality, and much more.

All human beings are regularly blocked. It is one definition of being human that we regularly fail to actualize our potentialities. Not only do we procrastinate, avoid challenges, take the easy path, and leap to the television or to the bottle to avoid our muses, but we generally live more dully than we might, blocked off from beauty and from our own wisdom.

Who wouldn't create—sing, make pictures, tell stories—if he weren't constrained not to? Who wouldn't try her hand at a hundred different art forms, from drumming to potting, from folk dancing to filmmaking, if she weren't constrained not to? But the constraints, the blocks, are practically numberless. There is the constraint of too little time. There is the constraint of having to make a living. There are the constraints of fear: fear that your voice will crack or that the audience will find your story boring. There are the constraints of belief: the belief that art is frivolous or useless, that

The ideal passes through suffering like gold through fire. The heavenly kingdom is attained through effort.

FYODOR DOSTOEVSKY

81

you are untalented, that forgoing art is a sign of stability or sanity. There are the constraints of personality: the inhibitions, doubts, anxieties, the characteristic style that each of us settles into, with its paranoid, depressed, shy, or antic edge to it.

You'd like to accomplish more, defuse inhibiting fears, and procrastinate less—but so would all people. You are sometimes, perhaps often, blocked and resistant to doing the work you want or need to do—but so are all people. It is in this context that we look at blocks in this chapter. Blocks are the constraints put on all of us by nature and by circumstances.

At a certain point, you have to go to the edge of the cliff and jump—put your ideas into a form, share that form with others.

MEREDITH MONK

SOURCES OF BLOCKS

The cognitive therapist tends to see creative blockage as the result of the maladaptive self-talk and rigid or inappropriate work rules that the artist adapts for himself; the artist is viewed as saying the wrong things to himself. The psychoanalyst tends to see creative blockage as the result of self-censorship and the repression of id material; the artist is viewed as blocking because of inner conflicts. Other psychologists have equated blocks with the artist's stupidity or laziness. The psychologist Edmund Bergler, for instance, argued that creative blocks were nothing more than "euphemisms for sterility of production."

I submit, however, that there is no single source of blockage but a multitude of sources, a multitude of constraints. Ultimately, yes, there *is* a single source of blockage: being human. Having said that, I think it's crucial for the artist to sort out the various causes of blockage in his life, even if only in a tentative way. We can't remove constraints if we don't know what they are, what they feel like, and something about where they come from.

It's important, after all, for the actress to know if she has stopped auditioning because she is tired of rejection, plagued by the introjected critical voice of her father, angry at the lack of strong roles available to her, or disillusioned with the art form of acting. It's important for the poet to know if he has stopped writing poetry because he happened upon a poem by another poet that he found to be too good, because his drinking has gotten the better of him, or because his outstanding debts are weighing too heavily on his mind.

I offer the following picture of 20 blocks (in no particular order) as a prod to your imagination. If you see your blocks here—if you can give them a name—you can begin the work of reducing them to manageable size or eliminating them altogether. They are:

1. Blocks from parental voices
2. Personality blocks
3. Personality trait blocks
4. Self-censorship
5. Self-criticism
6. World-criticism
7. World-wariness
8. Existential blocks
9. Conflicts between life and art
10. Fatigue
11. Pressure paralysis
12. Environmental blocks
13. Social blocks
14. Material blocks
15. Skill deficits
16. Myths and idealizations
17. Self-abuse
18. Anxieties
19. Depression
20. Incubation and fallow periods

BLOCKS FROM PARENTAL VOICES

As a child, you may have been told repeatedly that you were stupid, lazy, unworthy, untalented, or unimaginative. Now, at your easel or your computer screen, you hear your mother's or father's terrible voice and sit paralyzed. Or you no longer hear that hurtful voice but have nonetheless introjected it; the label has taken hold. It is no longer your parent's voice but your own voice that tells you you're untalented or stupid.

As a child, you may have felt that nothing you did was ever quite good enough. You couldn't please your parents; you couldn't begin to figure out what might please them. The resultant confusion, shame, anger, and self-doubt are practically bound to produce ambivalence that saps your motivational strength and makes you doubt that you have the wherewithal to proceed. You remember and are burdened by your parents' message: that they did not love you enough, respect you enough, or care enough.

PERSONALITY BLOCKS

Affected by experiences, raised in a certain family, living in a certain culture in a certain world, acting and being acted upon, the product of certain chromosomes, each of us ends up with a personality that seems—especially if we would like to make changes in it—all too immutable. You may come to possess a personality style, for instance, that is rigid, harshly self-critical, obsessive, or fearful. The fearful artist may effectively accomplish detail work, but may block when faced with the task of approaching a blank canvas. The paranoid artist may function well enough in isolation, producing fiction or practicing music, but may block at performing in public.

I honestly believed that if you gave guys who wanted to write a place to do it where they could live and eat free, then they would write. But it didn't work.

JAMES JONES

You've also acquired your own personal defensive structure, built around those defenses that were appropriate or valuable in childhood. Dissociation, for instance, may have helped you deal with an abusive or otherwise crazy-making family. But now you may dissociate in the face of the stress of producing art or dealing with the marketplace, so that you lose the very idea of what you intended to photograph or what you meant to say to your agent.

PERSONALITY TRAIT BLOCKS

In chapter 2, we examined the artist's personality in terms of the traits that appear to be needed in order for an artist to create. Persistent blocking can occur if one or several of these traits are relatively absent. Assertiveness, for instance, which is extremely valuable to the working artist and which I've dubbed the artist's necessary arrogance, is a quality that many talented, imaginative, but often-blocked artists possess insufficiently. An artist may be just a shade too much on the passive side, and that passivity can have far-reaching consequences. As the psychiatrist Lawrence Hatterer wrote, "An aggressive artist will make the most of a minor talent, while a more brilliant passive artist can easily be lost to the world."

SELF-CENSORSHIP

Blockage can occur because you can't or won't let out dangerous or disowned psychic material. Such material may be the stuff of

fantasy or painful historical facts, as for instance a childhood mo-
lestation or life with an alcoholic parent. Freud pinpointed this
source of blockage, and it's the one that has most interested psychoanalytic investigators. Creative and performing artists do have difficulty when their work puts them in touch with material they would
prefer not to explore.

> *If a character is brutal, it is
> because I am brutal. I take the
> blame and the credit.*
> MARIA IRENE FORNES

One client, who sang and acted, wanted very much to put together her own one-woman performance piece, but she found that
she couldn't begin. She seemed to be prevented from writing about
men and women in relationships, the intended subject of her show,
by the fact that her brothers had tormented and humiliated her as a
girl, a grievance that she remembered but had never addressed or
redressed.

Intransigent blocks are often related to this interior guarded-
ness. It is a special act of courage, in a context of danger, for an artist
with such a block to proceed with his or her art.

SELF-CRITICISM

Artists frequently criticize their art products and their marketing
efforts. This judgment, which may be accurate but harsh and self-
punishing, lowers the artist's morale and may ultimately paralyze
him. The artist who begins to believe, standing before a blank
canvas, that his first stroke will doom the painting, or the actor who
decides after some unsuccessful auditions that he is bound to botch
every future audition out of nervousness, is hard-pressed to proceed
with his art.

You may begin to judge yourself unequal to the task of creating
or performing. Your image of yourself as an artist loses more and
more of its luster. You begin to doubt both the quality of the specific
work or performance at hand and your ultimate worth as an artist.
This dual charge can render you artistically impotent.

WORLD-CRITICISM

Blockage can occur if you decide, at a conscious or unconscious
level, that the world is too sick, difficult, unresponsive, alienating, stupid, or bourgeois a place in which to do art. In a manner of

speaking, you judge the world a fraud or a failure. This judgment is often tied to your feeling unrecognized, unrewarded, rejected, and embattled. But the judgment may arise independent of your personal frustrations, independent of the cattle-call auditions you endure or the embarrassing smallness of the roles you win. It may come upon you simply because you chanced to watch the news.

It is easy to grow cynical or misanthropic, but it is harder to realize that such cynicism can become a source of blockage. The artist, angered or saddened by the world, may not understand that his blockage is more accurately his refusal to bring art products into a world that he does not love.

Hatred, rancor, and the spirit of vengeance are useless baggage to the artist. His road is difficult enough and he should cleanse his soul of everything which could make it more so.

HENRI MATISSE

WORLD-WARINESS

You can easily become paranoid as you pursue your art-making, experience criticism and rejection, and learn the hard lessons of the marketplace. You may come to mistrust others and approach the world warily. You may begin to expect that your performances will be negatively evaluated or that your peers will keep their contacts and connections secret from you. Feeling as if you're negotiating a minefield, you may remain continually alert and wary of the hidden agenda of others.

The artist wary of the world is less likely to want to put his products or his person out into it. Criticized enough, rejected enough, he may, like Melville after the poor reception of *Moby Dick,* not write for another thirty years. Criticized enough, the actress may stop performing, as Anjelica Huston did for six years after critics attacked her performance in *A Walk with Love and Death.*

The actor may be unable to face another audition; the writer, another editorial comment; the classical composer, another mixed review. The artist can grow so wary of these negative aspects of human contact that growing vegetables or sleeping seems like an excellent alternative to doing art.

EXISTENTIAL BLOCKS

The artist who becomes disillusioned and stops believing in the worth of his art, or in the intrinsic value of art, may experience the leakage of meaning from his art-making or performing. Albert

Camus wrote, "I have seen many people die because life for them was not worth living. From this I conclude that the question of life's meaning is the most urgent question of all." While firefighters may only rarely question the intrinsic value of firefighting or bakers the intrinsic value of baking, artists very often confront such debilitating doubts.

The actress who derives her income entirely from commercials may experience her life as depressing and empty. The writer who began with the intention of creating serious drama and who now makes a fine living writing soap operas may experience a similar meaning loss. Both may look successful but feel dejected.

A client, a young actor whose father was a successful television writer, described how such an air of disappointment and defeat hung in the air of his childhood home. His father masked his existential depression with cynicism and worldly intellectualizations, but the pessimistic message nevertheless got communicated to the son, who was battling his own depression.

What the unproductive artist describes as his failure of will or insufficient motivation may rather be an absence in his belief system of the meaningfulness of art or of the art-making he's presently doing. The most salient difference between the regularly blocked artist and the regularly productive artist may not be the greater talent of the latter, but the fact that the productive artist possesses and retains his missionary zeal.

Carlos Santana likened artists to "warriors in the trenches who have the vision of saving us from going over the edge." The artist who possesses this vision will pursue his art even if he sometimes blocks. The artist who is less certain about the sacredness of his profession or the value of his work is harder-pressed to battle for art's sake.

CONFLICTS BETWEEN LIFE AND ART

Severe conflicts arise for the artist as he attempts to apportion time and psychic energy between the regular demands of life and the regular demands of doing art. The artist is often convinced that he can't have a life *and* devote himself to art. If he wants, after his day job is done, to relax over a drink, visit friends, or put his feet up, there is no time left for art.

What a mad, inconceivable thing that a writer cannot—in any conceivable circumstances—be frank with his readers.
HERMAN MELVILLE

My slow painting, I tell myself, is like life; you don't know how it's going to end. But that doesn't release you from choosing from moment to moment, from point to point.
ANDREW FORGE

All the pressures that we human beings face—family and financial needs, inner compulsions, leaky faucets, sex drives, illnesses—conspire to throw us off course and make it seem that we need to make a choice between attending to life or attending to art. Often we feel that the decision must be an either/or one. If, consciously or not, we choose to attend to life, then our subsequent stabs at art-making are likely to be met with strong internal resistance.

FATIGUE

You may block because you are drained from your creative efforts, your marketing efforts, or both. You may simply be too tired after wrestling with the plot of your novel or the making of a hundred pounds of new clay to then write query letters to agents or locate markets for your art pottery. Each step of the way is taxing and can exhaust energy needed for the next step.

It may sometimes feel joyous and effortless to write, paint, rehearse, or go out on tour, but sometimes it feels like nothing but grueling work. It may sometimes feel like an exciting challenge to promote your novel, interest reviewers in your book, set up interviews and be interviewed, supply your publisher with a useful mailing list, and cajole a book-signing evening out of your local bookstore. But just as often you may find yourself tired before you begin.

Much of creating or performing is unglamorous, arduous, and sometimes maddeningly repetitious work. A symphony musician who plays more or less the same pieces for thirty years is typically burned out, and sometimes can only be provoked into really making music by a charismatic visiting guest conductor. Blockage here involves the artist subtly or not so subtly disconnecting from his art, practicing less, caring less, loving less. Real estate speculation becomes more attractive than music-making. The artist has not consciously disowned his art, but when he thinks about it he finds himself yawning.

Fatigue and the accompanying blockage also come with living the sort of marginal life that artists so often live. The effort required to put food on the table, to deal with an illness without benefit of a

It had been drilled into us that when an audience pays to see a performance, it is entitled to the best performance you can give. Nothing in your personal life must interfere, neither fatigue, illness, nor anxiety—not even joy.

LILLIAN GISH

Television demands a lot of material in a short time. Producers knock on your office door and ask, "Is it done?"— not "Is it funny?"

GENE PERRET

hospital plan, to pay the rent, to get a toothache treated, to attend to the needs of a spouse or children, can tire out the most passionate and dedicated artist.

PRESSURE PARALYSIS

How you perceive the importance of a given task or performance can easily cause you to block. A particularly crucial audition, book deadline, concert, or gallery show can induce the kind of anxiety that leads to total paralysis.

One flutist, appearing in her first major solo performance at Carnegie Hall, blocked on the first piece, left the stage, and the next day departed New York for good. Although she remained a musician, she no longer dared aspire to a career as a celebrated concert soloist. That one terrible moment of performance anxiety altered the course of her life.

The paralysis may not strike only in the actual moment of execution. Artists with an important event looming on the horizon can, out of mounting anxiety, easily fail to rehearse, write, or paint. Sometimes, after a long period of procrastination and blockage, they manage to avert disaster through last-minute heroics—the manuscript is delivered on time, the part is memorized, the piece rehearsed. These artists can even convince themselves that they need or like deadlines and the feeling of last-minute pressure. But nevertheless they know that the period before the heroics commence is one of frustration, depression, and self-criticism.

If an artist holds every one of his products or performances as desperately important, he may find this cycle of procrastination and feverish last-minute heroics becoming a way of life. He may then succumb to a stress-induced illness and burn out, or contrive to limit his opportunities in order to avoid the accompanying anxiety.

ENVIRONMENTAL BLOCKS

The artist often finds himself living in a noisy, chaotic, or uproarious environment. Because he lives marginally, he may have roommates. Because he lives in New York or Los Angeles, his cousins from the

The only people who claim that money is not important are people who have enough money so that they are relieved of the ugly burden of thinking about it.

JOYCE CAROL OATES

I would get paralyzed, once in an office, and would be unable to remember the name of the play I was trying to get a job in.

KIM STANLEY

Midwest will want to visit, just when he feels ripe to paint. Or, because he works so much in isolation in the country, he may desire a trip into town as an antidote to that isolation, at the very moment when he might write a short story instead.

The life of a writer is usually one of permanent insecurity.

JAMES T. FARRELL

Often the lives of artists are busily sexual, filled with considerable partying, drug-using, and much internal and external noise. In such a lively environment the artist encounters difficulty writing, painting, or rehearsing. If you spend too much time in such chaos you may begin to experience solitude as intolerable and find your moments of hard-won silence deafening and maddening.

SOCIAL BLOCKS

Many of us grow up learning social, cultural, or familial rules that can inhibit creative work. We may also block in the face of the social evaluations that come our way as adult working artists.

The female artist who learned rules about politeness and femininity may now find it difficult to adopt an appropriately assertive stance. She may defer to men and dislike herself for doing so, run errands and clean up rather than do her art, and in many ways play out stereotypical female roles. The male artist, for his part, may have been told that art was a feminine pursuit, unsuitable work for a man.

Or the artist may have grown up in a cultural environment in which hard work was not particularly valued, in which working at art was not prized, or in which the demands for conformity were overwhelming. The artist may have been encouraged to play an instrument, for instance, but in a context of great cultural conformity, so that practicing came easily as long as there were clear directions and strict teachers. When such an artist enters a conservatory where he must structure his own time and make his own decisions, he may falter.

Criticism and rejection are twin demons in the sphere of social evaluations. It takes courage and a persistent dismissal of the evaluative powers of others for the writer to resubmit his manuscript after a dozen agents have panned it, for the painter to send out slides of his paintings one more time after a hundred gallery owners have returned them, for the dancer to continue in a dance company even though every single day the director calls him fat.

Sometimes what fails the artist is not his courage but his ability to keep these critical evaluations from getting under his skin. He may then begin to believe that he really is too fat, or that his paintings really are too red, or that his novel really is too quiet, not because he's come to that judgment himself but because others tell him so.

Nobody can become perfect by merely ceasing to act.
BHAGAVAD-GITA

MATERIAL-SPECIFIC BLOCKS

The productive artist who rarely blocks will sometimes be stymied when he finds himself unable to answer a particular artistic, technical, or practical question that confronts him. The sculptor may face a commission larger in scale and more ambitious than anything he's tackled before. The novelist, having boxed herself into a corner with a new idea that she loves, may have no idea how to end her story. The violinist, examining the score of a rigorous competition piece he's planning to add to his repertoire, may see that he's chosen something at the outer limits of his virtuosity. He may block not because he can't play the piece, but because he fears he can't play the piece. The painter, deciding on an intellectual level to make a move from gestural abstract expressionism to figurative abstract expressionism, may not know how to translate that intent into art. The actor, used to bravely auditioning for any contemporary part under the sun, may flee from an offer to play an Elizabethan role.

Since the work facing artists is regularly challenging, and sometimes fiercely so, they frequently block as they attempt to meet that challenge. Proceeding up a rock wall just as sheer as the ones they tackled before, and maybe sheerer, they must create their own footholds and handholds. Every artist will sometimes dangle there, a thousand feet above the valley, without a clue how to get up or get down.

SKILL DEFICITS

You may have an idea of what you wish to create but may lack the technical skills necessary to get the job done. Until you acquire those skills through training and practice, or until you let go of the idea of doing that particular creative piece, blockage will occur.

The difference between this block and the preceding one is that in the former case the artist has the skills necessary to do the work—to tackle the large sculpture, difficult violin piece, or Elizabethan role. It is fear, doubt, inexperience, or confusion that prevents him from proceeding. In the present case proceeding is impossible, unless and until a certain skill is acquired.

I can't imagine getting up in the morning full of enthusiasm to make something that I already made the day before.

CAREL VISSER

Van Gogh, for example, deciding at the age of 28 not to commit suicide but rather to retire as a preacher and begin life anew as a painter, knew that he lacked the drawing skills necessary to paint at the level to which he aspired. Instead of blocking, he determined to spend the next two years teaching himself to draw. A less honest, rigorous, and dedicated artist would surely have ended up perplexed at his inability to paint to his liking.

I read once that F. Scott Fitzgerald saw a watch he wanted, so he wrote a short story, sold it, and bought the watch. It just seemed to me totally glamorous, to live hand to mouth.

RONA JAFFE

MYTHS AND IDEALIZATIONS

Myths about creativity, the creative process, the artist's personality, and the artist's life can all contribute to blockage. The artist who waits to be inspired before beginning work may wait a very long time. The artist who goes out searching for community, dreaming of finding a modern-day Paris-of-the-Twenties, may wander endlessly. The artist who romanticizes his drinking, his self-abuse, his eccentricities, his differentness may lead himself down paths he comes to despise.

Artists who idealize stardom, who believe they can't live without it, may block if stardom eludes them. Naturally, any artist is hard-pressed not to crave stardom. Attaining it is often the only way one can make a living at art. Our culture, for its part, encourages the idea that one is either a star or a failure. Consciously or not, you begin to label even your significant successes as failures, if those successes don't bring you stardom. Even a string of successes may not warm your heart much.

Thus the thought may intrude on you, even as you're working well on a short story, that the story won't make you famous—and you stop writing. Or you realize, even as you accept work in a good orchestra, that by accepting the position you're sealing your fate as an ensemble player and dooming yourself to obscurity, and so experience a panic attack as you write your letter of acceptance.

On the other side, the famous artist who has dreamed of fame and gotten it may, in turn, find fame an empty and unmagical commodity. For the person who has it, fame can lose its cachet entirely, leaving such an artist at an existential impasse.

Tolstoy, who achieved enormous fame by age 40 as the most revered writer in Russia, began to disparage the stardom he had always desired. He complained bitterly:

> Well, what if I should be more famous than Gogol, Pushkin, Shakespeare, Moliere—than all the writers of the world—well, and what then? I could find no reply. Such questions demand an immediate answer; without one it is impossible to live. Yet answer there was none.

People talk about Alcoholics Anonymous suddenly ending a bad habit, but it's really a question of the person himself coming to a slow but finally complete understanding of the nature of his own illness.
ROBERT YOUNG

Tolstoy could find no compelling myth, no adaptive illusion, to replace the myth of stardom. He wrote very little fiction for the next forty years of his life.

SELF-ABUSE

Substance abuse is rampant in the arts. You may abuse speed, alcohol, cocaine, heroin, or some other drug, including tranquilizers, sleeping pills, and codeine. Or you may be engaged in other ritualistic, compulsive, time-consuming, and self-damaging behaviors that give you a thrill or quell your anxiety, but that also leave you frayed and injured.

The artist-abuser can get a good deal of creative work done. He may even get to the top of his profession. But his affairs will not be in order, and time that he might have spent doing art will instead be spent making messes and cleaning them up.

One client, a musician, stopped while on his way to our counseling appointment to sell his instrument in order to buy smoking heroin. Another client, a performer, came to every early appointment on speed. To say that the musician bereft of his instrument or the performer on speed were blocked is simply to underscore the fact that blocks and problems of living are one-in-the-same thing.

Sometimes the artist is too busy scoring, too busy maintaining a drug habit, too busy recovering from excesses to even entertain the notion of working creatively.

ANXIETIES

Anxiety is the most prominent feature of virtually all creative blocks. Our anxieties—our nerves, doubts, worries, fears, sweats, panics—constrain us all the time. They control us to such an extent that they almost make the case for opponents of the idea of free will. If the anxiety is generalized the artist may feel himself troubled and unsafe everywhere: at his desk and on his way to his desk, at his easel and away from it, in the wings before a performance and at the cast party and the supermarket. One client, for instance, who complained of being too anxious to audition, also doubted that she could control her car and feared driving to my office.

Living is the source of my unease, because living means living anxiously.

EUGÈNE IONESCO

The anxieties that plague artists and prevent them from working are not invariably neurotic ones. Quite realistic worries can torment the artist, too. You may worry that your mate, who is unhappy at her job, will stop supporting you. You worry that playing a certain role will typecast you. You worry that your violent visual imagery will not fly in the marketplace. You wonder if it would be wiser to do graphics, which have a chance of selling, rather than your large-scale paintings, which rarely sell. You worry that the chemicals you use in your art-making are toxic. You wonder if it's too dangerous to write a book that ridicules the Moslem religion. Such questions naturally arise in your life, and with them comes blockage.

Moral anxieties may also confront you. As one contemporary writer put it, "I said to myself that if *People* magazine ever interviewed me, I'd fight to maintain my dignity. I'd refuse to let them photograph me sitting on the roof of my house, the way they like to photograph celebrities. Well, here's the photograph they took of me perched up in a tree."

You're often asked to do things, or decide it prudent or necessary to do things, that violate your principles. Your editor suggests that your novel would be much more readable if it had more plot. Should you agree? Should you add the kidnapping your editor wants? While struggling to decide whether modifying the plot would be a small sin, a large sin, or no sin at all, you may find it impossible to proceed. If you opt not to make the change, you experience the realistic anxiety that your editor will not like the book, and that she may be right about its chances of success. If you opt to add the kidnapping, you may experience pangs of self-hatred and self-disgust.

In either case, you may wonder why you're having so much trouble meeting your deadline.

An artist with a fertile imagination and a wealth of ideas, or an artist with several simultaneous work opportunities, may find his anxiety level rise as he attempts to choose among the possibilities before him. Such anxiety can produce the kind of blockage that prevents him from really choosing, either rationally or intuitively, a course of action. Instead he may let his agent or best friend make the decision; or spend the next two years of his life working on one novel rather than another simply because his penny came up heads. When, blinded by anxiety, you make decisions in this fashion, it is easy to later block as you try to execute your plan—a plan that came, after all, from nowhere except a coin toss.

A piece of iron is an idea in itself, a powerful and unyielding object. I must gain complete mastery over it, and force it to take on the tension which I feel within myself, evolving a theme from dynamism.

EDUARDO CHILLIDA

DEPRESSION

Depression, like anxiety, can prevent you from working. Like anxiety, it is probably present in the majority of cases of creative blockage. A depressive episode can stop even the most productive artist in his tracks. Depression has stopped artists as fiercely creative as Van Gogh and Beethoven for significant periods. A depressed mood may envelop the artist, preventing him from working. Or his inability to work, arising from some other source, may bring on the depressed mood. In either case, the artist is confounded by his case of the blues, or by his severe and intractable depression, and has little energy left to make art, to meet the marketplace, or to face life in general.

INCUBATION AND FALLOW PERIODS

If you're deeply and honorably wrestling with artistic questions out of conscious awareness, if you're doing the work of writing or painting but without pen or brush in hand, you may still in conscious awareness feel blocked and frustrated.

Ideas in art must incubate, just as ideas in science must incubate; but neither the artist nor the scientist feels fully content as he lets his unconscious do its work. Still, you must sometimes wait.

You may be in the minority and have symphonies come to you whole, as they came to Mozart. But even then you must wait, as Mozart did, for the propitious carriage ride during which the symphony courses through you. Or you may be in the majority, more plodding and less inspired, and believe in the necessity of hard work. Then, too, you must sometimes wait, for days, weeks, years, or even decades, as Beethoven sometimes waited for certain of his musical bits and scraps to come together as symphonies.

Creative people knock on silence for an answering music; they pursue meaninglessness until they can force it to mean.

ROLLO MAY

Even when you take a well-earned break between projects, you may feel so uncomfortable not working that you judge yourself blocked. Consistently creative artists, who despise unproductivity, may complain bitterly about their work habits, lack of discipline, or lack of imagination, even though they are turning out a novel every year or a record album every six months like clockwork.

THE MIRACLE OF THE CREATIVE ACT

Human beings are challenged to be creative, for dullness and blockage come much more easily than creativity. A multitude of constraints prevent us from making exceptional art.

You're challenged to make basic decisions about your art—whether to paint large or small, realistically or abstractly, with gouache on paper or oil on canvas. You're challenged to rethink those decisions when your art seems out of focus. You're challenged to deal with the small and often enormous blocks that prevent you from working well or working at all.

It does seem a wonder that anyone manages to produce excellent art. Carefully made and deeply felt art products and performances are, after all, miracles: gifts given against great odds. But it is also an incontrovertible fact that creative and performing artists regularly do break through their blocks and produce that long-bottled-up novel, suite of photographs, song, or performance piece.

STRATEGIES

Isolate the block that affects you and create a plan to eliminate it. If more than one block confronts you, prepare different plans of action to combat each.

A participant in one of my writing workshops said, "I was surprised how helpful it was to identify and 'domesticate' the blocks. The biggest step for me was owning my blocks. That galvanized me into working up a second draft on the piece I've been writing, which is a miracle."

Identifying and owning your blocks can produce important, human-sized miracles. To neutralize or combat each block, choose strategies from the following blockbusting menu. Experiment and trust that your honorable trial-and-error efforts will help you determine which strategies work best for you.

The excitement and joy I have after each success is always brief, while the hardship in writing is constant.

BAI FENGXI

Blockbusting Menu

Use guided writing. Working on step 7 of the guided writing program (see the Introduction), begin to zero in on the block or blocks that affect you. You may effectively narrow your focus by finding a word that captures the essence of your particular block. For one client, who was trying to write songs, that word turned out to be *embarrassment.* She was embarrassed to learn that the songs emerging from her were country-western songs, whereas she'd thought on a conscious level that she meant to do more "sophisticated" work than that. For another client the word was *fear.* Doing the work of sculpture for him was like standing too near the edge of a chasm. To help break through this block he decided to visit the Grand Canyon and actually stand at the edge of a chasm, to really feel the fear and confront the block.

Make a list of the 20 types of blocks described in this chapter. Work on numbering and ordering them, until you have a good idea of their relative place in your creative life. Isolate the blocks that appear most troublesome—the top half-dozen, say—and create one tactic to overcome each block.

If self-criticism heads the list, for instance, you might determine to meet with your inner critic. Seat him in the chair opposite you. What are his charges? That you're untalented? That you're too fat for a dancer? That you're too big a bundle of nerves to ever audition again? Listen to his charges. Think about them. Respond to them in writing—this is the very essence of your guided writing work. As you engage in this written dialogue, see if your inner critic can be transformed into a collaborator who has advice to offer, rather than a mean-spirited opponent with only complaints to lodge.

By proceeding in this fashion you can address each block in turn and also continue the personality integration work outlined in chapter 2. The ultimate goals are both to master the block of the moment and to become the sort of person who only rarely blocks.

Painting for me is a freedom attained, constantly consolidated, vigilantly guarded so as to draw from it the power to paint more.

ALBERTO BURRI

Other guided writing questions to consider:

- Is the source of my blockage something other than the 20 described in this chapter? How would I characterize my block?

- Is my problem a particular, recurrent combination of blocks? Can I tease the combination apart and work on each block separately, or does it make more sense to work on them all together? (Effectively using a behavioral contract, described in the Introduction, would be one way to work on all blocks at once. Such contracting demands certain behaviors on your part—a certain number of words written each day, a certain amount of time spent rehearsing—irrespective of the sources of blockage.)

- Do I block only on certain work? Is rewriting easier than writing, performing easier than auditioning, a face-to-face meeting with an agent easier than a telephone conversation?

- Do I block only in certain places? Can I write songs on the road but not at home? Could I paint in the larger studio I used to have, but have trouble painting in my present cramped work space?

- Do I block only at certain times of the day? Are there a certain few hours of each day during which I am almost invariably alert and creative?

- Do I block seasonally? Am I regularly unproductive in the spring, summer, fall, or winter?

- Is the blockage recent? What has changed in my life? Have my feelings about art changed? My feelings about the future? My feelings about myself? Has some event or series of events precipitated the blockage?

- What is one thing I can do to tackle my blocks? What is another thing I can do? Can I generate a whole list of things I can do?

Learn anxiety- and stress-reduction techniques. For example, combat pressure paralysis by learning to hold on to the importance *and* the unimportance of the task before you. If an audition is coming up, practice balancing these two positions by holding your palms out-stretched and weighing the importance of the audition in your left palm and its unimportance in your right palm. Is all the weight in your left palm? Learn to transfer some weight to your right—and hence to detach a little.

Practice meditation, learn progressive relaxation techniques, begin an exercise program. If you experience persistent or inca-pacitating anxiety, consult the strategies section at the end of chapter 3 and begin a comprehensive treatment program.

I need to touch music as well as to think it, which is why I have always lived next to a piano.
IGOR STRAVINSKY

Change your behavior. Introduce new habits and rituals into your life. Maintain a behavioral contract with yourself, as described in the In-troduction. Change your work environment, your routines, your customary practice times. Make schedules and honor them. Do art first thing Sunday morning, before you read the paper. Set goals and limits. A significant behavioral change—working four hours at your writing, say, instead of zero hours—is, in one sense at least, the ex-act equivalent of block elimination.

Use cognitive restructuring. Change how you think about yourself. Consider yourself capable rather than incapable. Consider yourself talented rather than untalented. Refuse to allow negative self-talk. For a fuller discussion of cognitive restructuring, consult the Intro-duction.

Use affirmations and visualizations. Visualize your goals. Affirm that you can work. Affirm that you can succeed and that success does not frighten you. Create simple affirmations that resonate for you, affir-mations as simple as "I can do this" or "It's time." There is a grow-ing literature on the power and use of affirmations (as well as a millennia-old tradition of their use) which you may want to consult.

Build a support system. Join or form a writers' group. Join a procras-tinators' group. Have lunch with your agent and brainstorm ideas. Collaborate with other actors on a project. Collaborate with other writers on a book. Invite an art buddy over for tea and generate ex-citement for your latest painting plans. Share an idea with your class. Ask your teacher for help. Assign your children the task of gently reminding you that a deadline is fast approaching.

Manipulate meaning. Construct and integrate into your belief system the adaptive illusion that your work is valuable. Reinvest meaning in your art-making and your vocation as an artist. Make challenges out of problems. Recast your beliefs so that your work looks more inviting. Weave your own meaning web, taking charge of the individual strands of meaning and of the completed existential fabric.

Educate yourself. Gather blockbusting techniques from books. Take a class to erase a skills deficit. Attend marketing workshops. Learn how to inoculate yourself against unwanted thoughts. Take an assertiveness training course and defeat your passivity. Educate yourself about your own personality and about the marketplace. Learn what resources are available and make use of them.

The only sound advice I can give to the young writer is to tell him to have faith in himself.

HOWARD FAST

I've finally come to the conclusion that you must accept what's bad about your work along with what's good. Maybe they are one and the same.

LILLIAN HELLMAN

CHAPTER 5

The Business *of* Art

An artist after many phone calls finally got an appointment with a local art dealer. The dealer kept him waiting for an hour, looked through his portfolio, and told him, "Come back when you're dead."

SAM PROVENZANO

Do you realize what would happen if Moses were alive today? He'd go up to Mount Sinai, come back with the Ten Commandments, and spend the next eight years trying to get published.

ROBERT ORBEN

YOU ARE TALENTED AND CREATIVE. You rarely block, and when you do block you know how to move yourself along. Your moods are not incapacitating and you haven't stepped over into madness. Your personality is sufficiently integrated that your necessary arrogance doesn't prevent you from having successful relationships, your nonconformity hasn't made you a pariah, and your skepticism hasn't bred in you a nihilistic darkness. You work happily in isolation but can also move into the world and have a life. You have, in short, met the challenges posed so far.

Are you home free? Unfortunately not. The next challenges you face are as great as any posed so far. They are the multiple challenges of doing the business of art: making money, developing a career, acknowledging and making the most of your limited opportunities,

living with compromise, dealing with mass taste and commercial-
ism, negotiating the marketplace, and making personal sense of the
mechanics and metaphysics of the business environment of art.

Many an artist grows bitter in this difficult arena. Many an artist flounders. Only the rare artist sits himself down to examine these
matters, for they are painful to consider. But you have no choice but
to examine them. If you are an artist, you want an audience. And if
you want an audience, you must do business.

ART AND THE MARKETPLACE

The business of art requires care and a significant amount of time.
Typically artists neither love this work nor do it well. But if you're
not your own supporter and promoter, coach, business manager,
market analyst, salesperson, best business friend, and maker of
luck, then you're likely to have a marginal career at best.

Many artists never admit that they are in business for themselves, even as they pursue their fiction sales or concert bookings.
Others admit that a marketplace exists, but argue that it shouldn't
be permitted to dictate to them. Both positions, the former a kind of
denial and the latter a kind of rebellion, stem not so much from the
artist's inability to do business—for in his day job he may work with
a budget of millions or a staff of twenty—but from a variety of
complicated factors, among them pride, anxiety, and sense of
mission.

How would your sense of mission, for instance, prevent you
from doing business? Your mission is to do art, not commerce. The
people who can promote you do commerce, not art. You know that
the publisher, the gallery owner, the network executive, the Hollywood producer are merchants. You know that the literary agent
looking for a romance novel or a mystery story is looking for a certain
kind of merchandise. As the painter John Baldessari put it:

> For a dealer, the only reality is the rent. A lot of ambiguities about
> artist-dealer relationships would be cleared up if art dealers were
> called art merchants. That's what they do. They sell art for money.
> They are not messengers from god with divine knowledge about
> what's art and what isn't. They show you because they think they can
> make money from what you do.

*There should be a single Art
Exchange in the world, to which
the artist would simply send his
works and be given in return as
much as he needs. As it is, one
has to be half a merchant on top
of everything else, and how
badly one goes about it!*

LUDWIG VAN
BEETHOVEN

You're also likely to believe that the public should be given what it needs, not what it wants. This vision flows from your love of your medium and your respect for traditions. You hold, in short, to a heroic ideal, or to a code of ethics. Zelda Fichandler, longtime manager of the District of Columbia's Arena Theater, said:

> While a theater is a public art and belongs to its public, it is an art before it is public, and so it belongs first to itself, and its first service must be self-service. A theater is part of its society. But it is a part which must remain apart since it is also chastiser, rebel, lightning rod, redeemer, and irritant.

You can't spend those unbelievable millions of dollars on something too risky for the kids who make up most of the movie audience now.

GEORGE CUKOR

This is the ideal; but for a regional repertory company, an orchestra, a dance company, or an individual artist, the reality remains that the audience pays the bills. In this regard Fichandler added, "The only real criterion for judging a production is the power of the impression it makes on the audience."

This is not so much a contradiction as a recognition that two positions exist, the artistic and the commercial. Between these two an abiding tension persists. The eighteenth-century American painter Gilbert Stuart complained, "What a business is that of portrait painter. He is brought a potato and is expected to paint a peach." The artist learns that the public wants peaches, not potatoes. You can paint potatoes if you like, write potatoes, dance potatoes, and compose potatoes, you can with great and valiant effort communicate with some other potato-eaters and peach-eaters. In so doing you contribute to the world's reservoir of truth and beauty. But if you won't give the public peaches, you won't be paid much.

Repeatedly artists take the heroic potato position. They want their work to be good, honest, powerful—and only then successful. They want their work to be alive, not contrived and formulaic. As the Norwegian painter Edvard Munch put it: "No longer shall I paint interiors, and people reading, and women knitting. I shall paint living people, who breathe and feel and suffer and love."

The artist is interested in the present and has little desire to repeat old, albeit successful, formulas. As the painter Jenny Holzer put it, "I could do a pretty good third-generation stripe painting, but so what?"

The unexpected result of the artist's determination to do his own best art is that he is put in an adversarial relationship with the public and with those who sell to the public. In that adversarial position he comes to feel rather irrational. For what rational person would do work that's not wanted?

The popular music scene today is unlike any scene I can think of in the history of music. It's completely of, by, and for the kids.

LEONARD BERNSTEIN

What rational theater director would put on plays that the public won't come to see? What rational filmmaker would make personal films no distributor will take? What rational composer would attempt a composition for full symphony orchestra, understanding that he'll never hear it performed unless he pays an orchestra to perform it? It appears more rational to sign a vow of poverty or to run full-speed into a brick wall than to engage in such frustrating activities.

The public, and players in the marketplace, smile indulgently at you, the artist. They, after all, are rational; you are irrational. They understand the bottom line; you are dense. But you understand, perhaps outside of conscious awareness, that their supposed rationality is a lie. Todd Gitlin, a student of marketplace dynamics and the notorious bottom line in television and publishing, wrote:

> Again and again, as I walked into corporate offices in Century City and environs, I was told to put aside my putative naivete and recognize that television was about making money, period. But often enough the success record compiled by such ostensible geniuses of economic calculation, by their own lights, is abysmal. Just because executives intone allegiance to their peculiar version of rationality doesn't mean that they deserve to be regarded as rational. Corporate publishers are always throwing money away—on giant advances, overprinting, glitzy salaries, slush funds, and bright ideas. Last year alone [1989] Simon & Schuster wrote down $150 million in losses.

Luchino Visconti, the Italian director, said of the Hollywood movie, "It is about money and the bogus morality. Always, they want to lower the picture, to make it pleasing to the most uneducated man in the smallest town in the most faraway state."

You may feel stupid as you process the advice you get. Judith Applebaum and Nancy Evans, authors of *How to Get Happily Published,* for instance, advise the writer that

> it is largely within your power to determine whether a publisher will buy your work and whether the public will buy it once it's released.

Failures abound because hardly anybody treats getting published as if it were a rational, manageable activity—like practicing law or laying bricks—in which knowledge coupled with skill and application would suffice to ensure success.

This advice, which, like bottom-line logic, wears the mantle of supreme rationality, is almost certainly false advice for the poet, for the writer working on her version of *Ulysses,* for the painter painting in a new idiom, for the screenwriter with a serious screenplay to sell, for the actress looking for serious roles in film. It is advice that can only be translated as "write peaches, not potatoes."

America is still a frontier country that almost shudders at the idea of creative expression.
JAMES MICHENER

Only if the writer's product is wanted in the marketplace are there rational ways of seeking a publisher and selling the work (although, as the author Peter Benchley put it, the matter still rests squarely in the hands of the "god of whimsy"). But it is largely outside the power of the writer attempting to create literature to determine whether a publisher will buy his work or whether his novel will do well in the marketplace once published. Serious fiction, like serious theater and serious music, simply does not sell well.

Serious work not only doesn't sell well, it's also judged by different standards than is commercial work. If the artist writes an imperfect but commercial novel it is likely to be published and sold. If the book is imperfect and also uncommercial it will not have that happy fate. If his screenplay is imperfect but commercial enough it may be produced. If it is imperfect and also uncommercial it will not be produced. If his painting is imperfect but friendly and familiar, it may sell. If it is imperfect and also new and difficult, it may not sell for decades, if ever.

Ironically enough, the artist attempting serious work must also attain the very highest level of distinction possible. He must produce *Crime and Punishment* and *The Brothers Karamazov* but not also *The Insulted and Injured* or *A Raw Youth,* two of Dostoevsky's nearly unknown novels. He is given precious little slack in this regard.

CAREER AND COMPROMISE

As you look around you, you see that commercial art not only sells, but even has permission to be bad. Noncommercial art not only doesn't sell, but must be singular to have even the slightest chance.

Understanding that such an enormous chasm exists between the commercial and the artistic, you frequently begin to formulate two different sets of career goals. You determine that, while you would love to make money from your cherished art, you will also pursue any other financial avenues available to you. You make an agreement with yourself to attempt just so much commercial work.

Probably the biggest bring-down in my life—it's so hypo-critical—was being in a pop group and finding out just how much it was like everything it was supposed to be against.

MAMA CASS ELLIOT

In making this inner arrangement you think of yourself as a professional. This is a new, additional, and frequently burdensome piece of identity to wear. The professional dancer determines to dance in anything. The professional actor determines to act in anything. The professional writer determines to write anything. You start on nonfiction or commercial fiction. You audition more for commercials than for live theater. Wanting to mold a band in your image, instead you take a job in an established band. You take advertising assignments and put your art photography away. You find your way onto a variety show, hoping to funnel the proceeds into the small dance company you mean to establish.

The artist's self-image changes a little or a lot the more he compromises and begins to see himself as a professional. In the extreme he lets go of art altogether. As the swing-era musician and arranger Sy Oliver put it:

> I was a professional arranger who used to do whatever the situation called for. There are different types of musicians. There's the story-book musician, the guy who loves music and hangs around all night and jams as long as there's someone to play with. Then there's the professional musician, who is in the business to earn money, period. That's me.

Naturally you feel uncomfortable as you work out your own brand of compromise. But compromise is necessary, and you are challenged to make peace with your decisions. The cynical artist, the unimaginative artist, the pragmatic artist have compromised from the beginning. If you agree at a late date to compromise, you are challenged to integrate that significant change into the web of your being.

At the same time you long to have your best work supported, recognized, and valued, even if it can't pay its own way. Henry F. B. Gilbert, the American composer, expressed this wish as follows:

True Art seldom pays for itself; at least not for a long time. And the finer it is the less likelihood there is of its paying for itself. Money, advanced to a composer to free him from the necessity of earning it, should be regarded in the light of an investment; not as a material investment which shall eventually bring returns in kind, but as a spiritual investment which shall eventually bring rich returns of an artistic or cultural nature.

Art that has to pay its own way is apt to become vitiated and cheap.
ANTONIN DVOŘÁK

But artists must usually compromise to survive. As one screen-writer said of his life in Hollywood, "They ruin your stories. They massacre your ideas. They prostitute your art. They trample on your pride. And what do you get for it? A fortune."

The visual artist Tim Rollins, describing his South Bronx neighborhood art program for learning-disabled, emotionally troubled teenagers, argued for his brand of compromise:

> We at the Art and Knowledge Workshop are a little like East Germany—we started out radical and ended up entrepreneurial. But I would much rather shake hands with the devil than be a martyr for some idea of purity. It's better to make certain political compromises than not pay the kids and lose them to the economy of the streets, which is mainly drug dealing.

The visual artist Sandro Chia argued that the artist, free to tackle any kind of work in the privacy of his studio, is still a slave to the system into which he is born:

> An artist is free to do whatever he likes in formulating his work, even the most extravagant things, but he is not allowed to say one word against the economy because the economy will punish him in the cruelest way. It has always been like this. At one time, it was the Pope or the emperor who chose the artist and decided how much he was valued. Now, it is done by a headless entity consisting of auctions, rumors, the media, newspapers, art magazines, interviews, and so on. If you're out, you're out—you simply don't count. There is no opposition, no different opinion. Anything that happens must happen within this system.

You set limits for yourself as to how far you will compromise. But when your editor tells you that your next novel could be your breakthrough book—a real bestseller—if only it possessed a tad more excitement, you must look at the line you've drawn in the sand and think hard about drawing it over again or carving it in deeper.

Is there a formula for how to compromise? Does the writer gain permission from himself to write a potboiler if he pledges to do a serious novel next? Does the successful actor keep his star in ascendancy in pop movies but determine to make every fourth movie a significant one? The pressure to compromise is enormous. A Pablo Picasso self-portrait sells for $47.85 million. Two books by Ken Follett are bought for $12.3 million, and three by Jeffrey Archer are bid on at $20 million. Jack Nicholson makes a fortune on *Batman* and Steven Spielberg makes a fortune on *E.T.* Whether these figures are generated by astounding art or by astoundingly commercial art, they send shock waves through the artist's system. And so the artist is sorely tempted to draw the line closer to mammon.

Of course it may then hurt the artist's feelings to be labeled commercial, for he understands that he is being criticized for selling out. Even an artist with the tiniest audience can find himself having to dodge this charge, even as he starves to death. As Herbie Mann, the jazz musician, put it, "If you're in jazz and more than ten people like you, you're labeled commercial."

The artist may unconsciously determine to avoid this tense business of compromising by doing art for which there is no commercial market whatsoever. He may guarantee that he will not have to deal with the world of commerce by choosing, say, to write poetry. Of course he writes poetry because, first of all, he loves it and needs to write it; but he may also harbor the understanding that his choice allows him to remain apart from the fray. He may then entertain the role of uncompromising artist with a certain smugness and a certain sense of relief.

Because the marketplace frustrates you, you may simply avoid attending to business. Because the challenges you face in taking care of business are taxing and complicated ones, you may feel exhausted and defeated before you begin. You know that to have a career you must negotiate a maze full of obstacles, a maze designed, it would seem, to test your courage, principles, heart, and soul. This is a dizzying prospect that you approach with a touch of vertigo.

It is true that making a dollar is hard for everyone, artists and nonartists alike. As the performance artist Eric Bogosian put it, "The artist today has it harder but so does the truck driver and the

I looked around and I saw other jazz musicians who were limited, guys who wouldn't compromise their talent and wouldn't search for an audience. I don't think I ever compromised my talent, but I did search for a newer audience.

GEORGE BENSON

doctor because, economically, it sucks out there." For the artist the path to a dollar is a particularly mystifying proposition. Is it more important to be good, to be mediocre in a certain sort of way, to be well connected, to be white and male, or to be lucky?

Such questions confound and infuriate the artist. But you are nevertheless challenged to come to grips with the fact that the answers to these questions matter. In so doing you will see that your business has two sides to it: the mechanical side, which many artists' self-help and marketing books address, and the metaphysical side, which this chapter addresses.

If I go into Universal and even mention the word art, security forces will come and take me away.

TERRY GILLIAM

THE MECHANICS AND METAPHYSICS OF ART AS BUSINESS

The mechanical and the metaphysical come together for each artist as that artist's particular career path. That path is a function of the artist's personality, the product he determines to sell, the goodness or appropriateness of that product, the array of compromises he is willing to make, his historical moment and cultural milieu, his group associations (as a Chinese-American actor or an African-American painter, for example), the decisions he makes (about teachers, mentors, and so on), and luck.

Let's look at a painter's career first. On the mechanical side, you attend an art school or a university art program, have art school shows, learn to send out slides of your paintings and contact gallery owners. You maintain mailing lists and attempt to find fair and regular representation for your work. You frame your paintings if you can afford to. You try to become known to purchasers of art. You prepare for shows, sign contracts, garner commissions, deliver your paintings to buyers, and the like.

On the metaphysical side are all of the following considerations: *What* are you painting? Is it the right moment for what you're painting? How many painters can your culture sustain, and how many painters are vying for the available slots? How does your personality help or hinder your ability to sell your art? In quelling your anxiety about the demands of the marketplace, do you rush away from contacts or rush toward them? In your historical moment, is it providential to be a woman painter, a Midwestern painter, a Primitive

It is impossible for ideas to compete in the marketplace if no forum for their presentation is provided or available.

THOMAS MANN

painter, or an Italian-American painter? How do you hold art—as craft, decoration, entertainment, sacred product? How are your stars crossed or uncrossed?

The metaphysics of the matter combine into a prescription for failure or for success. You may be the wrong person doing the wrong art at the wrong time. On the other hand, you may be thrust by accident into a museum exhibit that becomes the hottest show of the decade. This happened to Nathan Oliveira in 1959, when, at the age of 27, he found himself included in the Images of Man show at the Museum of Modern Art with Jackson Pollock, Willem de Kooning, and Alberto Giacometti.

The luck of having talent is not enough; one must also have a talent for luck.

HECTOR BERLIOZ

Because you are painting in a style, a size, and colors that are popular, you may find yourself (by accident or design) at the forefront of a movement to which attention is paid. At a certain propitious moment, your work is reviewed by the right reviewer or appears in the right show. The impact is not lost in the next instant but, because of your personality or connections or sheer luck, you capitalize on the opportunity. All of a sudden you matter, and your soup cans, black abstractions, or superrealistic images of cordless telephones become all the rage.

For the suddenly successful artist everything may come together in a kind of synergistic explosion that catapults him from anonymity to celebrityhood. Caroll Michels describes this synergistic moment as follows:

> Curator tells dealer that critic wrote an excellent review about artist. Dealer checks out artist and invites artist into gallery. Dealer tells curator that artist is now part of gallery. Curator tells museum colleagues that artist is part of gallery and has backing of critic. Curator invites artist to exhibit at museum. Curator asks critic to write introduction to exhibition catalog in which artist is included. Dealer tells clients that artist has been well reviewed and is exhibiting at museum. Clients buy.

Can this success happen unless you are calculating, unless you put yourself in the right spot at the right moment with the right product? It can and has. But the moment is altogether more likely to happen if your personality is such that you naturally think of hiring a publicist to keep your name alive, if you naturally stir up controversy, if you understand trends and fashions, if you offer up peaches, if you enlist everybody's aid in your cause.

Now let's look at the novelist. From the mechanical point of view, you attend a creative writing program, begin to send out your first stories, and get published in your student magazine. You work on your first novel, try to interest a literary agent in it, submit clean manuscripts and appropriately stamped return envelopes. You study the market, network at writing conferences, sign contracts and meet deadlines, work with editors, publicize your work, struggle to move from your small press to a larger publisher or from the mid-list to the front of the list.

But what is your first novel about? That is a matter of first principles. Is it meant to be frankly commercial? Is it a genre piece in a popular style? If it is neither commercial nor in an established genre, will it have the luck to strike that synergistic moment where reviews and reader interest come together in a kind of firestorm of publicity?

For one writer, the greater part of success may be calculation. He will frankly write commercial mysteries, will understand the formula and the market, will give each story its own spin but not spin it away from what's expected of the genre. For another writer, success will be a matter of fortune. The right agent accepts his imperfect manuscript, the right publisher buys it, the right editor supports it, it has something in it that ignites interest in just that historical moment. Reviewers fan the flames, and the public chooses his novel as the one serious novel they will read that year.

This sort of fortune is recounted too often in the biographies of well-known artists to be ignored. You may have the fortune, for instance, to have the sort of roommate Dostoevsky had. Upon reading Dostoevsky's first short novel, *Poor People,* the roommate literally ran with it to the preeminent literary critic in Russia, Vissarion Belinsky. Belinsky read it, loved it, and single-handedly made Dostoevsky's name.

But the Russian author's fortune was not just to have that helpful roommate or to be championed by that powerful critic. It was equally to have written a naturalistic and conventional novel first. *The Double,* Dostoevsky's second novel, was stranger, modern, existential, and psychological, and gravely disappointed Belinsky. It was too fantastic, Belinsky complained, "and the fantastic can have

I do have to declare in all candor that no one interested in being published in our time can afford to be so naive as to believe a book will make it merely because it's good.

RICHARD CURTIS

its place only in lunatic asylums, not in literature; it is the business of doctors and not of poets."

Had *The Double* come first, it would not have been championed by Belinsky, and Dostoevsky might have had no early successes, nor, possibly, any later ones. Norman Mailer confesses to this same kind of luck at the beginning of his career. By writing a conventional novel about World War II, *The Naked and the Dead,* which had no real voice and so could be readily accepted in the marketplace, he became famous overnight. He then had permission to write in his own voice and be published.

The classical musician's career, taking the mechanical and the metaphysical together, revolves around his early choice of instrument, early virtuosity, early support, early teachers, and early chance connections, as well as his later teachers and successes in conservatory and at the right competitions, his ability to carve out a concert and recording career as a soloist or to win a seat in a first-rate orchestra. It may include university teaching, conservatory teaching, or the offering of private lessons. It may involve the soloist in a hundred or more nights on the road each year. He may experience tremendous performance anxiety or little, learn new repertoire pieces slowly or quickly, obtain a Stradivarius or Guarnerius, nurse lingering wrist and elbow injuries. But, as with painters and writers, in all cases the metaphysical mixes with the mechanical.

If, for instance, he learns from his teacher to hold his fingers and move on the piano bench like Glenn Gould, and playing in Glenn Gould's style is out, he has hurt his career. If he learns to play with flat fingers, and flat-finger playing is out, that style will hurt him at competitions. Even more important, if his teacher is influential, that connection will vitally help his career. The young musician who is the protégé of a well-connected teacher may be said to have a significant leg up on his peers. As Robert Bloom, the oboist and oboe teacher, put it:

> If one teacher is a little more persuasive than another, his student gets the orchestra job, and if one teacher gets a reputation for having his students get the jobs, then students go to that teacher. It is a very, very uncomfortable and commercial situation.

The career path for the actor, the metaphysical and the mechanical together, often has at its center what Julius Novick called "the

People don't realize that the "big break" is an accumulative thing. The "big break" comes from small fractures.

JOHN KAPELOS

temptations of fame and fortune, of Broadway, television, and the movies." The young actor imagines himself striking it rich. While he is attending the right classes in the right city, working in live theater and on the outskirts of film, television, and commercials, gaining agency representation, making personal and professional connections, and auditioning, his eye is fixed on the gold ring: on discovery, on breakthrough opportunities.

He may also want the opportunity to act steadily. He is then faced with a decision about where to live. Should it be New York, Los Angeles, or a city with good regional theater? The actor who opts for life in regional theater may work more regularly and in more interesting pieces than his brothers in New York or Los Angeles, but may naturally feel that he is missing his chance at stardom. Howard Witt, an actor with nine productive years in a regional theater, wrote:

> There are certain things you have to give up when you come into a regional theater. You have to give up the idea that you're going to become famous, that you're going to become rich, that you're going to be recognized, even in the profession. I have an old saying that my mother had two sons, one joined the Foreign Legion and one went to Arena Stage, and neither was ever heard from again.

As a matter of principle, would you rather act regularly or be a star? Which decision more naturally flows out of your personality?

The way you attend to your business can only be understood in the context of your real life. It is fatuous to demand of the introspective, imaginative, agitated, alienated painter that he chat up dealers at parties. To be sure, you can be helped, if you so choose, to better understand the mechanical matters of doing business. You can learn from Paul McCartney:

> The main downfall is that we were less businessmen and more heads, which was very pleasant and very enjoyable, except there should have been the man in there who would tell us to sign bits of paper. We got a man in who started to say, come on, sign it all over to me, which was the fatal mistake.

You can learn from John Hill Hewitt, the nineteenth-century American composer:

My ballads are (or rather *were*) well known throughout the country; for I have not published for many years. Why? the reader may ask. For the simple reason that it does not pay the author. The publisher pockets all, and gets rich on the brains of the poor fool who is chasing that *ignis fatuus,* reputation.

You can learn the rules of the game. You can learn from Rodney Gordy of Motown Records: "Knowing who needs what is a key to success." You can embrace or recoil from the advice offered to young songwriters by Tom Vickers of Almo-Irving music: "Bathe the listener's ears with pleasant sounds that people will want to hear over and over, don't scrub them with abrasive material."

You can learn these and a hundred other lessons from books, from history, from your own experiences and the experiences of your peers. But to understand the metaphysics of the matter you must look into your own soul.

TWO WRITERS' PATHS

It's worth our while to stop here and examine the differing paths of two hypothetical short-story writers. The first writer doesn't secure a career for himself; the second does, although not the one he would have predicted.

Let's take it for granted that both writers are talented and creative. From the details given, we can't judge who is the more brilliant. Talent and creativity are not the issues. The issue is squarely the metaphysical one of the interrelationship among product, personality, and marketplace.

Joseph K.

Our first writer, Joseph K., decides as a young man that it's necessary for him to write short stories. He loves the stories of Zamyatin, Joyce, Borges, Paley, Welty, and Kafka, loves the compression and precision of the form, doesn't much revere poetry or the novel, and isn't interested in literary criticism or nonfiction writing. He calls himself a short-story writer and determines to spend his life writing.

From a business point of view, the path he has chosen is an unfortunate one. How much can a short-story writer expect to earn? How much do even the highest paid short-story writers earn? But these are not questions Joseph K. puts to himself.

His own stories, as he begins to write them, bear a family resemblance to the stories of Kafka. We may guess that he is not a people-pleasing sort of person. We would not expect him to have a calculating way about him with respect to the marketplace. We would not expect him to agree with Truman Capote, who said, "I never write—indeed, am physically incapable of writing—anything I don't think I will be paid for." We would not expect him to agree with Samuel Johnson, who said, "Sir, no man but a blockhead ever wrote except for money."

Rather we expect him to be a wounded, depressed, and lonely fellow with an excellent imagination and a fine way with words who, like Kafka himself, is more than a little ambivalent about interacting in the marketplace. Our writer likely neither knows nor cares whether this is a good or bad time to be writing Kafkaesque short stories. He is writing the stories that flow out of his imagination and soul, without calculation. His dreams of fame, recognition, and respect, which he does harbor, do not influence in the smallest measure what he writes or how he writes it.

Through college and afterward, Joseph K. spends a lot of time at his desk, in coffeehouses reading and writing, and on his sofa thinking. He works at odd jobs, goes to the movies, has a friendship or two, is shy with and estranged from women, has a stormy relationship with his overbearing father and polite mother, sleeps a good bit, is fonder of marijuana than other drugs, writes letters, and continues to polish his stories.

When his car breaks down for the final time and his teeth hurt so much that he really must find a dentist, he sets about looking for a steady day job. But because he considers himself no better at the game of academia than the game of publishing, and because there are relatively few teaching jobs anyway, and because, a little arrogant and a little hurt, he despises teachers, he chooses not to pursue an advanced degree in English with an eye toward teaching. Nor does it seem to him wise to seek out a job that might violate his principles or might get under his skin too much—say, a job in advertising. He decides, instead, to find work in a bank.

A year or two later, with three complete and several incomplete

The gift turned inward, unable to be given, becomes a heavy burden, even sometimes a kind of poison. It is as though the flow of life were backed up.

MAY SARTON

stories to his credit, he picks up his first copy of *Writer's Market* or *Novel & Short Story Writer's Market.* Reared on the classics and with too many of them still to read, he knows little contemporary fiction and has no ready way of distinguishing one little magazine from another. With some care but still with only half an eye, he selects several magazines and sends them his stories. They are rejected. A few of the rejections are personal and encouraging. A few are vitriolic. Most are form letters.

He writes more stories. Several years pass. He now has a book-length collection of stories. A co-worker at the bank, one of the few who know that he's a writer, reminds Joseph K. that her sister is an editor with a medium-sized literary press. Our young writer ignores this, for by this time he does not believe in the ability of editors to recognize the worth of his stories and is tired of rejection. Although not aware of it, he is made extremely anxious by his co-worker's suggestion.

Our writer's only good friend offers him much sound advice about how to market his manuscript, and Joseph K. listens. He tries certain publishers who seem likely, varying his query letters and altering the sequence of his stories. He gets only form letter rejections.

After the manuscript is rejected ten times, he puts it away and begins to work on a novel, harboring the not-quite-conscious idea that novels, at least, can sell, and when his novel sells then his short stories will be wanted.

When his dark, brooding, and strange novel is finished he sends it out. It is rejected ten times. By this time he is 32 years old.

Everyone in the trade knows that Joseph K. is to be pitied. Edwin McDowell, writing in the *New York Times,* said, "The odds against an unknown writer getting a manuscript published by simply sending it directly to a publishing house are astronomical." This sentiment is echoed in a *Time* magazine article: "It is virtually impossible for an unknown author to break into print through the U.S. mails with what is known in the trade as an 'over the transom' manuscript." Walter Powell wrote: "Few of the major trade publishers will take a chance on a manuscript from someone whose name is not known."

Does Joseph K. in his studio apartment know this? Does he realize that blindly and hopefully sending out his collection of short stories or his first novel is a nearly futile gesture, the equivalent of

Always we come upon this feeling, ridiculous, senseless and baseless—that it is beneath the dignity of an author to manage his business matters as a man of business should.

WALTER BESANT

buying a lottery ticket? In a way he does, for he has at least his own experience to guide him. But in an important way he doesn't, for first novels and collections of stories *are* regularly published. On balance he continues to think that his marketing strategies, minimal as they are, must be sound.

He does, however, make one new decision. Some experts contend that with an advocate in the marketplace the odds of Joseph K. getting published would change from one in a thousand to one in ten. One day Joseph K. realizes this, and begins to send his collection of short stories and his dark novel out to literary agents rather than to publishers. He gets many personal and pleasant responses, all of which boil down to a categoric rejection: his work would be too hard to sell. (Roger Straus, president of Farrar, Straus & Giroux, said, "It's harder for a new writer to get an agent than a publisher.")

Over the next few years, two or three of Joseph K.'s stories appear in literary magazines. One is anthologized in a collection of neo-Kafkaesque stories. But his own collection and his novel will not sell. He reads a newspaper poll that asserts that Stephen King is considered America's greatest living author, followed in descending order of greatness by Danielle Steel, James Michener, Louis L'Amour, and Sidney Sheldon. One 47-year-old female fan explains why she adores Danielle Steel's novels: "It's pure escapism. Her heroine is always beautiful, the men in the novels are always handsome, the people are rich and everything turns out fine, unlike life." None of this upsets or educates Joseph K. He simply doesn't take it in.

But our now not-quite-so-young writer is perplexed that two different universes seem to exist in the same time and space. He has a shelf full of books that inform him that if he puts his manuscript together neatly, researches the market, and sends out a solid query letter to the correct publisher, he has a good chance of being published. At the same time he understands that to operate in such a fashion feels like a pathetic waste of time and looks like lunacy.

He turns 40. His best writing goes into the letters he writes to a woman he has never met who lives on a dairy farm in Eastern Iceland. She is the cousin of a co-worker at the bank. He begins to tell her that he loves her.

Finally he stops writing stories altogether. He stops reading fiction. Instead he reads books about early Christianity, especially about early Christian martyrs. By the age of 60 he is an expert on the

The artist, the person concerned with artistic endeavors, must show an assertiveness in fields that are not his or her own.

JOHN KENNETH
GALBRAITH

subject, and what began as a modest monograph on an obscure martyr has turned into a thousand-page manuscript. Once or twice he sends the manuscript out. But of course no one wants it.

Something in each of us wants to pity, ridicule, and laugh at Joseph K.—even if, as artists, we may not be so different from him. Something in each of us wants to call him blind, foolish, and weak. And yet, with respect to his writing career, all he has done is carefully and conscientiously write what he thought it important to write, and then market his writing in (exceedingly) quiet fashion, according to textbook advice. To be sure, he ignored some opportunities and the basic demands of the marketplace, but he nevertheless operated rationally enough, in ways dictated by his personality makeup.

We can call him a failure, as he can't help calling himself, but we would be wise to understand that he did not fail as a writer of excellent fiction. He failed to negotiate the maze constructed by his own personality and the demands of the marketplace. He failed, that is, to understand how he was fated to travel along a certain path, unless and until he changed himself and revisioned his role in the universe.

Authors do detailed research on their subject matter but seldom do any at all on which publishing house is appropriate for their work.

WALTER POWELL

Robert F.

Our second short-story writer, whom we'll call Robert F., is not that much different in personality from Joseph K. He, too, is introspective, thoughtful, imaginative, and sensitive. He, too, loves the stories of Zamyatin, Joyce, Borges, Paley, Welty, and Kafka. He, too, is essentially a proud, arrogant, antisocial loner. In fact, our two writers look rather alike during their twenties. They work at odd jobs, write stories, frequent cafés, send out their stories, and have their stories rejected. Neither attends marketing workshops nor experiences much internal willingness to meet the marketplace.

But there are major differences between them. We could draw the differences in any number of ways. We could say that Robert F. is the less impaired one—less wounded by his childhood, more able to form relationships, more flexible, or less anxious. We could postulate that Robert F. has been better supported by his parents, has higher self-esteem or a better self-image, or is less romantic and more shrewd than Joseph K. Maybe he is less uncompromising, more self-aware, or more able and willing to listen to the advice of others.

However we draw the differences, they are sufficient that Robert F. is able to enter into an intimate relationship with a woman, marry, and have children. In this new context Robert F. arrives at a crucial turning, for it begins to seem to him like an act of bad faith to stoically identify himself as a short-story writer and thereby contribute so little to the household income.

At this existential extremity, Robert F. tackles the question of choice. How should he fashion his life? What will appropriately serve his wife and children as well as himself? What can he do in addition to writing short stories—or even instead of writing short stories? How should he change? What should he do with his life?

The answers do not come overnight, but the questions remain alive within him. He thinks about them, makes plans, makes decisions. He goes out into the world more and more often, in strategic fashion, to see what's happening and what's wanted. He battles his own antisocial tendencies and works to keep his artist's necessary arrogance in check.

He discovers, over the course of a year or two, that the themes he has been writing about in his stories resemble the themes being addressed by the burgeoning men's movement. It dawns on him that he could probably offer a men's workshop. He thinks about this, works on the idea, and eventually presents his first workshop, which draws only three men. But he does a better job of marketing the second workshop, and the third. His fifth workshop earns him more money than all of his previous short-story sales put together. Just as important, it strikes him that his new path is not a repudiation of his dreams or a violation of his principles but rather a hitherto unforeseen way to do good work and gain recognition.

Over the course of a year he writes a nonfiction book based on his workshop materials and experiences. This book interests an agent and is quickly sold. It does quite well, and his nonfiction career is launched.

By 40, Robert F. no longer considers himself a short-story writer. He no longer *is* primarily a short-story writer, although he returns to his first love whenever he reasonably can. He finds his

Literature is like any other trade, you will never sell anything unless you go to the right shop.

GEORGE BERNARD SHAW

identity hard to pin down. If asked, he sometimes calls himself a writer, sometimes a teacher, sometimes a group facilitator.

New business challenges continually arise for him. Some of the compromises he makes are harder for him to swallow than others. Some of his choices turn out to be misguided. But on balance he is pleased to have a career and proud that he has squarely faced the issue. If asked, he would refuse to call himself better than Joseph K. But neither would he accept, even for a minute, the purist's charge that he had sold out by revisioning his career in this particular fashion.

For every person who will say yes, there are twenty who will say no. For a positive response you must find the twenty-first person.

CHUCK REAVES

THE CHALLENGES NAMED

The hard truth about art is that you must think about it as a business. What is wanted, what is not wanted? Who are the players in the game? How does the marketplace operate? You must spend real time thinking about the business end of art: how it operates, what you need to learn so that you can operate in it more effectively, what movement you must make in order to transform yourself into a smarter businessperson.

You must deal, on both the practical and psychological levels, with the high probability that your art will not earn you a living. As a young artist it may be impossible and even undesirable to acknowledge this probability. But the day will come when it begins to dawn on you that the odds are heavily stacked against you. Reconsider then the rightness of your choices: your choice, for instance, to work any sort of day job no matter how demeaning or debilitating. Might a second career be a better idea? A willingness to do more commercial art? A relationship with a supportive wage-earning gentleman or lady?

At every stage of your career you must consciously do business, if you want a career. If you are an actor you must do business as a 20-year-old actor and, 30 years later, as a 50-year-old actor. If you're a novelist you must do business as a neophyte and as a mature artist with six novels behind you. At each stage of the game you must understand the marketplace and make decisions based on that understanding. You must handle the hundreds of small and large details that are an integral part of plying your trade—the mechanics of the business.

You're likewise challenged to examine your career path to see if, metaphysically speaking, there are crucial turnings to take. Above all, you're challenged to retain your spirits as you go about your business. Especially if you produce potatoes rather than peaches, you can be certain that your business road will be a rocky one and that you will get bruised as you journey along it.

STRATEGIES

Every actor goes through periods when he has to earn a living in a routine way.
CEDRIC HARDWICKE

How can you better conduct your business and make sense of the business of art? The most important strategies to employ involve the creation and implementation of a personal business plan of action, one that takes into account both the mechanics of doing art business and the metaphysics of your life in art.

Your business action plan won't look like a recipe or an agenda. What concerns you is too complicated to allow for simple, linear solutions. Your approach is more like the juggler's, who launches five apples into the air and keeps them all flying. Even as the juggler grabs one apple in order to take a bite out of it, he is aware of the other apples. Sometimes he needs to take a small, hurried bite because a distant apple is falling. Sometimes he can take a more leisurely bite. The items you are juggling in your business action plan are the following seven. None should slip entirely from your awareness even as you pay closer attention to one or another of them.

Artist's Business Action Plan

Perform ongoing self-assessment. Your first step is to engage in a general assessment of your present relationship to the business of art. Consider the following questions in conjunction with step 7 of the guided writing program (narrowing your focus).

1. Am I willing to create peaches, not potatoes?

2. How effective am I at doing the business of art?

3. How effective am I at mastering my resistance to doing the business of art?

4. How effective am I at meeting the fears and anxieties that well up in me when I contemplate business situations or attempt to negotiate business situations?

*In terms of survival, for anyone
who's a painter or a sculptor,
I would really recommend
becoming a printmaker also,
because it's such a tremendous
way to earn some money from
your art.*

JUDITH BRODSKY

5. What have I learned from my past selling experiences and how have I built on that knowledge?

6. How much time do I devote to the business of art? Is it enough time?

7. How much psychic space do I turn over to the business of art? Is it enough space?

8. What are my business goals and aspirations?

9. How would I like my career to look? Modest but solid? Immodest and dramatic?

10. What tools will I use in assessing how I do the business of art? Will I read the trade magazines and learn to comprehend the realities of my business environment? Will I engage in quiet conversations with friends and ask them how they see me as a seller of art? Will I bring the matter up in my individual therapy?

Engage in ongoing assessment of your personality as a seller. Consider the following in an effort to assess and improve your selling and marketing skills.

1. What in your personality can you enlist to enhance your ability to sell? Your intelligence? Your intellectual playfulness? Your sense of curiosity? Your slyness or sense of whimsy?

2. What in your personality must you better manage in order to enhance your ability to sell? Your stubborn, nonconforming side? Your aloof, distant side? Your sarcastic side? Your estranged, hurt, defensive side?

3. Learn to empathize with a potential buyer. Get into his shoes. What is he thinking? What demands are placed on him by others? What does he need? Why should he deal with you and not someone else?

4. Insofar as your products make this possible, have a polished sales pitch. Present graspable ideas—that you are saving Celtic harp music from extinction, that your self-portraits are in the Expressionist tradition, that your

collection of stories are linked by their Arizona desert setting. Try to be as clear as are the Ten Commandments.

5. Be able to say why your work should be wanted. Self-advertise. Become the expert, the master. Give workshops on what you do. Create the demand for your work.

6. Set aside time to do business. Schedule time for it.

7. Create a team. Collaborate. Encourage writers to write about you and interviewers to interview you. Make and maintain significant professional connections.

8. Have selling awareness. Look for opportunities to sell. Network. Exchange business cards with others. Bring your strengths and not your insecurities to the cocktail hour, the gallery opening, the network party. It's not a sin to sell—only to sell out.

9. Make yourself accessible and visible. Go out. Nurture your extrovert side. Be present. Make small talk. Watch to see if you self-sabotage. Are you drinking too much? Hiding in a corner? Can you manage your boredom, your arrogance, your shyness?

10. Acquire business savvy. Learn about contracts. Honor deadlines. Negotiate a nonexclusive deal with your gallery owner. Spot the trends early. Learn to read between the lines. What is really being said in comments about your work? "Your paintings are very large" may mean "My gallery makes most of its money from graphics." "You lost me when your character went to Finland" may mean "You violated the genre formula." "This doesn't seem very focused" may mean "This is too painful to read." Try to intuit the real message and respond to it.

11. Practice your new skills. Practice exercising your personality in the selling arena. Practice pricing your art. Practice asking for what you want. Videotape yourself asking and answering questions. Interview yourself. Practice being a businessperson and a professional with a career in the arts. Rehearse business situations. Role-play them with friends. Arrive at ideas about what you want and what the other person might want before you set off for a meeting

It's important who you meet— after all, if you meet forty or fifty people, the one person who will produce your first film might just be there.

MARTIN SCORSESE

with a curator, a collector, an art dealer. Step into the other person's shoes. Walk around the block in them. Be prepared for his agenda and his savoriness or unsavoriness.

Practice ongoing anxiety management. Doing business raises the anxiety level of most artists. You may feel anxious contemplating the business you have to do, anxious because you doubt yourself as a salesperson, anxious because you have no clear idea how to proceed with your business. To handle your anxiety you will need to assess it, learn general anxiety-management techniques, and specific techniques that apply to you as an artist. Answer the following questions, and others you'll need to frame for yourself, so that you really learn how anxiety operates in your business life.

- How do I presently manage anxiety? With drugs and alcohol? By avoiding situations that make me anxious? By denying that I feel anxious? By acting self-deprecating, agreeable, or nice? By acting out aggressively and sabotaging myself?

- Which business situations make me most anxious? Discussing my product? Negotiating contracts? Making decisions about who to hire for my band or my play? Choosing between the options in front of me? Studying trade magazines to learn about trends? Talking on the phone with agents or curators? Meeting in person with directors, gallery owners, publishers? Auditioning? Entering competitions?

When you have assessed how anxiety affects you, make use of the following general anxiety-management techniques:

1. Meditation and yogic breathing

2. Exercise, diet, and rest

3. Biofeedback and autogenic training

4. Medication (tranquilizers)

5. Stress-reduction practices incorporating guided visualizations and affirmations

6. Behavioral and cognitive approaches: learning new thoughts and inoculating yourself against old thoughts; and systematic desensitization to anxiety-producing situations

7. Rehearsal and role-playing in preparation for anxiety-producing situations

Specific anxiety-reduction techniques for artists include the following:

1. Have a marketable product. If you do highly personal art that has a questionable chance of reaching an audience, diversify.

2. Disidentify from your product. You are not your painting, novel, or performance. When your agent asserts that your novel is not working for him, he is really talking about your novel—he is not calling you incompetent or a failure. Be able to step aside and hear what your agent, your director, or the curator is saying.

3. Demystify the process. Ask questions of friends. Read books. Learn what to expect and what not to expect. Listen to the players in the game. How are things done? When do you turn to your agent and when do you consult your entertainment lawyer? How much must you socialize? How important are personal contacts and personal relationships? What does a good contract look like and what does a bad one look like? Arm yourself with a dose of reality.

4. Acquire advocates. A room is less intimidating with a friendly face in it. People who have already bought your paintings are on your side. An agent who has sold a book of yours is on your side. A playwright whose play you lit up with your performance is on your side. You may approach these people with confidence.

5. Prepare for business events. Rehearse. Ask yourself potential questions and answer them. Meet potential objections. Role-play with an art buddy, your intimate other, or your therapist.

Engage in ongoing market analysis. This applies to both the practical and metaphysical sides of your art. Analyze what exactly is selling in your field. For example, is it regional art but only from a certain region? Mysteries but only British-style atmospheric mysteries,

I'm one of those guys who got real sacred about writing and wanting to write my own songs, when I really should have been out there looking for a great song.

AL JARREAU

police procedurals, stories featuring an old-fashioned, hard-boiled private eye, or cozy mysteries featuring a female amateur detective? New Age music but only on one or two certain labels? The students of a certain teacher? The clients of a certain agent? Artists represented in certain galleries?

It will be necessary to yield to the world. What the crowd wants finally becomes law.

GEORG PHILIPP
TELEMANN

If someone is selling in your field, what exactly is that artist doing? Is he adhering to a certain formula? How does he market himself? How does he keep himself in the public eye? Who represents him? With whom does he network? If his product is essentially uncommercial, how has he managed to obtain an audience? How has he managed to get his symphony performed or his quirky film financed, produced, and distributed?

Perform ongoing audience analysis. Who is your audience, in general and specifically? What are some of the characteristics of audience members you know personally? Do they come to all modern dance performances or only to see certain companies? Do they like all live theater or only feminist theater, drawing-room comedies, or plays by playwrights with name recognition?

What do they claim to like in general? Are surveys available to you? Questionnaire responses? Can you take the audience's pulse? What do they say they like with respect to your work? Do they have clear favorites among your paintings, books, songs, or repertoire pieces? Do they say that your fiction is difficult but that your nonfiction is useful. Do they say that your watercolors are charming but that your paintings are scary? Do they say they could listen to your Mozart all day but can't really tolerate any modern music? Do they like your ballads, angry message songs, or upbeat tunes the best?

Work to acquire a small respectful and knowledgeable audience (in addition to any other audience you may have) by searching out one or a few art buddies. Is there someone who really understands and appreciates your work? The person who holds Greek drama and Russian literature in the same high regard you do may be your most valuable reader.

Accept that, insofar as you have an audience, you are a public figure. Have a public face. Accept that there will be misunderstandings—that your fans will not really know you, that they may not understand your message, that sometimes you and they will get caught up in the unreality of your status as a known artist.

Work to retain your audience. Insofar as it's in your heart to do so, play your hits, produce your trademark work, repeat yourself, be recognizably you. When you want to stretch or change, plan strategies to minimize the risks involved in offering your audience what they are not expecting. Help them understand.

Do ongoing product and portfolio analysis. Be able to talk about your products in detail. Get to know your products. Prepare a written statement, as for example: "I paint large-scale abstract Expressionist paintings in primary colors, with a recent emphasis on cobalt blue and cadmium red. I paint in two scales: roughly five feet by eight feet and three feet by five feet. In feeling my paintings are like those of Hans Hofmann or Nicolas de Stael, but my inspiration is drawn from the look of contemporary Los Angeles."

If *you* are the product, be able to talk about yourself as a dancer, actor, or musician. Practice by preparing a written statement, as for example: "I've worked in the theater for the past dozen years. During my time with the One Act Repertory Theater I've performed in more than twenty contemporary plays and a dozen revivals. My performances in Simon Gray's *Butley* and Wendy Wasserstein's *Uncommon Women and Others* were singled out for praise, as was my performance in the revival of Bertolt Brecht's *Mother Courage*. My strengths are my voice (both speaking and singing), the conviction I bring to roles, my discipline, and my look, which reviewers have called 'exotic' and 'extraordinary.' "

Think about which of your products have been commercially successful. Why were they successful? How can you repeat those successes or make use of what you learned from them?

How might your present products be altered—without sacrificing too much or compromising too much—to better meet the demands of the marketplace? Might you paint in a smaller scale? Add more plot to your fiction? Tailor your songs to a certain market? Can you do private, idiosyncratic, charged work *and* commercial work?

What other products might you attempt that would allow you to diversify? Nonfiction along with fiction? Mysteries along with poetry? Multiples along with single images? Solo performance pieces you write and perform? Music of your own composition? Might you audition for unaccustomed roles? Would you accept commissioned pieces? Send your band in a new direction? Create

When Pavlova came out to thank the people, this was a moment as great as the dancing itself. It was like a benediction—a blessing.

MURIEL STUART

products in another medium? Accept trends and fashions? Produce both passionate products and dispassionate products?

Prepare answers to the following difficult questions.

*Confidence is preparation.
Everything else is beyond
your control.*
                RICHARD KLINE

- In what tradition do I work?
- Which famous or popular artist is my work like?
- What makes my work unique?
- Of what am I the master?
- Why do I paint or play the way I do?
- Why is my work important?

*It is better to have a permanent
income than to be fascinating.*
                OSCAR WILDE

- Who has loved my work and will vouch for it?
- Who collects me? Who reads me?

Dream up other difficult questions and answer them, too.

Do ongoing financial support analysis. There are essentially eight sources of income available to you as an artist. You may want to treat them as if they make up a buffet meal from which you select according to what's available and most palatable. These eight sources are:

1. Art products and performances
2. Commercial products (including commissions, genre work, commercials)
3. Grants, residencies, gallery stipends
4. Related careers (including tutoring, teaching, producing, agenting, editing, doing art therapy)
5. Unrelated secondary careers (lawyer, doctor, psychologist, etc.)
6. Unrelated day jobs
7. Income from a mate or spouse
8. Income from family and friends

Although you might prefer to live on income from the first category only, that's not generally the most plentiful source. Accept that perfect solutions are rare and that psychological fallout comes with any financial survival program you put together.

Obscurity *and* Stardom

Any writer who says he doesn't worry about fame, who says he has never, from time to time, gauged his success against that of other writers, is lying.

SEAN ELDER

MOST ARTISTS DESIRE RECOGNITION, and the persistent lack of it may be a bitter pill to swallow. The artist who is too-soon recognized, as Norman Mailer felt himself to be, might argue that early fame is harder on the artist than years of obscurity. But the composer with a score for a powerful symphony locked away in his drawer, and the actress who has never found her way into a great drama, are hard-pressed to agree with Mailer. Similarly, the painter who has her entire output of paintings to enjoy for herself because she cannot sell them may praise her fortitude and applaud her accomplishments but still experience great sadness.

Hardly any of the names of ancient artists are recorded, even though they did more for the happiness of their people than the pharoahs, generals, and world rulers whose pride filled the world with sorrow.

EMIL NOLDE

If you are not honored with real, appropriate recognition, you struggle not to consider yourself a failure. You may argue that it is the world that has failed you, for any of the many metaphysical reasons discussed in the last chapter, but it is hard to take comfort in that knowledge. You need recognition more than you need an accurate understanding of why recognition has eluded you. And as you deal, during your years in the trenches, with what may turn out to be a maddeningly insufficient lack of recognition, you are challenged to find ways of maintaining your faith, courage, good cheer, and emotional equilibrium.

RECOGNITION AND GOOD WORK

I decided that my painting would never be the equivalent of that pseudo-Cuban music for nightclubs. I refused to paint cha-cha-cha.

WILFREDO LAM

All of the critics engaged in a personal free-for-all, one even going so far as to review my baby, to whom I had given birth two days before the opening.

GWEN DAVIS

The first implicit assumption about recognition is that the artist wants to be recognized for the goodness of his work. It does not do to gain fame for the badness of your art, for your publicity stunts or drinking habits, for your affairs or because you run with celebrities.

Take, for instance, the case of Jean Cocteau, the fabulously notorious French playwright, novelist, filmmaker, and artist. No man could hope to achieve greater fame than did Cocteau, whose career was likened in its brilliance to that of Merlin's. But Cocteau complained bitterly that he was never really recognized. He called himself "the most invisible of poets and the most visible of men." He saw that he possessed celebrityhood, not real recognition. Others saw that, too. Jean Genet, Cocteau's protégé, charged his mentor with "having done nothing but be a star for ten years." Cocteau, stung by the sense that recognition had eluded him, confided in his diary: "My fame derives from a legend consisting of gossip and carelessness. No author is so known, so unknown, so misunderstood as I am."

The contemporary star, even more than Cocteau, is caught in a great blizzard of publicity, gossip, and myth-making, so that it becomes nearly impossible for a Christo to know if his wrapped bridges and buildings are bringing him recognition or notoriety; nearly impossible for a painter like R. C. Gorman to know if his reputation is based on his stylized paintings of Indians or on the fact that celebrities like Elizabeth Taylor regularly visit him in Taos; nearly impossible for Cher to know if she is respected as an actress and performer or held in ridicule as the embodiment of low culture.

In order to warm the artist's heart, it's necessary to assert that he is doing good work. Random or wrong-headed praise won't do the trick, but will only exacerbate the artist's feeling that he is unseen and misunderstood.

RECOGNITION, CRITICISM, AND REJECTION

Even wrong-headed praise is the exception rather than the rule in the artist's search for recognition. More often than not your recognition will consist of criticism, not praise. You may be criticized for not attempting work you have no desire to attempt, for pandering to

mass taste, for working too exotically or too narrowly, for not sounding like Pavarotti, Willie Nelson, or Aretha Franklin—or *for*
sounding like Pavarotti, Willie Nelson, or Aretha Franklin. You
may be criticized for being too parochial or too catholic, for being
out of fashion or for being in fashion. You may be attacked in a
mixed review that purports to praise you. In short, you may be criticized for everything and anything under the sun.

Can you escape this criticism as you struggle for recognition?
No. The journalist Elbert Hubbard said, "To escape criticism, do
nothing, say nothing, be nothing." You simply can't escape the
"venomous serpents that delight in hissing," as the writer W. B.
Daniel called them, or the "drooling, driveling, doleful, depressing,
dropsical drips," as the conductor Sir Thomas Beecham characterized his critics. You can't escape criticism, you can't tame your
critics. You may not even be able to rid your dreams of them. Igor
Stravinsky wrote: "I had another dream about music critics. They
were small and rodent-like with padlocked ears, as if they had
stepped out of a painting by Goya."

The artist will be criticized as an individual; his whole group,
once he is considered part of a group, will also be criticized.
Whether the criticism is directed at French surreal poets, New Age
musicians, Soviet realist painters, performance artists, African-
American filmmakers, photographers who work large, watercolor-
ists who work small, too-handsome actors, or tuba players, the artist
discovers that he must defend himself against criticism leveled at
artists whom he is told are his brothers and sisters.

It is disheartening to hear it said that only postmodernist writers are worth reading, or only Japanese prints are worth collecting,
or only European filmmakers are really doing art. You may find
yourself, in addition to cultivating and protecting your own reputation, protecting the whole genre, style, or idiom in which you are
working. George Inness, the nineteenth-century American artist,
for example, felt compelled to write:

> Nothing is considered good without a foreign name on it. Why,
> when one of our biggest dealers on Fifth Avenue was asked to pro-
> cure for a gentleman two American pictures for one thousand dollars
> each, he said he could not take the order because there was not a pic-
> ture produced in America worth one thousand dollars.

*How seldom do we meet
with a proper amount of
sympathy, knowledge, honesty,
and courage in a critic.*
CARL PHILIPP
EMANUEL BACH

One does a whole painting for one peach and people think just the opposite—that that particular peach is but a detail.

PABLO PICASSO

When you must also fight to have your genre recognized—modern dance, or poetry, or live theater—an extra burden falls on you, one you don't want to shoulder but can't avoid.

Nor do you possess many effective ways of responding to criticism. If your mother shudders as she views your latest work and wonders aloud why you persist in painting screams, what can you say in defense? If your mate, viewing your latest work, finds herself without a response, how will you address what feels like her silent criticism? Can you cry out and demand, "Say you love it, damn it!"? You may not even know if you love it yourself. Is it really a successful work, or is it flawed by the black in the corner, or pretty but lifeless, or lively but ugly? Your own doubts are magnified by the shudders and silences around you.

In pain, you may make an occasional retaliatory gesture, as the writer did who rented an airplane to buzz the office of an editor who'd rejected his manuscript. If you have the money, time, and an inclination to do battle, you may counterattack, as the Broadway producer David Merrick regularly has. Merrick, for instance, placed a full-page ad in the *New York Herald Tribune* peppered with raves for his latest show from people with the same names as the critics who'd panned it. Another time he offered up ads with references to his critics' love lives. Is such revenge sweet, or futile and embarrassing?

As often as the artist is criticized, he's probably still more often rejected. If you produce a product for which there is only a limited demand, if you ignore the requirements of the marketplace, if you're unlucky and unconnected, if you do work that is objectively inferior to the work of other artists in your territory, if you venture into new territory, if your message isn't a bland one, then you're more likely to experience rejection. The producer Don Simpson described life as a production executive at Paramount: "You're tired all the time, and you're never in a great mood because you have to say no to 200 people a week. Ninety percent of your judgments are no. You offend people, you hurt people, you may damage people."

There are a thousand varieties of criticism, much of it implied, and of rejection, much of it covert, in the lives of artists. The writer's novel is published, but in a small and careless printing. The dancer moves from the corps de ballet and debuts as a soloist; but the next time the ballet is performed she is back in the corps. The actress or musician who has been steadily—and heroically—working is asked in an interview, "Where have you been all these years?"

The playwright's play is booed off the stage opening night and canceled after five performances, as Chekhov's *The Seagull* was. The composer's concerto is rejected by every famous soloist, as Tchaikovsky's violin concerto at first was, then finally performed, only to be castigated in the manner of Edward Hanslick's review: "The violin was yanked about, torn asunder, beaten black and blue. Tchaikovsky's violin concerto brings us for the first time to the horrid idea that there may be music that stinks in the ear."

The artist may be criticized and rejected in tragicomic ways. The following news item came from Derby, England:

> Seven metal sculptures, representing one year's labor by artist Denis O'Connor, were sold as scrap for $16 by his landlord while he was on vacation, the artist told a civil court hearing this week.

The landlord told the court that he thought the sculptures were junk. Perhaps he did think that. Or perhaps he had merely found the perfect expression of his antipathy for the artist. How better to reject the sculptor and cast him in a ridiculous light than by mistaking his images of birds and trains for junk?

I have had an inordinate and painful concern for the audience in my writing career. I get to the theatre and think, "Oh my God, these poor people, now they have to go through this."

MARSHA NORMAN

If everything is measured against what that friend you went to college with is doing now, lose you will.

DAVID ROSEN

RIVALRIES AND ENVY

In this highly charged force field, in which each artist secretly longs for recognition, attempts but only sometimes accomplishes excellent work, and is battered by criticism and rejection, terrible antipathies between artists, and between artists and players in the marketplace, smolder and sometimes erupt.

Truman Capote, himself only wanting to be praised, characterized Jack Kerouac's work as "typing, not writing." John Lennon attacked Paul McCartney. Dostoevsky criticized Turgenev. One poet asked of another in an open letter in *Small Press Review*, "I am often puzzled how someone could write all those highly sympathetic poetic biographies and be so vicious in his criticism of his fellow writers."

The painter Mary Cassatt criticized all the paintings she viewed at a visit to Gertrude Stein's—and all the people there as well. The dancer Igor Markevitch described the ballet impresario Diaghilev's sadistic glee in humiliating Prokofiev:

Competition is for horses, not artists.

BELA BARTOK

> One day, I visited Diaghilev in his hotel. As I entered the lobby, I met a man who had just been to see him. The man was in tears. When I saw Diaghilev minutes later, I asked him who that poor fellow was. He smiled diabolically, and said, "Oh, that was Prokofiev. He burst into tears because I asked him to change the finale of his score for *Le Fils Prodigue.* It was the third time I requested the change." Diaghilev seemed to take a sadistic pleasure in making his artists suffer.

Take, as a last example of the genre, the following item, reported by San Francisco columnist Herb Caen:

> The literary round table that meets monthly at Trader Vic's includes such illuminati as Arthur Hailey, Paul Erdman, Oakley Hall, Henry Carlisle, Barnaby Conrad, Herb Gold, Blair Fuller and Martin Cruz Smith. Among the very few women writers ever invited, rather condescendingly, was Miss Danielle Steel, who looked around the table and said sweetly, "Y'know, I've sold more books than all of you put together." A simple fact that caused a terrible silence to fall over the distinguished group.

The psychologist Peter Salovey wrote, "Everyone feels some envy or jealousy, but only in those domains that matter the most for his own view of himself. You feel envy or jealousy in those areas where you stake your reputation and pride."

Even real but limited recognition likely feels insufficient to the artist who invests his whole being in his reputation as an artist. Not only is such an artist challenged to live without the recognition he craves and challenged to experience his fellow artists as something other than rivals, but he's also challenged to master what may turn out to be his own insatiable appetite for recognition.

OBSCURITY AND INJURY

Who emerges from this picture of rejection, criticism, and envy? An artist, first of all, who feels himself unfairly treated. Forty years

...ize for literature and still ... the award took too long ... *Review:*

...years. The first half of that ... or the second half my ap- ...tle magazines that pay in ...n letters, pamphlets, and ...character. It feeds resent-

In the arts there are no A's awarded for effort.

JOHN BRAINE

...ng to go unpublished or ... of a big press. The poet ...pecting to self-publish. The pianist does not start out expecting to play at weddings and bar mitzvahs. The actress does not start out expecting to see door after door close in her face.

The realization comes gradually. It may take years coming. Sometimes the artist will feel closer to realizing his dream, sometimes farther away. For some a full measure of recognition will come one day. As the columnist and novelist Anna Quindlen, on tour with her first novel, put it, "One of the best parts is when people say, 'Oh, you must get so tired of signing books.' On the contrary, I've been waiting all my life to do that!"

IF SUCCESS COMES

A ballerina's life can be glorious. But it does not get any easier. I don't think anyone must ever think about it getting easier.

ALICIA MARKOVA

Few artists achieve the success they dream of. Even the artist with several gallery shows, mid-list novels, or records to his credit likely neither reaps rich rewards nor feels singularly successful. And yet it may be an even greater challenge for the artist who achieves immense success to survive his own stardom. The singer Pat Benatar said: "I wasn't prepared for stardom. I wasn't prepared for everyone wanting a little piece of me, literally and figuratively. The first year was so hard, going from a nobody to a somebody."

The artist who isn't a star laughs at such problems. "Just give me stardom!" he cries. "I'll try my hand at it!" But stardom can and often does injure the celebrity artist. As the actor Charlton Heston put it: "Celebrity is a corrosive condition. Fame literally destroys actors. It has crippled a score or more and it has left none unmarked. You can't be a celebrity and remain a normal person."

Once an artist wins a little approval from the world, once he becomes even a little known and acquires even a little audience, certain challenges come into play. At the extremity of stardom, failing to negotiate them isolates the artist, overwhelms him, or causes him to change in disturbing ways. Why should this be the case? The following examination of the challenges that confront the successful artist gives us a taste of the issues involved.

The Freeze Frame Reaction

I can't stand to sing the same song the same way two nights in succession. If you can, then it ain't music, it's close order drill or something, not music.
BILLIE HOLLIDAY

The audience perceived me in a certain way, and it was in an insecure attempt to please the audience that I lost myself.
ARTIE SHAW

Once an artist is successful, his audience typically expects a certain kind of work from him. He has little permission to grow or to change. He's supposed to remain frozen in the position they met him in and in which they presume they like him best. As Artie Shaw, the bandleader, put it:

> In 1938, I was the highest-paid bandleader in America, and yet I was beleaguered. The audience would not support me if I did what I wanted to do. I had to do what they wanted me to do. Music to order. How do you do the same tune every night the same way? How many years can you play "Begin the Beguine" without getting a little vomity? I got to a place where they said, "Stop, don't grow anymore." That's like telling a pregnant woman, "Stop, don't get more pregnant."

The singer Paul Simon said:

> Having a track record to live up to and the history of successes had become a hindrance. It becomes harder to break out of what people expect you to do. Nobody encouraged me to break with Art Garfunkel. Everybody said, "What the hell's wrong? Why don't they stay together?"

The composer Igor Stravinsky complained: "I cannot compose what they want from me, which would be to repeat myself. That is the way people write themselves out."

To expect that the artist doesn't want to grow once he has gotten successful is to think of him as mercenary, in it only for the money and the tangible rewards success brings. But a mercenary feeling is not usually the motive in the artist's heart. In love with his medium and believing himself to be full of astounding possibilities, he wants to grow, to experiment, to stretch limits. Repeating himself bores and frustrates him. But his audience is unwilling even to permit his fictional detective to start smoking a pipe, let alone get married or move to Tangiers.

The artist is thereby challenged to find ways to make fame less stifling than it can easily become. For instance, some artists have announced early on to their fans: "Love me, love my changes." Some have done two kinds of work, one of which remains familiar and unchanging, and one of which is less formulaic. The Belgian writer Georges Simenon, for example, produced an array of comfortable Inspector Maigret mysteries but also a number of psychological novels not restricted by a recurring character. Film stars return to the stage, sit-com actors stretch by going against type in film, and rock musicians, tired of electrification and drum machines, join together to play acoustic music.

Deceitful Compromises

The path to stardom may involve the artist in significantly compromising situations. Compromise is a well-nigh inevitable component of doing business in the arts or anywhere else. But some compromises are more likely than others to deflect artists from their original intentions and creative aspirations, more likely to diminish their self-esteem and sense of moral worth, and more likely to injure them.

I can definitely recognize greed. I know when a man is playing for money.
COLEMAN HAWKINS

We might suppose that among the worst compromises are such deceits as the desperate or cynical writer who has his books ghost-written, the artist who allows others to paint his paintings, or the lip-syncing "singing" team of Milli Vanilli. The reputed production of hits by the Monkees without their participation, the recording of the Crystals' hit "He's a Rebel" by the Blossoms (so as not to inter-fere with a Crystals tour), along with the current ubiquitous deceit of musicians lip-syncing their own music in concert, may strike us, because they are outright frauds, as the worst sorts of compromises. But these flagrant deceits, like the sit-com laugh track, are perhaps only the loudest examples of moral and aesthetic sacrifice.

There's no real excuse for being successful enough as an actor to do what you want and then selling out.

CLINT EASTWOOD

How much must you compromise? What will you do to secure and maintain your popularity and income?

We may think, in this regard, of the case of Sir Arthur Conan Doyle, the creator of Sherlock Holmes. Coming to hate the fact that his historical novels, like *The White Company,* could not compete with the immense popularity of his Sherlock Holmes stories, Doyle up and killed Holmes off. Outraged, Doyle's public and his pub-lishers brought intense pressure to bear on him to resurrect his fic-tional detective.

Clearly, Doyle could not meet his public halfway and write half a Holmes story or write about Holmes from the waist up only. Doyle, wishing Holmes dead but pressured to revive him, made what we may suppose was the painful decision to bring Holmes back from purgatory. He maintained, however, that the detective would have only a brief, limited second coming.

We might dub this particular solution the compromise of the limited sequel. Like the "freeze frame" phenomenon, it speaks to the fact that the successful artist, like the successful retailer, has cus-tomers whose needs and expectations he fails to satisfy only at great peril to his career. That peril is not only to the artist himself, but to his family and his "stockholders" as well—his publishers, agents, producers, collectors, dealers, and the rest. He may expect pressure to be exerted from all sides as he mulls over a decision, pressure to keep doing the popular and lucrative thing until the public tires of the sequels.

Plateauing or Stunted Growth

Often the successful artist harbors the sentiment, as did Doyle, that the work that has made him famous isn't his best work. Even the most heroic, iconoclastic artist can find himself trapped by his own image, popularity, and fame, so that he comes to feel that his work has stagnated, plateaued, and never had the chance to mature. Pablo Picasso wrote:

> Today I am famous and very rich. But when I am completely honest with myself, I haven't the nerve to consider myself an artist in the great and ancient sense of the word. I am a public entertainer who has understood his times. This is a bitter confession, more painful indeed than it may seem, but it has the merit of being sincere.

If even a Picasso feels thwarted by fame in fulfilling his artistic potential, we see how corrosive a condition stardom can be. Did Hemingway, Tennessee Williams, Arthur Miller, and many other of our most famous novelists, poets, short-story writers, and playwrights produce their best writing early in their lives because fame derailed their artistic journeys? As the actor Maximilian Schell put it: "I'm not happy about winning this Oscar for my role in *Judgment at Nuremberg.* Fame only rewards its recipients with pain. An actor is happier when he's still making his ascent."

Topping Oneself

The famous artist is under great pressure to continue to please and draw an audience, especially by repeating himself and doing his signature or trademark work. At the same time he is expected to outdo himself. He feels this pressure and his audience and stockholders feel it as well. If his next book, album, or movie sells only as well as his last, he may appear to be in decline. Everyone is disappointed.

The American artist especially is caught in such an unfortunate trap, because he is bound up in the potent but rarely articulated American root metaphor of the ascending spiral. The ascending spiral, one of the central images of early American letters and employed especially by Emerson, is probably an unconscious piece of every American's personal mythology. Its shorthand name is progress. We expect the next generation of stove to cook our meals automatically, the next generation of refrigerator to bring us ice water where we sit. And we expect our artists to steadily ascend, as if on their way to heaven.

But, as the writer William Saroyan put it, "You write a hit the

What I found myself writing, after the success of my first book, was a second book based on what I thought various people wanted—something fairy tale-like, or exotic, or cerebral, or cultural, or historical, or poetic, or simple, or complex.

AMY TAN

Q. How do you rate your music?

A. We're not good musicians. Just adequate.

Q. Then why are you so popular?

A. Maybe people like adequate music.

THE BEATLES

same way you write a flop." All the artist can do is do his work, some of which will succeed, some of which will fail. The superimposition of an upward spiral on top of the more sine-curve-like reality of the creative process presents the artist with a tormenting paradox.

Success is what sells.
ANDY WARHOL

Survivor Guilt

In this case, the artist may wonder why he has been singled out for success. Did stardom come because of his talent or his true grit, because of sheer luck, or as the result of one or another sellout? Is he really that much better than his peers? Is he really worth the astronomical amounts of money he may be making? The bandleader Artie Shaw wrote:

> At the peak of the '38 band, I was making $60,000 a week, which is the equivalent of $600,000 today. It seemed insane. I began to ask myself, "How can I be getting $60,000 a week when the first clarinet in the philharmonic only gets $150 a week?"

When the extremely successful artist reminds himself that hundreds of thousands of his peers are drowning, when he reminds himself that he, too, might have drowned had not the god of whimsy nodded in his direction, he may feel both guilty and estranged from his fellow artists.

What, after all, can he say to them? How can he make amends? Is it his duty to make amends? Such questions do not necessarily torment the successful artist on a conscious level. But, like the last Jew out of the liberated concentration camp or the last Iraqi out of the bunker, he knows that he is a fortunate survivor, no more meritorious as a human being than the many others who did not make it.

This understanding may subtly color his relationships. Survivors, it would seem, are internally pressured to side with the vanquished, with the victor, or with both. Having lost the possibility of a comfortable neutrality, the famous artist is more likely than his less famous cousins both to believe it his duty to help his mates, and to take, at the same time, an arrogant and intolerant stand vis-à-vis their putative failure.

Bursting Balloons Syndrome

The successful artist may also worry about how fragile a commodity is his fame. Will his balloon burst at any second? The sting of the journey and an appreciation of the realities of the world may conspire to make him live in fear of losing his fame. As the singer John Cougar Mellenkamp put it: "Somehow I always think that the record company is going to drop me next week, that the next record is going to come out and sell five copies, and I'll be back to pouring concrete."

The artist is not wrong to fear the possibility of such a loss—it is a realistic apprehension. The public may turn away from him; tastes may change; his drinking may begin to lose him roles. The artist may be a Bach, but history shows that Bach fell into obscurity. The artist may be a Faulkner, but history shows that Faulkner fell into obscurity.

Fame is often fleeting. Very few artists manage to spend a lifetime in the public eye; very few acquire the sort of name recognition that persists from year to year and decade to decade. Writing a bestseller or winning the Academy Award guarantees no lasting fame. Even the artist whose name we instantly recognize may be out of work for longer stretches than he would like us to know.

The artist may also harbor the irrational fear that he will be exposed as a fraud. Or he may simply not *feel* successful, doubting his success at a gut level. As the actor Jack Lemmon put it, "Success is always someone else's opinion, not your own."

The artist may fear that fashions will change and that his music, painting, or writing will no longer be wanted. Something new will win the hearts of collectors or of the few patrons of live dance or theater. The marketplace will exert its special brand of tyranny, and suddenly raw work, which was thought to be beautiful, will now be considered ugly; or subtle work, which was thought to be beautiful, will now be considered insipid. As the German artist Hermann Albert put it, "People used to demand beauty, grandeur, and such-like from works of art. Later they wanted the opposite, and that's a form of dictatorship, too."

If the artist is in one of the arts where he is racing against the clock, he may fear his balloon bursting as he grows older. The dancer, like the athlete, is especially confronted by the specter of a

Every year there's a whole new crop of performers.

SHERRY EAKER

time-bound career. Age also alters the standing of the leading man or woman and the rock musician. When will the rock singer finally look too silly breaking his guitar over his knee and cavorting as the last angry old man? As the singer Grace Slick put it, "There's nothing more ridiculous than old people on the stage."

The only power an actor has is the ability to say no.

KATHLEEN TURNER

The artist may also fear that he'll prick the balloon himself. The successful artist has almost too many chances for self-sabotage, considering that his perch is a precarious one, that his art is difficult to do, and that he faces enormous pressures. As a result he frequently does burst his balloon himself. As the pianist Claudio Arrau put it:

> We artists suddenly fall sick before major appearances. We create frightful emotional upsets, we risk losing what we hold dearest. We fall and break an arm. We have car accidents. Singers suddenly become hoarse, can't make their high notes, and often tighten their neck muscles into such a vise that it is amazing that their vocal cords function at all. Instrumentalists suddenly lose the use of some fingers or suddenly can't play the simplest (or the most difficult) passages.

In this regard we must remember that the successful artist, like his less famous brothers and sisters, is confronted by all the challenges discussed earlier, including blocks and disorders of mood. The artist who salutes his audience with a big smile and a clenched fist as he is applauded may in fact be severely depressed before, after, and even during his performance. The following newspaper account catches some of this flavor:

> The dramatic intensity of Rachmaninoff's "Third Piano Concerto" took an unexpected turn at UCLA when soloist Norberto Capone suddenly stopped in the middle of a solo passage, rose to his feet, and announced that he would play no more.
> As a stunned Mehli Mehta looked on from the podium, the 34-year-old pianist calmly told the hushed crowd Sunday night, "This is a crisis I've been dealing with. I don't want to play in public anymore. I'm sorry." And he sat down on the piano bench.

As Claudio Arrau recalled his early career, he explained: "I won the Liszt Prize twice in succession at sixteen and seventeen, but hardly a day passed when I didn't think of death."

In part out of insecurity, the newly crowned star may also loathe saying no. He may try to please everybody. Having waited years for his art to bring him recognition, and now suddenly surrounded by apparent well-wishers, he is challenged to remain true to himself, to refuse some invitations, to carefully examine all of the contracts he signs. As a poet friend warned the painter Marc Chagall: "Do you realize that you are famous here? Just the same, don't count on the money Walden owes you. He won't pay you, for he maintains that the glory is enough for you!"

For a great many people the activity of becoming successful is more rewarding than the success itself. It's certainly true of the novelists I know.

JOSEPH HELLER

Cult of Personality

The star is hard-pressed, once he achieves stardom, to feel like a normal person, to act like a normal person, or to be treated like a normal person. Stardom has about it such a pervasive air of unreality, and so changes the artist's relationship with other human beings and with himself, that he may wonder if he'll ever be able to get his feet back on the ground.

Especially during the first months and years of stardom, a loss of inner tranquility can easily occur. This sudden and severe disequilibrium can disorient, upset, and block the newly famous artist. Some artists seem never to recover, never recapture the qualities of absorption out of which their art flowed. Naguib Mahfouz, the Egyptian Nobel Prize–winning author, upon tasting worldwide fame for the first time at the ripe age of 77, lamented: "I can tackle small things as far as my health condition permits. But even for this I do not have the psychological tranquility."

Tennessee Williams wrote an eloquent essay, called "The Catastrophe of Success," which first appeared in the *New York Times* and was later employed as an introduction in the New Classics edition of his play *The Glass Menagerie*. In it he writes:

> [After the great success of *The Glass Menagerie*] I was snatched out of virtual oblivion and thrust into sudden prominence, and from the precarious tenancy of furnished rooms about the country I was removed to a suite in a first-class Manhattan hotel. [After some time] I found myself becoming indifferent to people. A well of cynicism rose in me. Sincerity and kindliness seemed to have gone out of my friends' voices. I got so sick of hearing people say, "I loved your

play!" that I could not say thank you any more. I was walking around dead in my shoes and I knew it.

The artist is both pleased and disturbed by the new attention he receives and feels pressured from within to make instant decisions. He is pressured to lock up the next giant role, to quickly capitalize on his fame, to secure the next big book contract. Whom will he let interview him and at which openings will he appear? How will he invest or spend his money? Will he move from his small apartment behind a factory to a grand house on the hill or by the ocean?

In making these quick decisions he may alter his life, perhaps without improving it. He may find himself madly on the go, a party animal and performing seal, the recipient of gifts of designer drugs and sexual adventures and praise. He may find himself living in a town he had never even meant to visit, in an enormous house with servants and guard dogs, more isolated than he ever was as an aspiring artist. As the singer Johnny Cash reflected: "I still don't know why I ever moved to California. I liked it there, had worked out there quite a bit and thought I'd love living there. But I didn't really belong out there. I never really felt at home there."

Life in solitude is no longer the same and life out in public is even more greatly transformed. The newly famous artist is noticed, pawed, and scrutinized. His former anonymity, from which he had been able to view and study the world and which he thought he would willingly give up for recognition, begins to feel like too great a commodity to have lost. As the actress Meryl Streep put it: "The soul, the source of what I do, is observation. But since I became famous I can't watch people—because they're watching me."

A pimple on the cheek of the unknown artist is a pimple. On the celebrity's cheek it is something of a stigma. The unknown artist need possess no arsenal of witticisms or pat responses with which to fend off interviewers. But the celebrity will look foolish or aloof if he doesn't respond glibly. The unknown artist need take relatively little care about what he says or how he says it. But the celebrity will be quoted, and a few quotes will go a long way toward defining for all time how the world thinks of him.

The celebrity's utterances suddenly have value—as do his underwear, his used car, his garbage. He becomes in no time both a symbol of the great riches that elude the many and an entrée into that world of wealth. No aspiring actor can forget that the celebrity director across the room can change his life overnight. No aspiring writer can forget that the celebrity writer is deep inside the castle, while he remains outside. Contact with the star feels both dreadful and wonderful—two words that together are a definition of awe.

The star is easily experienced as a kind of god, not because of who he is, but because of what he possesses and what he represents. At the same time many in the artist's sphere rebel at deifying him. So the artist will find himself surrounded by a gleeful multitude who are happy to notice that he has gotten fat, that his last picture was a stinker, or that his wife has run away.

If a man be without the virtues proper to humanity, what has he to do with music?

CONFUCIUS

The star—loved, feared, despised for succeeding, wooed, envied, seduced, and invisible as a real human being—is on everybody's trophy list and target list. In a sense and sometimes literally, he is marked for destruction. As Truman Capote put it: "The people simply cannot endure success over too long a period of time. It has to be destroyed."

The artist who becomes a cult figure, who is possessed by the public and carries the burden of a public mythology, can grow angry with his audience and the world. He may, at the same time, feel embarrassed by his own bellyaching, because he understands as well as anyone what a statistical rarity his success represents. He may work hard to quell his feelings of anger, believing them unseemly. But the feelings are likely to persist and to finally leak out, as they leaked out of the singer James Taylor's lips:

> They don't want to see an album cover without my face on it, the record company says. They want *Sweet Baby James.* And the audiences may want *Sweet Baby James,* too. So I thought, the next cover I make, I'll get someone with an airbrush; I'll get a tan on my ass, and I'll get someone to photograph it with one of those lights that makes a halo around you, and I'll call it *James Taylor—Like You Like Him.*

The artist isn't glad that he appears sour and ungrateful. But especially when he finds himself trapped by an alien, false, or inhuman public image—as a ladies' man when he is gay, as a sex god when he is simply human, as a sweet young man when he is angry and unruly inside—he can't help but despair at the discrepancy between his cult image and his real self. It is no easier in this regard to be James Dean or Beaver Cleaver. As the writer Joel Selvin observed about the singer Ricky Nelson:

> I discovered a deeply troubled young man who hated the TV show that had made him famous. He acted out his resentment in every way he could—drugs, motorcycle gangs, car crashes, music—but he couldn't stop what made him Ricky Nelson, which was the very TV image his father had created.

The Misuse of Power

If the artist sometimes experiences his success as terrible and burdensome, he may also experience it as a special and wonderful kind of arrival. At those dizzying heights he may fulfill all of his material ambitions, hobnob with princes and billionaires, wield interpersonal power, and seduce and conquer. In partaking of that magic he is challenged not to grow tyrannical.

The editor William Feather wrote, "Success makes us intolerant of failure, and failure makes us intolerant of success." Just as the unrecognized artist may despise all stars, the star may come to despise all unrecognized artists. He may begin to deny his own failures, growing intolerant of them as well. He may become the one whom no one can criticize—not his stockholders, for whom he is making money, and not his fans, for whom he is a cult figure. This regal, lofty, and icy insulation distances and may demoralize the celebrity artist, who, like the king, is challenged not to grow corrupt as he rules his kingdom. Erik Bruhn, the dancer, explained:

> When you become a box-office name, nobody dares to tell you anything. They don't realize that sometimes there is a need to be told that something is still working or that something is bad. You hear neither. I'm sure Rudolf Nureyev never hears any criticism from anybody. The point is, fellow dancers are afraid to say anything. Even more so, directors or managers never say anything—as long as the house is full.

It is in the arena of interpersonal relations that the star can especially abuse his power. The tyrannical director, the dictatorial conductor, the star in any art discipline wields undeniable power. The choreographer George Balanchine, for instance, demanded that

If my father {Otto Preminger} didn't get his own way, he'd throw the same kind of temper tantrum he'd thrown as a 3-year-old. For the person on the receiving end, these explosive outbursts were a horrible, devastating experience.

ERIK PREMINGER

his dancers not marry. He defended his position in the following way:

> For a female dancer, marriage means the end of her individuality. Men don't lose this individuality. Take a promising eighteen-year-old girl. She is beautiful. She dances like a dream. She becomes a star. Suddenly, from being a star she becomes Mrs. So-and-So, married to a doctor. She runs around like mad being a dancer and being a wife—and, of course, it's all over. I say dancers should have romances, love affairs, but not marriages.

In no other legal line of work could a man exercise the supreme control that Balanchine exercised over the 12- and 13-year-old girls whom he selected to teach. While admonishing them not to marry, and firing them if they did, *he* felt entitled to marry them. He married four of his star ballerinas and lived with a fifth. It seems not the least bit farfetched to suppose that Balanchine desired to possess all of his female dancers, soul and body. His position of power and prestige provided him with the means to that end.

The dancer Sallie Wilson described studying as a young girl with the choreographer and dancer Anthony Tudor:

> He was an inspiration, but he tinkered with people. He liked to get into their hearts and break them, thinking that made you a better person or a better dancer. He toyed with people's emotions—anyone he was interested in. He told me when it was time for me to lose my virginity. I set about doing that. I told him when I had done it and he gave a dinner party for me.

For all artists, stardom brings with it a new round of control, authority, and dependency issues. One artist may discover that he is suddenly dependent on invitations from the rich and experience his stardom as a new kind of slavery. Another artist may discover in stardom the potential to control others, score victories, and practically fulfill the fantasy of becoming God.

Albert Camus wrote, "When he is recognized as a talent, the creator's great suffering begins." To you this may sound like a lie or a romantic exaggeration, and yet it's clearly the case that many of our celebrity artists appear ravaged and done in by their fame. We must

As any young artist would, I made all the necessary efforts to enter the system and be recognized by it. Once I was in the system, my only problem was how to get out of it.

SANDRO CHIA

suppose that fame really is as dangerous as it is thrilling. The wise celebrity artist will take precautions against burning himself to a cinder in the great glow of his long-awaited stardom.

STRATEGIES

For Dealing with a Lack of Recognition

A great deal of talent is lost to the world for the want of a little courage.

SYDNEY SMITH

Use self-assessment and guided writing. Try to determine why you haven't gained the recognition you desire. Consider the following questions in connection with step 7 of your guided writing practice.

- Am I ambivalent about gaining recognition? What do I see as the dangers or drawbacks of being recognized?

- Am I uncompromising? Am I locked into one path or one product? Am I locked into an oppositional stance with regard to the marketplace?

- What is the relationship between my lack of recognition and my answers to the questions I posed to myself at the end of chapter 5? Am I producing a product that is not wanted? Are my business strategies poor? Is my lack of recognition more related to my personality or to my product?

- Do I need to do better work? Have I been working too superficially or uncreatively? Do I do too much of my work in my head and not enough in my sketchbook or in the practice room?

- How have I defined recognition? How will I know that I'm recognized "enough"? What do I consider an acceptable level of recognition, given the sort of art I do?

Test your willingness and challenge your unwillingness to move in a new direction. If and when you come up with strategies to increase your chances of success, the question will remain as to whether you want to make changes. Do you want to continue doing your most personal, important art, even though you've calculated that a turn to the commercial will offer better chances of gaining recognition? Will you make a compromise today that was anathema to you yesterday?

Test your willingness, and if you're willing, engage in new business practices, produce new products, self-promote, make and consult your business action plan, try everything you can. Work harder at realizing your art and at marketing it.

Challenge your unwillingness to make changes. If, finally, you remain unwilling, accept that you turned the matter over and decided to make potatoes, not peaches. Honor your decision.

Engage in detachment training. While you remain unrecognized, and even after you gain recognition, it's extremely valuable to learn how to balance a healthy disinterestedness against your ambitiousness and need for recognition. It is not a renunciation to acknowledge that there is unfathomable whimsy at work around us—that the role you're auditioning for may be earmarked for the producer's cousin, that the orchestra seat you're trying out for may be reserved for a student of the conductor's old violin teacher. In the face of such realities, it's crucial that you learn the art of detachment.

Get and have a life. It's imperative that you maintain a life outside of art that is rich in meaning and in relationships. Consult the discussion of parallel life at the end of chapter 7 for a fuller description of this point.

Be realistic about the recognition you can achieve. Artists envision themselves in different roles—as artist but also as teacher, activist, rebel, entertainer, classicist, recluse. What may feel like too small an audience to a popular singer may seem like an excellent audience to a singer striving to keep the madrigal form alive. Try to evaluate what constitutes a reasonable amount of recognition, given the role or roles you've chosen for yourself. If, say, you want to stretch limits, solve artistic problems, uphold a cultural tradition, or manifest your spiritual nature, isn't it wise to revel in the audience you acquire and not expect to be as well known as Madonna?

Find joy in the process as well as in the product. The issue of recognition is in part the issue of process versus outcome. Insofar as the process brings you joy, insofar as constructing a paragraph, painting shafts of sunlight, or playing a passage fills you with awe and delight, for that hour the issue of recognition vanishes. Insofar as the effort to construct that paragraph or to master that passage is a heartfelt struggle, welling up from deep sources, for that hour the issue of

Every great and original writer, in proportion as he is great and original, must create the taste by which he is relished.

WILLIAM WORDSWORTH

recognition vanishes. Notice your joy in the work, so as to remind yourself why you embarked on this journey.

Modestly define success for yourself and redefine it as necessary. What would make for a successful day, week, month? Having the opportunity to write? Producing one excellent story? Producing important fragments of one story? Pleasing yourself with your efforts? However you determine to define short-term success, invest meaning in your definition and work to achieve it in that time frame.

The applause of a single human being is of great consequence.
SAMUEL JOHNSON

Strive to gain a small audience—even an audience of one. Has someone responded to your work? Has someone advocated your work and sought to advance you? Reestablish and maintain contact with those important persons. Invite them to a private showing of your new work or to hear your new polonaise. Cultivate a relationship with and make time for anyone who respects your work.

My enthusiasm and my capacity to give are more important than the magnitude of the reception.
ROBERT PLANT

Engage in inner work and self-therapy to mitigate the pain that a lack of recognition may bring. Ventilate and accept your feelings. Strive to reconstruct your life in such a way that your emotional well-being does not depend on whether and in what measure you are recognized by the world at large. Learn to recognize yourself and appreciate and respect your own efforts.

Consider a career change. If it hurts too much for too long to go unrecognized, or if you otherwise determine that it's in your best interests to make a drastic change, entertain the idea of making a transition out of art. You may be able to manifest your creativity, remain true to your sense of mission, and satisfy your needs to be recognized and respected in a hitherto undreamed-of career. For a fuller explanation of this point, please consult the 10-step transition program described in Appendix 1.

Strategies for Dealing with Success

Use guided writing. Consider the following questions in conjunction with step 7 of your guided writing practice.

- What new challenges have arisen now that I've become successful? Is one particular challenge the most pressing?

- Can I create a tactic to handle each new challenge? How, for instance, will I choose among the many projects being offered me? What plan or procedure will I use to help me choose? (One client, a writer, visualized an ideal shelf full of her books, past and future, and determined not to write a book unless it appeared on that shelf. In this way she kept alive the idea that she was producing a body of work she could love and respect.)

- What challenges, which previously confronted me, have not disappeared in the aftermath of success? How will I handle them?

- Do I feel successful? How high must I rise? Can I do work that I love, or must I only do work that will make me more successful?

- Am I losing *me* as I gain more recognition and make more public appearances? Am I remaining true to myself? Am I more frightened than ever, more full of myself, more phony? Is personality integration an even greater issue than it was before?

When the film is finished, it is never the film I said I wanted to make.

FEDERICO FELLINI

Go slowly. Success is a kind of energy field. You vibrate in it like a charged particle. There are new demands on your time and talents, new interview requests and business questions, new possibilities and opportunities. In this context, when you have a free half-hour you may continue spinning like a top. Walk, breathe, stretch, meditate. Do the mundane: scrape a carrot, sweep the patio. Calm down.

Manage your money. You may or may not have paydays like this again. Study a book on money management. Learn your options. Think before you hire a full-time personal trainer or buy a car that corners tightly at 100 miles an hour. Think before you find yourself in the position of needing to earn half a million a year in order to cover expenses and feed your vast retinue.

Protect your privacy. Begin to calculate how public and accessible you mean to be. Learn how not to give yourself away. Be able to say "Thank you" and "I don't have an answer for that question." Have an interview persona and a public persona. At the same time be able to access your humanity.

Watch your impulses. You may feel a powerful urge to give money away, to indulge in the excesses suddenly available to you, to accept the drugs and sexual opportunities offered you, to wield your new power carelessly and tyrannically. Practice impulse control.

I don't like my music, but what is my opinion against that of millions of others?

FREDERICK LOEWE

Manage your opportunities. What will you do next and why will you do it? How will you choose your next movie, next book, next tour? Count to 100 before committing to anything, even though you experience the powerful desire to strike while the iron is hot each time an opportunity is offered. Express your excitement but don't commit until you've engaged yourself in real dialogue.

Build your professional support team. Engage, as necessary, an entertainment lawyer, accountant, business manager, publicist, investment specialist. Keep up cordial contact with peers and business associates. Send a card to the editor with whom you no longer work, the gallery owner who no longer represents you, the director who directed you in your first film.

Guard against feeling like an impostor. You may have persistent doubts—that you're really a marvelous director or writer, that you can really create powerful sculpture or memorable music, that you're as stunningly beautiful, sexy, or talented as your publicist claims. Having doubts, even legitimate ones, does not make you a fraud. Accept that you're not your publicist's fantasy or the projection of your producer's wildest dreams, and not an impostor either, but an entirely human being.

Manage your anxiety. New stresses exist in your life. More is expected of you. The ante on each project rises. Success is not a magic pill that allays anxieties. Consult the Recommended Reading list for chapter 3 and embark on an anxiety-management program.

Expect setbacks. The next book you write after your bestseller may disappoint you, your publisher, or your readers. The movie you direct after your blockbuster may bomb. But even if your stock is lowered in the eyes of the world, it need not sink in your own eyes. Virtually no artist experiences one success after another. Determine to come back. If doors have closed to you, consult your business action plan and analyze ways to reopen them. Demonstrate your courage all over again.

Guard against the internal pressure to continually top yourself. Watch out that you don't grow insatiable. How high must you rise? Above the clouds? So high that no one in your field can consider himself your equal? So high that no one sells more albums or more books than you do? No feast is so sumptuous that an insatiable appetite won't find it wanting.

Guard against existential discomfort, despair, and depression. After half a million people have come to hear you perform, what will your new goals be? Will one million satisfy you next time? It may be more important to play for a few close friends in the warmth of your living room. Having approached or attained your goals, what will matter next? Redefine your future, allowing for the possibility that new meaning will reside in unexpected places.

Remain human. Guard your privacy and your person; decline to become a stereotype or a frozen icon. Be more than the bad-boy rock singer, the sex goddess, the reclusive dancer, the brilliant violin virtuoso. Remember that you have a heart and a mind as well as a reputation.

> *I'm ambitious, in the way that Matisse said that it is a painter's job to introduce new things into the world.*
> JOHN WALKER

> *The artist has to make the viewer understand that his world is too narrow. To do this is a task for the humanist.*
> ANTONI TAPIES

PART TWO EXERCISES

The Artist's Work

No question may be more difficult for you to answer than this deceptively simple one: What is your work as an artist?

This is not an academic or trivial question but a core question whose answer the artist undertakes to live. Artists without a sufficient answer to this question, even if they never articulate their doubts and uncertainties, are likely to block and flounder. But even artists who do possess a rich, sustaining understanding of their work will sometimes face crises of doubt, developmental change points, and other natural road markers on their journey. Therefore all artists can profit by taking time to examine this question, a question which can be reframed as, "Why am I an artist?"

Exercise 1. Starting Out

Reflect on the following questions. What is your work as an artist?

- Is it the novel you're working on now, the play you're in, the preparations for your upcoming concert tour?

- Is it attending gallery openings, reading the latest psychological fiction from Eastern Europe, learning audition monologues?

- Is it everything that you are and do, everything art-related and life-related, so that your work and your life are quite inseparable?

- Is it as much negotiating the six months between shows as the two months that the show runs, as much surviving the two years of trying to get your novel published as the two years of writing it?

- Is it only your personal work: your performance pieces but not your voice-over work, your experimental novels but not your genre fiction?

- Is it maintaining a certain stance as outsider, rebel, witness, trickster, charmer, wise woman?

- Is it in large measure networking, self-promoting, marketing, wheeling and dealing?

- Is it more your inner process or more your products or performances?

- Does it defy description or understanding?

Without music, life would be a mistake.

FRIEDRICH NIETZSCHE

Exercise 2. The Artist's Path

Why are you walking the artist's path? Please expand on any of the following that seem true to you.

1. Because I must.

2. Because art has tremendous value.

3. Because every other job pales by comparison.

4. Because it gets me or may get me what I want, like sex, recognition, power, money, love, adulation, glory.

5. Because it allows me to communicate what's in my heart.

6. Because I'm talented.

7. Because other pursuits seem ordinary and run-of-the-mill.

8. Because doing art work suits my personality.

9. Because it's a family tradition.

10. Because it helps me heal myself.

11. Because it's great work for a deranged person.

12. Because it was expected of me.

13. Because, as a child, I fell in love with my medium.

14. Because I'm not really suited to do anything else.

15. Because it is the very embodiment of freedom.

16. Because it has social utility.

17. Because the bug bit me.

18. Because it's as noble a calling as a saint's or a hero's.

19. Because it lets me get up late.

20. Because . . .

Only when he no longer knows what he is doing does the painter do good things.

EDGAR DEGAS

Exercise 3. Varieties of Work

You may never have attempted to define your work before or tried to think about it in exactly these ways. You may even believe that such exercises are wrong-headed. If so, you still may profit from learning why you feel this way. Try to spend some time looking at these issues with a fresh eye.

Can you define your work with a single adjective? Look at the following list and select any phrases that resonate for you. For each one you select, personally define it and give an example, either from your own work or from the work of another artist.

It is my opinion that art lost its basic creative drive the moment it was separated from worship.

INGMAR BERGMAN

• dignified work • sacred work • courageous work • idiosyncratic work • willful work • socially relevant work • escapist work • existential work • commercial work • playful work • entertaining work • professional work • passionate work • career-oriented work • important work • culturally relevant work • useful work • innovative work • marketable work • personally relevant work • beautiful work • political work • true work • controversial work • my work

Exercise 4. Work Paradoxes and Contradictions

The very definition of your work may include apparent or actual paradoxes and contradictions. Comment on whether any of the following seem to you contradictory or paradoxical. For those you select, answer the following two questions: 1) Is the contradiction only apparent or is it real? 2) If it is real, should I embrace it or work to unravel it and effect changes in my life?

1. I want to do highly personal art that nevertheless reaches a large audience.

2. I am both a truth-teller and a trickster.

3. I want to do work that is socially relevant and that is also entertaining.

4. I want to work in solitude but I also want to be part of a community.

5. I want to be on the road as much as possible but I also want a home life.

6. Performing makes me very anxious but I want to perform as much as possible.

7. I am not sure about the value of art but I also think that there is nothing more valuable.

8. I want to do the art of my choosing but I also want to make money.

9. I want to do classical art that nevertheless reaches a contemporary audience.

10. I see the following as a contradiction or a paradox . . .

The artistic process is more than a collection of crafted things; it is more than the process of creating those things. It is a chance to encounter dimensions of our inner being and to discover deep, rewarding patterns of meaning.
PETER LONDON

Exercise 5. A Mantra for Your Work

A mantra is an incantation, inbued with meaning, that resonates powerfully. In traditional Hindu practice brief hymns or portions of Veda text were chanted as mantras. Try out the following phrases, making each into an incantation, and see which have power and meaning for you. The goal is to hit upon a mantra that points to an important source of your work and that will serve to remind you of that source. Make use of any of the following mantras that have meaning for you by memorizing them and practicing them or by writing them down in your journal and referring to them as needed.

• "I have something to say" • "We must never forget" • "See me" • "Come with me" • "Beauty matters" • "I stand with the believers" • "Truth matters" • "I am a mystic" • "I stand alone" • "You are in me" • "I am a hero" • "Be happy" • "I sustain life" • "What I do is needed" • "I serve in this fashion" • "I will be no less than fully alive" • "I am unafraid" • "If not me, then who?" • "I must" • My own mantra . . . •

Exercise 6. Personal Needs

What must you possess within yourself in order to do your work? Develop strategies to meet the needs you select from the following list.

1. I need sufficient peace of mind in which to work.

2. I need fewer worries about how I'll survive financially.

3. I need a better idea of what art I want to create.

4. I need to be more consistently creative.

5. I need to be more deeply motivated.

6. I need to take more risks.

7. I need to take fewer risks.

8. I need to feel more connected to like-minded people.

9. I need a willingness to do commercial work.

10. I need a more competitive attitude.

11. I need to accept the flaws in my work.

12. I need a more critical (but not self-critical) attitude.

13. I need to better balance my commitment to art and my commitment to life.

14. I need to learn to accept praise.

15. I need to learn to tolerate criticism.

16. I need to better manage my impulses.

17. I need a better understanding of the art marketplace.

18. I need to begin to recover from my addictions.

19. I need a more assertive attitude.

20. I need a less cocksure attitude.

21. I need to find my voice.

22. I need a better understanding of my own personality.

23. I need a better understanding of my place in the world.

24. I need limitless faith and courage.

25. I need . . .

The best advice I have is to keep spiritually sound and be persistent. Persistence is the key. Just never stop believing in your dream.

DEBORAH AQUILA

Exercise 7. Practical Needs

Artists in all disciplines have many practical needs that must be met. They need canvas and gallery representation, quiet time and a receptive publisher, appropriate head shots and a well-connected agent, a singular violin and a recording contract. Can you name your practical needs? Can you say how you mean to meet each one? Select at least ten needs from the following list and indicate how you might meet each one.

Need List

I am so rich that I must give myself away.

EGON SCHIELE

1. more business savvy
2. practical coping skills
3. an art buddy
4. new business opportunities
5. inexpensive suppliers
6. some inspirational reading
7. a college degree
8. an advanced degree
9. marketable products
10. a computer
11. better technical skills
12. agency representation
13. a schedule
14. more training
15. an assertiveness class
16. an advocate
17. ongoing financial support
18. good books on the business
19. career counseling
20. a work space

21. a better filing system
22. a better mailing list
23. an award
24. a break
25. a change of place
26. less clutter
27. a residency
28. a grant
29. a mentor
30. a new teacher
31. health insurance
32. a second career
33. a teaching job
34. new markets
35. more connections
36. a financial planner
37. a sponsor
38. a union
39. like-minded friends
40. more time
41. short-term goals
42. a new long-term plan
43. a golden opportunity
44. ??????????????????

Exercise 8. What Is Your Job Description?

Write a one- or two-page job description that takes into account the many aspects of your job (or the job you want) as a writer, dancer, photographer, painter, actor, director, singer, etc. What does it take to be effective in your art discipline, both as an artist and as a salesperson? Include all of the following:

- skills needed (including marketing skills)
- training needed

- experiences needed
- personal qualities needed

Exercise 9. Create a Tentative Definition of Your Work

Look back at your responses to the exercises in this section. Highlight the most important points. Incorporate your conclusions into a single tentative definition:

My work as an artist is . . .

The Challenges of Relationships | PART THREE

CHAPTER 7

The Rewards *and* Perils of Isolation

I am glad I chanced on a place so lonely and so still
With no companion to drag me early home.
Now that I have tasted the joy of being alone
I will never again come with a friend at my side.

BAI

In solitude
What happiness? Who can enjoy alone,
Or all enjoying what contentment find?

JOHN MILTON

ARTISTS SPEND A GREAT deal of time living and working in social isolation. Artists in all disciplines are confronted by this need, and for some, like novelists or painters, isolation may constitute the very essence of their lives, as it is the essence of the hermit's life.

One not only writes a book. One lives it. Upon completing it there are certain symptoms of death.
JOHN CHEEVER

In this chapter we'll examine the important benefits and serious dangers to the artist of prolonged isolation. Without such isolation, creativity cannot exist. An artist can't pore over negatives, learn a sonata, or write a novel while chatting with friends. An inability to seek out isolation, to love and make use of it, is a crushing impediment to the creative process. By the same token, there is no greater peril to the artist's mental health than failure to realize how risky a business prolonged social isolation can become.

Because artists are well aware that isolation is both necessary and desirable, on the one hand, and perilous, on the other, they are often conflicted about whether to seek it out, or else too quick to leave it. In a way this is territory we examined previously in chapter 4, the territory of creative blockage. Artists who leave their work too soon may say they are blocked, but are they leaving their work or fleeing some sudden sense of aloneness? It is also the territory of chapter 3, for prolonged isolation is the ground for mania, depression, and virulent acting-in. Artists who stay with their work around the clock will master their craft, but will they also grow disturbed as a result of their avoidance of other human beings and their preoccupation with their own thoughts?

One must not eye oneself having an experience, lest the eye become an evil eye.

FRIEDRICH NIETZSCHE

Additionally, since many of the artist's personality traits, especially his habits of mind, draw him to solitude, we must consider that the artist's need for social isolation flows directly out of the demands of his personality. Consequently, when he avoids isolation because, for one reason or another, he is afraid of it, he is doing violence to his own soul. He may indeed manage to avoid the risks of prolonged isolation, but at the same time understand that he is not living authentically.

This preliminary discussion is meant to underscore the fact that the benefits and perils discussed in this chapter are of the greatest moment to artists. In solitude, and only in solitude, do artists create. But in isolation artists despair and sometimes go mad. It is an issue that artists must address.

THE VALUES AND BENEFITS OF SOLITUDE

Solitude is the ground of creativity. As the psychiatrist Anthony Storr described in *Solitude: A Return to the Self:*

> The creative person is constantly seeking to discover himself, to remodel his own identity, and to find meaning in the universe by means of what he creates. These moments are chiefly, if not invariably, those in which he is alone.

The French philosopher Montaigne wrote, "We must reserve a little back-shop, all our own, entirely free, wherein to establish our true liberty and principal retreat and solitude."

While the benefits of solitude are in one sense self-evident, it is also important that we specifically name them. There are two reasons for this: as a reminder as to why artists must spend such a significant portion of their lives in isolation (and why they're unhappy when they don't spend enough time there), and because each specific benefit has its shadow side—carries its own warning label, so to speak—and points the way to an understanding of the hazards of prolonged isolation. The benefits of solitude, then, are the following ones.

Personality Fit

The artist is often a loner, a solitary introvert. This is generally as true for the performing artist as for the creative artist. As the actress Linda Hunt expressed it:

> I think most of my life I have thought of myself as a solitary figure. Over and over again, I express that solitariness onstage and on film— over and over again. I want to see myself as solitary in the landscape. It's the story I tell.

The introversion of the actor as he works among other actors on a stage or of the musician as he sits among 20 other violinists is at first glance less obvious than is the introversion of the painter or the writer. But all artists appear to have a personality makeup on the introverted side, and as a rule prefer solitude to social interaction. They desire to be alone with their work; often they just prefer to be alone.

The psychoanalyst Donald Winnicott wrote in a paper entitled "The Capacity to Be Alone":

> It is probably true to say that in psychoanalytical literature more has been written on the *fear* of being alone or the *wish* to be alone than on the *ability* to be alone. It would seem to me that a discussion of the *positive* aspects of the capacity to be alone is overdue.

Creative and performing artists generally have this capacity. However, they may fear isolation, because they expect to find in it aloneness and not solitude. They may avoid the studio or practice room. They may avoid their art altogether. But such avoidance doesn't alter the fact that, as a matter of personality fit, they really do prefer solitude to social interaction.

Contact with the Work

My interest in the theater was always in being alone *with the play.*

LILLIAN HELLMAN

In the bubble of absorption that is the most precious aspect of solitude, artists can be together with their love—their medium, their art, their work. They can connect with melody, meter, or color. They wake up dreaming about the work they'll get done in the solitude that a new day brings. As the painter Alice Baber put it, "I wake up in the morning and feel the need of a color and I begin to work."

By becoming thoroughly absorbed, thoroughly lost in the moment, artists can do sublime work. This is as true for the performer as for the poet or sculptor. The musician practicing his instrument is no more engaged in a merely mechanical enterprise than is the painter with his brush or the writer at his computer screen. The musician's rehearsal activity is larger, more profound, richer than that. As Pablo Casals put it, the musician is out to "make divine things human and human things divine," and that is work he does in solitude as much as in public performance.

Free Play

In solitude artists can experiment, make a mess, sustain notes for the joy of it, imagine themselves on any stage in any play. In the studio or practice room, they are not on public display and need not wear their public face. They can be their secret selves, their best selves, their worst selves. If there is unfreedom on stage or in the gallery, there is freedom in the studio. As the visual artist Allen Kaprow put it, "Artists' studios do not look like galleries, and when an artist's studio does, everyone is suspicious." Galleries are for show; studios are where messes are made and where the real work happens.

Working Out One's Life

In solitude artists are also ordering and organizing their experiences, making connections, traveling through time and space, wrestling with the abuse heaped upon them in childhood, searching out the color of the sunlight that once warmed them, listening to the sounds that once thrilled them. As the French writer François Mauriac explained about his moments of solitude:

> [During these times] I don't observe and I don't describe; I rediscover. I rediscover the world of my devout, unhappy, and introverted childhood. It is as though when I was twenty a door within me had closed forever on that which was going to become the material of my work.

It's not a conscious preoccupation for me to expose loneliness in my films—it just happens that way.
LOUIS MALLE

Artists are working out their lives in this silence that they are compelled to seek. While they fix a print in a chemical bath, play a passage a hundred times over, study to become Oedipus, or create the biography of their protagonist's father, they are reaching for answers to the questions that most interest or trouble them.

It is the deep need for spiritual fulfillment which makes the role of art vital today.
YEHIEL SHEMI

Contact with Others

Artists, when they are absorbed in their work, are also deeply connected to other human beings. The theologian Matthew Fox said, "The journey the artist makes in turning inward to listen and to trust his or her images is a communal journey." The psychologist Otto Rank argued that "the collective unconsciousness, not rugged individualism, gives birth to creativity."

To be sure, artists are not making real contact with living human beings as they work in the studio, but they are making contact in the realm of the spirit. The absence of the pressures real people bring to bear on them allows them, in solitude, to love humankind. Whereas in their day job they may hate their boss and at Thanksgiving they must deal with their alcoholic parents, in the studio their best impulses and most noble sentiments are free to emerge.

Spiritual Journey

In many religious traditions contemplation in solitude is considered an important—sometimes the most important—path to spiritual growth and understanding. A dictum of Buddhist teaching has it that no one can teach another to become a Buddha; all must learn for themselves. In this way, the artist who is sincerely working is engaged in a spiritual activity very like that of the religious contemplative—he is becoming a Buddha. For many artists, this spiritual enlightenment is the central purpose of the time they spend in solitude. For others it is a by-product of their devoted creative efforts.

Safe Haven

Only when I experience do I compose—only when I compose do I experience.

GUSTAV MAHLER

In solitude it is eminently possible to avoid painful or uncomfortable social interactions. Artists can drop their social masks and necessary social pretenses. They can stop smiling politely. They can let down their hair, put up their feet, and do what they please. In their study no one can criticize or reject them, demand that they patly describe their work, or badger them with questions. Solitude is an island of safety in a dangerous world. As the fourth-century Chinese Taoist poet T'ao Ch'ien put it:

> In my empty rooms are time and space.
> I return to be myself
> Unfretted and unfettered
> in this self-like place.

Integrity and the Existential Encounter

In solitude, artists confront life with all the integrity, passion, and intensity they can muster. These existential encounters are the very essence of authentic living.

As discussed in chapter 2, artists may work in a state of tense concentration or else in a trance, deeply absorbed and utterly lost in the moment. They may feel as knotted as a Beethoven, building laboriously with musical scraps, or as weightless as a youthful Mozart or Mendelssohn pouring out music whole. They may be able to say, as E. M. Forster did, that they always find writing pleasant and easy; or they may resemble the Cézanne described by Rousseau:

> He spent many more hours looking and thinking than he did painting. People who watched him say that he sometimes waited as long as twenty minutes between two strokes of his brush. He himself said that there were days when he looked at his subject so long that he felt "as if his eyes were bleeding."

In either case, they are working with integrity. As long as they remain in contact with the work—whether their brow is clear or furrowed—they consider that they are spending their time honorably. The poet Stephen Spender wrote:

> In my own mind I make a sharp distinction between two types of concentration: one is immediate and complete, the other is plodding and only completed in stages. A poet may be divinely gifted with a lucid and purposive intellect; he may be clumsy and slow; that does not matter, what matters is integrity of purpose.

I have always been the cat that walks alone.

ARLETTY

Aliveness

For a great many artists solitude is the time when they feel most real and alive. It is when they have their most intense experiences, when they can vicariously live out any adventure, any dream. Tennessee Williams said, "I'm only really alive when I'm writing." The painter Robert Motherwell wrote, "I feel most real to myself in the studio." The young, exuberant Russian painter Marie Bashkirtseff exclaimed at the end of the last century:

> In the studio all distinctions disappear. One has neither name nor family; one is no longer the daughter of one's mother, one is oneself and individual, and one has before one art, and nothing else. One feels so happy, so free, so proud!

We may think of this aliveness as the accumulation of all the above-listed benefits, as the artist working out her life, manifesting her creativity, suiting her personality, playing, avoiding unwanted social interactions, working authentically and with integrity, living intensely—as the artist being her grandest self.

THE DANGERS OF PROLONGED ISOLATION

While the time artists spend in solitude is of incomparable value to them, isolation carries with it tremendous dangers as well, including all of the following ones.

Lack of Relationships and Social Savvy

It is difficult for the artist who remains too long in isolation to forge or to adequately maintain real relationships with other human beings. Artists who spend too much time in isolation not only experience grave difficulty in forming friendships, intimate relationships, social contacts, and community but also remain insufficiently practiced in the ways of the world. They find themselves painfully ill-equipped to handle the interpersonal moments they do seek out. At such times they stand shyly apart or passionately charge about, speak too bluntly or speak too little, and in a hundred other ways demonstrate their lack of interpersonal skills and social savvy.

I'm death grip on abstractions, but I forget living people.

ISAAC ASIMOV

Lack of Knowledge

If we think back to the stories of Joseph K. and Robert F. presented in chapter 5 and consider them in the present context, we see that Joseph K. gains little new knowledge of the world as he works on his stories in severe social isolation. Robert F., who also loves solitude and is quite capable of making use of it, purposefully ventures out into the world, learns about the men's movement, and makes use of that information to create a product that is widely wanted.

Artists, because they spend such prolonged periods in isolation, frequently fall behind the times. They may gain great self-knowledge, spiritual insight, and understanding of their media as they work in private, but at the price of a lack of vital knowledge of the world around them.

Minimal Personality Challenge and Real-World Challenge

Because solitude provides artists with a safe haven, fits their personality, and offers them a kind of communal contact with other human beings through their work, it can also serve as a breeding ground for stagnation. Without ever quite realizing it, artists can grow flaccid in isolation and begin to experience their solitude as deadening. The studio can become too easy and unchallenging a place.

The world outside the studio offers unmatched opportunities for growth and for the expression of authentic and courageous behavior. Artists often miss these opportunities and, remaining relatively untested, handle themselves poorly when they do venture out.

Workaholism

Artists, because of the demands of their personality, their sense of personal mission, and their need to create or perform, are driven people. Mixed with the love of work can be a terrible pressure to work. For many artists, and especially for the most productive ones, the line between love and obsession and between effort and compulsion blurs or disappears entirely. Are such artists free or are they slaves to their work?

In *The Artist and Society* the psychiatrist Lawrence Hatterer said of such an artist:

> His most recognizable trait is his recurring daily preoccupation with translating artistic activity into accomplishment. The consuming intensity of this artistic pursuit brooks no interference or obstacles. His absorption with the creative act is such that he experiences continually what the average artist feels only infrequently when he reaches unusual levels of creative energy with accompanying output. He appears to be incapable of willful nonproductivity.

This is Picasso working for 72 hours straight. This is Van Gogh turning out 200 finished paintings during his 444 days in Arles. The artist who is "incapable of willful nonproductivity" is a workaholic for whom little in life, apart from his artistic productivity and accomplishment, may have any meaning.

Prolonged Unreality

Because artists feel alive when they encounter their work in solitude, and because that work is real and important to them, they can easily make the mistake of believing that they can successfully live without ever venturing out of the studio. But for such artists, life becomes unreal and their cherished studio turns into a prison.

Prisoners in penal institutions have written eloquently about their slide, after years of isolation, into a dark world of distorted reality. One prisoner, who had served 14 years at England's Durham Prison, wrote:

> Can you imagine what it is like being a prisoner for life? Your dreams turn into nightmares and your castle into ashes, all you think about is fantasy, and in the end you turn your back on reality and live in a contorted world of make-believe.

This is the danger Freud pointed out in his writings about the artist's life. In a characteristic passage he noted:

I must be careful and not do too much acting, because there is always the danger that I might forget my own life.
SIMONE SIGNORET

The artist is an incipient introvert who is not far from being a neurotic. He is impelled by too powerful instinctive needs. [He] turns away from reality, and transfers all his interests, his libido, too, to the elaboration of his imaginary wishes, all of which might easily point the way to neurosis.

The moment a man feels or realizes himself as an artist, he ceases to belong to any milieu or time.
PERCY WYNDHAM LEWIS

No play is finished without an audience in attendance.
MIA DILLON

Freud went too far in calling the artist's time in the studio invariably a substitute for life and in portraying the artist as an essentially dissatisfied and incompetent soul. What the artist does in isolation is serious and important real-world business. To call it a substitute for life is both to misunderstand what is in the artist's heart and to make an unjustified claim for the preeminent value of the world outside the studio. But Freud was right to note that a very real danger exists for those artists who so turn away from the world that their self-enforced isolation takes on a pathological look. For such artists solitude has a nightmarish feel to it and life is experienced as a prison sentence.

Mental and Emotional Disturbances

We discussed in chapter 3 the mood and anxiety disorders, emotional disturbances, and psychoses that afflict many artists. Prolonged isolation is the ground for such disturbances, and meaningful social interaction is their cure.

The painter Jim Dine said, "I do not think obsession is funny or that not being able to stop one's intensity is funny." Much that goes on for the artist in isolation is unpleasant and unfunny, for in isolation obsessions build; rejections, rivalries, and grievances are rehashed; and wounds fester. It's altogether harder to obsess while folk dancing or playing softball, building a barn or baking bread with others. It's all too easy to brood and obsess if you live cut off from the world, your shades drawn tight, entirely alone with your preoccupations.

Aloneness, Alienation, and Estrangement

The aloneness we're describing here is the chief theme of existential literature and as important a psychological challenge as any that confronts us as human beings. Its other names are alienation and estrangement. It is also sometimes called the problem of the outsider.

Artists are particularly likely to experience this estrangement. They regularly ask the question, "Is life worth living?" They demand personal answers to the question, and frequently they can find no satisfactory answers. One moment the artist feels connected to others, to his god, his ancestors, his descendants. He contemplates human happiness and, like Beethoven, attempts to find fitting music to accompany Schiller's *Ode to Joy.* Then, in the very next second, he finds himself utterly alone and empty. In this sudden coldness he contemplates suicide, as did Vincent Van Gogh, Sylvia Plath, and Ernest Hemingway.

Unbearable solitude—I cannot believe it or resign myself to it.
ALBERT CAMUS

This existential aloneness should not be confused with loneliness. Loneliness can be ameliorated by human contact. Aloneness, however, is a problem that roughly translates as "Life is meaningless," "I do not matter," or "Nothing matters." It inevitably cries out for a spiritual solution. Aloneness is experienced by the artist as a terrible lack—a chilling lack of purpose, a frightening lack of direction, a sudden, despairing lack of interest in the work at hand. It can strike in the blink of an eye.

When this terrible coldness does strike, artists stop working. If they force themselves to continue, out of a sense of discipline or an inner compulsion, the results are often inferior. Too much of their consciousness has been distracted by the coldness. Their world becomes a mess—not the happy mess that a child makes, but the unhappy mess of unrealized art, because they have lost contact with the work. As Jackson Pollock put it: "It is only when I lose contact with the painting that the result is a mess. Otherwise there is a pure harmony, an easy give and take, and the painting comes out well."

The easy give and take is gone. The work the artist has just accomplished feels inferior or worthless. He feels awful, discouraged, frightened.

The need to fill the void becomes insistent. A common solution—the one chosen by Pollock and countless thousands of creative and performing artists—is to take to the bottle. They may seek out drugs or engage in other distracting mischief. If the artist is practiced at intellectualizing, he may invent fine arguments to wrap around the moment. Denying that he's suddenly frightened, he may argue himself into the belief that it's a certain book that he wants, which he can get across town. As a character laments ironically in one of Margaret Switzer's *Existential Folktales,* "What means we go to to fill the emptiness!" The coldness and emptiness are incontrovertible feelings, and the artist must do something.

This is a matter worth addressing at length. In the context of the present discussion, however, the point to remember is that artists often experience life as outsiders, that in prolonged social isolation such feelings grow stronger, and that even for less estranged artists a chilling wind of existential malaise may suddenly blow through the studio.

Fiction, even at its best, is remarkably useless in the world of events.

WRIGHT MORRIS

FINDING A PERSONAL BALANCE

You're challenged to find and maintain a balance in your life between necessary isolation and necessary human contact. In order to work, you must be alone. But you must also get out and meet what the writer Suzi Gablik has called our human needs "for relatedness, for rootedness, for a frame of orientation and an object of devotion."

What will the right balance be for you? Twenty percent of one and 80 percent of the other, or 50 percent of each? Certainly opting for 100 percent of either—for the extreme of complete social isolation or a complete lack of meaningful solitude—constitutes an unfortunate and dangerous choice.

Speculate, for instance, on the possible differences between the journeys of two people who from an early age loved art, one of whom became an artist and the other of whom did not. In the context of the present discussion, it may be that the latter individual experienced isolation more as aloneness than solitude, dreaded isolation more, and reasonably chose a more social path. Such people, however, may forever feel that they failed to manifest their own creativity, and may come to despise the fact that they've involved themselves in doing other people's work and not their own. This may be an example of the one extreme, of the person who was called to art but who saw such dangers in that empty room that he swore off solitude altogether.

Likewise the blocked artist, the artist who is unhappy, the artist who is unwilling or unable to confront his art, the tired or anxious artist, the artist driven by a desire for sex or drink, may find remaining alone in the studio a fearsome, impossible task. He leaves his solitude too soon and draws the balance too near the extreme of artistic inactivity. When, however, he escapes to the café up the street or picks up the phone to call a friend, he's likely to instantly regret his decision. He knows that his flight is a loss of nerve, an uncourageous act, and his subsequent time out in the world is tainted by a secret sense of failure.

At the other extreme is the artist who remains in self-imposed isolation around the clock. He may sometimes go out, but he still contrives to bring his solitude with him. He may go for long walks alone, go to the movies alone, and congratulate himself on having been out in the world. There is no doubt, for instance, that the Paul Klee of the following diary passage, although out of the studio, is nonetheless still alone and at work:

I consider that every artist who isolates himself from the world is doomed. I find it incredible that an artist should wish to shut himself away from the people.
DIMITRI SHOSTAKOVICH

> Yesterday afternoon I took a nice walk. The scene was drenched in a sulphur yellow, only the water was a turquoise blue—blue to the deepest ultramarine. The sap colored the meadows in yellow, carmine, and violet. I walked about in the river bed, and since I was wearing boots, I was able to wade through the water in many places. I found the most beautifully polished stones.

All artists are caught on the horns of this dilemma. If they spend too little time in isolation, they do not get their work done and feel guilty and ashamed. If they spend too much time in isolation, they feel lonely, unhappy, and estranged, and may also grow unbalanced. How will you strike a balance? How will you reorder your life so that you get enough of each and not too much of either?

STRATEGIES

You're challenged to find time for your solitude and to make real use of it in order to reap its potential benefits. You're likewise challenged to avoid or minimize the dangers of prolonged isolation. By making use of the strategies presented below and by creating others of your own you'll do a better job of maintaining effective solitude, combating existential coldness when it strikes, and engaging the world.

Engage in guided writing. There are several interrelated issues brought up in this chapter that you might focus on in your guided writing practice. They're broken down below into five groups of questions.

On gaining solitude:

No great work has ever been produced except after a long interval of still and musing meditation.

WALTER BAGEHOT

1. Do I have a place to go that is all mine? Do I have a room of my own, a sacred space, a sanctuary?

2. How much do I love my solitude? Does solitude fit my personality? If I seem to love it insufficiently, or if it does not fit my personality, what strategies will I employ to gain the solitude I need? Will I contract with myself or change my environment by unplugging the phone or moving from the living room to the basement?

3. Do I make enough time for my working solitude? Do I set such time aside at the end of the day, when I'm too tired to make use of it? Can I instead begin each day with a period of solitude?

4. Have I prepared myself to make use of solitude? Do I have work to do? Am I really engaged in and committed to my art?

On maintaining solitude:

1. How long do I generally remain in my working solitude? Can I stretch out that time by taking brief, strategic time-outs and then returning to my work, rather than entirely fleeing my solitude for the day?

2. Will I work on the blocks that prevent me from maintaining my working solitude?

3. What distracts or derails me as I try to work in solitude? My own thoughts? My sense of aloneness, loneliness, or estrangement? My doubts about the goodness or importance of the work I'm doing? What specifically derails me and what plan can I devise to combat the problem?

4. How much solitude can I tolerate? How much aloneness? If I can tolerate a great deal of solitude but relatively little aloneness, what will I do when I flip from one mood to the other? What strategies will I employ to regain my sense of solitude?

On addressing the dangers of prolonged isolation:

1. By remaining in isolation too long and too often, am I failing to really challenge myself? Am I failing to gain new, needed knowledge? Am I failing at the business of art?

2. Am I estranged or alienated from the world? Do I consider myself an outsider? What, for me, is the relationship between alienation and social isolation?

3. Am I a workaholic? What, for me, are the dangers of workaholism?

4. Is there a connection between the social isolation I seek out and any emotional disturbances I experience?

Sometimes when I sit down to practice I have to stifle my impulse to ring for the elevator man and offer him money to come in and hear me.

ARTHUR RUBINSTEIN

On determining when to leave:

1. What are good, legitimate, or sufficient reasons for me to leave my solitude? That I've got enough work done and met my daily goals? That I've spent all the hours I set aside and now have other important things to do? That, by staying longer, I will grow disturbed?

2. Have I made any rules about leaving—for instance, that I mustn't leave if it feels like I'm running away? Should I create a few such rules and test them out?

3. What are bad, illegitimate, or insufficient reasons for me to leave my working solitude? Is it bad to leave if nothing more has happened than that I've grown distracted or don't know how to proceed with the musical passage, portrait, or paragraph at hand?

4. Might I create a ritual or ceremony of leave-taking in order to slow the process down, ensure that it's time to go, and celebrate the completion of a period of work?

On calculating the balance:

1. Am I severely endangered by my social isolation? Must I dramatically reduce the time I spend entirely alone?

2. Am I severely hampered by spending an insufficient amount of time in solitude? Must I dramatically increase the time I spend alone working on my art?

3. Am I bound to a myth about how solitary I should be? Can I dispute that myth? Can I picture myself more in the world and work to effect that change?

4. What seems to be the right balance between social isolation and social interaction for me? Can I calculate a rough percentage or tentatively determine how many hours I should spend alone with my work, on the one hand, and how many hours engaged with other people and in the affairs of the world, on the other?

Whether you're working or not, you must have another stimulus, something that is fulfilling. To me this is a wonderful living, but not if I'm eating my insides out.

TONY CALL

Engage in parallel-life work. You can best avoid the dangers of prolonged isolation by having available to you a robust and meaningful life apart from art. This life outside the studio also helps prevent existential coldness from striking because it reminds you, unconsciously but clearly, that you have something to look forward to after work.

Begin now to cultivate a life full of real meaning apart from your life as a creative or performing artist. If you do not have such a parallel life presently in place, start by making small but real changes in the direction of new relationships, new community efforts, and a new belief system. I am not proposing that you disavow your present life as an artist, but rather that you take steps to procure for yourself a volunteer activity, second career, new friendship, or other useful out-of-the-studio interest.

This parallel life, of course, produces its own tensions and carries its own risks. Won't a second career, even one lovingly entered into, bring disappointments and frustrations? Won't a mate and children provide more than a few distractions? Won't giving some energy to a needy cause bring with it burnout and depression?

These are risks worth taking. You may come to possess more energy, suffer fewer depressions, feel less concerned about the success of a rival, enjoy the art of other artists more, and despair and doubt less as you work in your studio. You become freer to live life if you supplement your identity as artist with other real and important identities in the world.

People will begin to matter to you in ways in which you've been prevented so far from caring about them. Albert Camus said of his fictional painter Jonas in the short story "The Artist at Work": "For human beings and the ordinary circumstances of life he merely reserved a kindly smile, which dispensed him from paying attention to them." But Jonas does not fare well in the loft he builds for himself; his perfect isolation finally paralyzes him.

The artist whose investment in art is so great, who is so obsessed with art-making and art-brooding that he is prevented from having a life, is likely to feel cheated. It's one thing to be on a mission, and every artist is on a mission. It's another thing to martyr oneself to the cause of art.

The following elements, then, enter into the process of creating a parallel life.

Outside of music, my life is a strange mixture of academic science, biology, husbandry, and entrepreneurial flair. That's what fish farming is all about. I could be Ian Anderson, salmon farmer, and not have to talk about music all the time, which was exciting.

IAN ANDERSON

1. Get permission from yourself to produce fewer art products or give fewer performances than you otherwise might. Set more modest daily, weekly, or monthly goals. Rest for a day on your laurels. Incorporate into your schedule both in-studio and out-of-studio time.

2. Redefine success so that accomplishments outside of the art arena count. Call it a successful morning if you write a letter to your foster child, have brunch with your sister, and pack up old clothes to give to the Salvation Army.

3. Redefine productive time and wasted time. It's important that the afternoon you spend at a town meeting, in the waiting room of your son's orthodontist, or on a crisis hotline feels like time appropriately spent.

4. Pay new and better attention to other people. Do this not because they are fascinating creatures and make for good stories or good conquests, but to enter into sincere and sometimes loving relations with them.

5. Expand your repertoire of activities. Will you graciously host Thanksgiving dinner? Play with a child? Protect a principle? Make barbecued chicken wings for a picnic? Just enjoy leisure in great spirits?

The pursuit of a parallel life, the contours of which will be different in each artist's case, is the single most important self-help strategy available to the artist.

Take strategic time-outs. Even having inoculated yourself against existential coldness by obtaining a parallel life, icy moments will intrude. What will you do?

The basic antidote is simple: take a strategic time-out. Do something pleasant, of short duration, that isn't harmful to you, while holding the conscious intention of returning to your work in a very short time. Take a brief, pleasant time-out only—don't run away. For instance:

- make a bowl of popcorn
- take a hot shower
- play with your child's hamster
- take a memory tour and recall a grand encounter from last summer
- shoot one rack of pool on your miniature pool table
- read one chapter in the book by your bed
- call a friend
- melt cheese on a tortilla
- engage in a brief, ritual ceremony you've devised for such occasions
- visit your rock garden
- take a brisk walk
- meditate
- sit in the sun
- watch a foreign-language television show for ten minutes
- play a dozen hands of go fish with your children
- chat with your mate
- play soccer up and down your hallway
- read the ads in a glossy magazine

It's queer for a live human animal, endowed with intelligence, to spend waking hours of a very mortal life cooped up in a room, not talking to anybody, just scribbling words on a page.

JOHN BARTH

Prepare a whole array of brief, fanciful strategies. Plan for a minimum of disruption and a minimum of self-destruction. Such coldness may be better banished, at less cost, by a hot shower or a brisk walk than by drugs or alcohol, a misadventure at the local tavern, or a bout of depression. If a brief time-out proves inadequate, turn to the rich parallel life you've been cultivating and let go of art for as long as you must.

CHAPTER 8

Social Interactions *and* Community

THE ARTIST BRINGS his complex and contradictory nature with him when he ventures out into the world, and while his personality may serve him extremely well in the studio, it may just as easily fail him in social situations. Each of the artist's personality traits produces social effects, as do each of the artist's moods. Even the artist's vitality and passion can prove an impediment in the social arena. He may fly out of his studio full of passionate, manic energy, his vitality hardly spent by two hours of painting, writing, or practicing, and fly into the company of others. The dancer John Prinz recalled, "I was like a volcano. In fact, everybody called me the 'Volcano.' I had all this incredible energy that kept exploding."

How do *you* come to the interpersonal moment? Does one aspect of your personality predominate? Are you consistently ironic, assertive, frightened, silent, or prideful? You may find it immensely profitable to determine what sides of yourself you present to the world—to determine, in effect, how others see you—with a view to discovering whether there are changes you'd like to make in your public persona.

In this chapter we'll look more closely at artists' social interactions and relationships. Whether it's the relationship with a parent, sibling, or spouse; with a teacher, mentor, or business associate; or with a colleague, fellow artist, or rival, there are five specific areas that are important to reflect upon in determining how successful you'll be at establishing and maintaining relationships. This discus-

An artist is not an isolated system. In order to survive he has to continuously interact with the world around him.

HANS HAACKE

sion will also naturally lead us to an examination of the important topic of whether or not artists can find community amongst themselves.

OUTSIDER FEELINGS

The atmosphere of the Existentialist Outsider is unpleasant to breathe. There is something nauseating, anti-life, about it: these men without motive who stay in their rooms because there seems to be no reason for doing anything else.

COLIN WILSON

Most artists are not quite as estranged from their fellow human beings, as bereft of reasons for existing, or as alienated from the common values and enthusiasms of the world as are the outsider characters created by existential writers like Kafka, Camus, and Sartre. But insofar as artists do regularly feel different from other people, a differentness experienced both as a sense of oddness and a sense of specialness, they identify with the outsider's concerns and come to the interpersonal moment in guarded or distant fashion.

In part, artists are outsiders because of the personal mythology they possess. This mythology is a blend of beliefs about the importance of the individual, the responsibility of the artist as a maker of culture and a witness to the truth, and the ordained separateness of the artist. Artists often stand apart on principle, like Napoleonic figures perched on a hill overlooking the battle.

The artist may also find himself speechless in public. Around him people chat, but he finds he has little to offer. Too much of what he knows and feels has gone directly into his art and too much has been revealed to him in solitude—infinitely more than he can share in casual conversation. In this regard he is not unlike the biblical figure Zacharias, who is described in the Gospel according to St. Luke in the following way:

> And the people waited for Zacharias, and marveled that he tarried so long in the temple. And when he came out, he could not speak unto them: and they perceived that he had seen a vision in the temple: for he beckoned unto them, and remained speechless.

How can the artist communicate or paraphrase what has transpired in the studio? And if he isn't to communicate that, what is he to speak about?

The artist is also aware that he was born into a ready-made society. He didn't choose it and he can see clearly much that he doesn't like about it. But by the same token he can't live the life of a Balinese composer, a Pueblo Indian potter, or a Greek dramatist; he must make do where he is, in an avid, heterogeneous, fragmented, disharmonious, mercantile society, a society he perhaps doesn't respect. This disrespect easily translates into a disdain for the people he finds himself with, for implied in every social gathering (except a protest event) is a shared acceptance of the status quo.

How much of an outsider do you feel yourself to be? Do you demand that you take that stance? How much outsider energy do you bring to your social interactions? Do you feel certain that other people see less clearly than you do and fall far short of the mark? What sorts of relationships are possible for someone who interacts as a stranger in a strange land?

It is well worth your effort to address these questions anew and perhaps even to cross-examine yourself about them, for outside in the cold is where the outsider finds himself.

Here, in America, we become virtuosos to gain a name, but there, in the Andean festivals, they try to lose their identity, and they do: they become part of the collective whole.

QUENTIN HOWARD

I should compose with utter confidence a subject that set my blood going, even though it were condemned by all other artists as anti-musical.

GIUSEPPE VERDI

ART OBSESSIONS

To put it simply but accurately, artists are often lost to the world because of their obsessions with their art. They may be just as lost as they prepare to work or incubate a new idea as in those feverish days when they make their final cuts on a film or race toward a publishing deadline. They may obsess about artistic questions and feel bursts of creative energy day or night, alone or in the company of others, in the middle of the work week or on vacation in the Bahamas.

Lost in time and space, the artist may feel more connected to Picasso, Emily Dickinson, Ingmar Bergman, Gertrude Stein, Handel, or Tennessee Williams than to the people in his immediate world. The living past holds extraordinary meaning for him. He travels elsewhere, removing his spirit and attention from the present. He may reside, as he works on his novel, in the childhood of a character, walking the garden paths and living the household dramas there. He may come upon a Rembrandt drawing and find himself wrenched, not to any particular place or time, but just *elsewhere*, as he reexperiences the greatness of his traditions, measures himself anew, and dreams again of his future.

One musician explained to me that when he heard his first Beethoven symphony as an adolescent he experienced a tremendous disruption of his life that lasted two full days. He knew that his life had changed; he felt agitated, awestruck, in love. To the world, however, he seemed preoccupied, inaccessible, and self-involved. While connecting with a new, powerful, and hitherto unknown universe, he disconnected, in both subtle and obvious ways, from the world of everyday affairs. Artists often lose the present moment this way and live surreally.

Thus obsessed by their art, artists find it difficult to make room in their lives and in their psyches for flesh-and-blood human beings. Fyodor Dostoevsky's wife Anna said of her husband, "I even think that he is incapable of love; he is too much occupied with other thoughts and ideas to become strongly attached to anyone earthly." Lucy Audubon, wife of the ornithological painter John James Audubon, complained, "I have a rival in every bird!"

The relationship between the artist and his or her art is a central one, a core relationship. The visual artist Eleanor Antin said, "For art I could do anything." The dancer Starr Danias said of herself, "During layoffs, I miss dancing the way I would miss a person." The composer Georg Phillip Telemann claimed that "music requires a man to give himself entirely to it." The novelist William Faulkner advised, "The writer's only responsibility is to his art; he will be completely ruthless if he is a good one." The playwright George Bernard Shaw echoed the sentiment: "The true artist will let his wife starve, his children go barefoot, his mother drudge for his living at seventy, sooner than work at anything but his art."

Are you willing to care about other people more than this? Are you willing to practice really letting go of art? Can you make an effort to avoid snubbing those around you, even if it means losing an idea or an image? Can you interrupt your work when someone needs you? Can you let a human being matter more than your art? Not every artist is able or willing to answer these questions in the affirmative, but every artist should at least consider the implications of a string of responses in the negative.

Dependency, Authority, and Control Issues

Artists consider themselves to be independent people. But the artist's independent, rebellious, nonconforming nature, coupled with his introspective habits of mind, also make him wary of social interactions. Whereas the fireman, for example, has no reason to believe that keeping company with other firemen will diminish his ability to fight fires, the artist, keenly aware that his journey is a personal and independent one, often fears that contact with his peers will slow him down, detour him, contain him, limit him, or unduly influence him.

I don't think that I'm a collaborator by nature—nobody else thinks I am, either.

LILLIAN HELLMAN

He knows that other artists are opinionated and have their own agendas. Won't he be distracted, he wonders, by those opinions and agendas? Is it realistic painting that's ridiculous or is it abstract painting? Should the modern dancer avoid ballet training or embrace it? Should the actor thumb his nose at commercials or accept them as life-savers? Is the novel dead or only in its infancy? Is painting sexist and knitting not, or is knitting pathetic and painting heroic? Is it moral or immoral to write novels in which women are skinned alive? Should the sculptor accept a commission from a city council that is racist? Is a teaching job a useful avenue or a dead end? Is a soup can art? Is an opera ticket too expensive?

Because the artist must know for himself, do for himself, and believe in himself, he is unwilling to mindlessly agree with his peers or placate them when they disagree with him. If they say New York is the only place for an artist to live, but his journey is about to take him to Santa Fe, Arles, or Nepal, he will buy his ticket anyway. If he's leaving his regional theater for Los Angeles, or leaving Los Angeles for a regional theater, he will leave. If he means to photograph in black-and-white, he will photograph in black-and-white. He will not let other artists define or deter him. Similarly, he will resist attempts to label him as a member of their particular school, for that, too, is a blow to his ego and to his freedom.

But, by the same token, artists simply can't live as independently as they would like. At the simplest level, they are often financially dependent on parents, a mate, or on a day job. They also depend on publishers, film distributors, curators, producers, and similar industry professionals to put their work before the public.

Because there is such a sizable discrepancy between the way

artists view themselves and the realities of the situation they find themselves in, conflicts arise. On the interpersonal level, these conflicts emerge as issues of dependency, authority, and control. These issues generally become more troubling over time. For example, in the first years of the artist's career, through school and in his first steps away from school, the question of financial independence may not strike him as of paramount importance. He works and gets some help from his parents. Maybe he receives a partial scholarship or uses his savings. His art may bring in a little money. Perhaps he enters into a relationship where he is dependent on his mate's income, but that dependency isn't much of an issue yet, because both partners believe that one day he'll break through and make money.

Listen! There was never an artistic period. There was never an art-loving nation.
JAMES MCNEILL
WHISTLER

The contours of this life will be different for each artist. The black female dancer will have a different experience from the white male painter; two black female dancers will also have significantly different experiences. Each, though, will share the artist's common experience: that art does not produce enough income to live on.

The artist becomes less and less eager to think about his finances or to talk about how he's supporting himself. As the painter Susan Schwalb put it, "Most artists don't like to talk about money, and how they survive. Most artists don't like to admit how they make a living, or who helps them."

Even as he tries not to think or talk about money, he continues to worry. How will he be supported if he doesn't achieve stardom? Will the average person buy his oil painting for $4,000 when a plastic-framed Monet or Warhol print can be purchased for $20? Craving entertainment and a good read, will the average person pick up his small-press-run, difficult novel? Committed only to a yearly visit to *The Nutcracker,* will the average person support his attempts to start a modern dance company? Expecting the production values of a $50-million movie, will the average person rush out to see his grainy, $40,000 epic?

As a rule, the average person will not. Nor will society's representative, the government, help the artist much. As the Israeli artist Zvi Goldstein put it, "Western society never pays a cultural tax." The few pennies each citizen puts into the pot to support the entire range of creative and performing arts can't go far toward sustaining artists.

Eventually the artist gets tired of this lack of financial reward.

He may begin to demand of himself that he do more commercial work, that he compromise to meet the demands of the marketplace. He begins to realize that the odds are stacked against him. What was an appropriate and even charming life of poverty for the art student and young bohemian artist wears thin as the artist leaves his twenties. It is no longer charming that his car doesn't run, that he has no medical insurance, that he's still waiting tables, transcribing court trials, or driving a cab. As Eric Bogosian, the performance artist, put it:

There is only one success—to be able to spend your life in your own way.
CHRISTOPHER MORLEY

> It's not fun to be poor. We used to romanticize the artist's life; we used to romanticize poverty. We spent years in art school studying the lives of artists, learning how to live like an artist. It was going to be cool to come to New York and live on the Lower East Side next to dope dealers. But we became frightened by the squalor and the poverty. I didn't want to live in a slum the rest of my life.

The composer Philip Glass, describing the early decades of his music career, underlined the point:

> The first problem an artist has is how to survive. I began writing music when I was fifteen and was not self-supporting as an artist until I was forty-one. So for over twenty-five years I could not entirely support myself through the work that I wanted to do.
>
> To begin as an artist means to take on a life of struggle, so that at forty-one you can finally make a living as an artist. My European artist friends say, "My gosh, it took you so long!" But in this country you'd say, "You mean, you did it so quickly?" It can just as easily never happen.

The artist's social interactions are sooner or later affected by this real lack of independence. He may find it hard to take from anyone . . . or hard not to take from everyone. He may maintain a feeling of independence by rebelling in any small way he can—by walking out of his acting class when the teacher criticizes him, by writing an angry letter to the small-press editor who has rejected his poems. His social interactions—with his mate, his business associates, with other artists in the café—may show a volatility that can be traced to his need to retain a feeling of independence. Some of his interactions, which may look self-sabotaging and may otherwise seem incomprehensible, can be roughly taken to mean "You can't do that to me!" or "I'll do what I damn well choose!"

Many of the rivalries and unpleasantnesses in the arts stem from the unhappy feelings associated with this lack of real or felt independence. The artist, his pride wounded, is hard-pressed not to consider anyone who appears successful or who occupies a position of authority an enemy. He may see every social interaction as a kind of threat, and attempt to maintain control in the most trifling matters.

As writers we are guilty of treason in the eyes of history if we do not denounce what deserves to be denounced.

ARTHUR KOESTLER

Both subtle and flagrant battles over control may pepper his private and public life. The battles may be loud, ugly, and perverse; the artist, fighting for control, may connive, challenge, manipulate, attack. He may adopt a passive-aggressive stance and agree in principle to everything demanded of him by his agent or his mate but then make sure to arrive late, forget the milk, or break a vase. He may take a heroic (or heroically foolish) stance in order not to feel pushed around by circumstances; he may become, as Whistler said of himself, "the Quixote in the battle fought by painters."

The artist, motivated by a sense that he's a caretaker of culture, certain that it's his right to be free, is at once less likely to achieve independence and more likely to mourn the fact that independence eludes him. But since no person can be as independent as romantic mythology and two centuries of idealization of the individual have led him to think he can be, each artist is obliged to reassess his ideas about independence and interdependence.

SELF-ESTEEM ISSUES

An artist with low self-esteem or one whose self-esteem is eroded over time enters into social interactions burdened by his inferiority feelings. The fact that his art happens to be appreciated is no hedge against these feelings. As one celebrated rock musician put it, "I believe in what I do, but not in who I am."

Much can erode the artist's sense of self-worth. Even a successful career as a member of a good symphony orchestra may bring with it a sense of failure. As the musician Carl Fischer put it:

> The tragedy of the orchestra violinist's career is that his activity from the very first is equivalent to a renunciation, that it does not

represent a beginning supported by joyous hopes, but in most cases forms the close of a period of painful disappointments and hopes destroyed. Nearly every orchestra violinist, once upon a time, has dreamed of becoming a celebrated soloist.

When an actor, dancer, or musician is led into group activity, he may struggle, ultimately unsuccessfully, to hold on to his artistic identity. He may blend into the group effort even while fighting to retain his individuality in the face of the efforts of the conductor or director to maintain control and provide direction. This tension frustrates him and wears him down, and finally he may submit to the demands of the institution in which he finds himself. As the author Donald Henahan put it:

> Without anyone's willing it, an orchestra bends to its common purpose (some would say flattens) all the diverse human types that enter it. There comes to be a recognizable symphony orchestra personality, an orchestra level of talent, an orchestra temperament. Like any walled city, the orchestra demands of its inhabitants submission to authority and unquestioning response to a leader.

Pride may prevent the artist from sharing with others this central experience—that he has fallen far short of realizing his dreams. Because his self-esteem is being eroded, because every day he feels less whole and less adequate, he may experience ever greater difficulty in entering into relationship with anyone he supposes to be healthier than himself. In fact, he may find himself drawn to the dregs of society, so as to feel superior to them or because he identifies with them, thus descending another notch and further eroding his already tarnished self-esteem.

Fame, experience, and success do not necessarily mean that an actor knows what he is doing, or that he feels secure with his proven talent.

DAVID BLACK

Envy and Competition Issues

Our discussion of the reasons why creative and performing artists find it so difficult to interact in satisfactory ways would hardly be complete without an acknowledgment that artists typically compete fiercely and envy one another. It is a problem expressed by Alex Gross, founding editor of *Art Workers News,* in the following way: "It would seem that there is no sum of money so small, no crumb of reputation so paltry, no opportunity to show one's work so uninviting, that it will fail as the reason for one artist to stab another in the back."

The young actor has a painful thing to realize: that the theatre does not support its own people, even those who have been successful enough to have their talent recognized.

EDITH ATWATER

Although many important dynamics operate between artists—including fellow feeling and mutual respect, a sense of shared purpose and joy during the run of a play, for example—as often as not it is the dynamic of envy that defines the relationship between two artists. As the actress Danielle Brisebois put it: "I was in *Annie* about three years. All of us kids were jealous of each other, even though we never let the others know it. No one wanted any of the other kids to have more than them."

It's not that the artist sits at home making lists of his rivals. When he's absorbed in enjoying a fellow artist's work or absorbed in his own art-making, he has no rivals. At such times his fellow artists are his spiritual companions. But at other times he finds he can't stop comparing his lot to theirs. They are getting the parts he covets, they are having important shows, they are being rewarded for their dull acting, flat singing, amateurish painting, or sloppy writing. Their novels occupy the few spots on the bestseller lists. His own good friends withhold information about grants and group shows. His own good friends attend parties and rub elbows with people whose elbows they would invite him to rub if they were really his friends.

Artists are often aware of their envious feelings but not aware of how deep they run. An artist may claim, for instance, to hate realistic painting (or abstract painting, figurative painting, installation pieces, environmental art, miniatures, photographs, or murals), not realizing that this position may be a way of simply dismissing out of hand an army of potential rivals. Their successes become irrelevant to him because their work doesn't count. By taking a dismissive stance, the artist reduces the area in which he competes.

An artist's envy may manifest itself in any number of ways. In the past he may have loved to read; now he avoids contemporary fiction completely. All living authors have become his rivals. Or he may avidly read contemporary fiction, but only to assure himself that it's bad. Or he may read only the works of an author he knows is an alcoholic or near death—a rival he can pity or feel superior to.

How is an artist to alter this unfortunate relationship with his peers? We live, after all, in a society and a cultural milieu that foster envy. Because there are relatively few jobs in art, the ones that do exist are precious. For an artist to unilaterally work on quieting his feelings of envy is like unilateral nuclear disarmament—a noble idea with many risks attached. If he undertakes to love and respect his fellow artists, to support them, to attend their shows, to buy their books, and to judge them generously, will they return the favor? Will they notice and be transformed themselves? Or will they exploit his generosity?

Each artist is challenged to make sense of this dilemma. The artist has great gifts to offer her fellow artists—love, appreciation, and understanding among them. But these gifts will be withheld by the artist disabled by envious feelings.

IS COMMUNITY POSSIBLE AMONG ARTISTS?

The need for innovation in art exists as much as ever, but its challenge at this point surely lies in more comprehensive goals that link the personal with the global.

SUZI GABLIK

The above discussion inevitably leads us to the observation that only rarely do artists establish or maintain meaningful communities. While they can and do join groups—orchestras, bands, repertory companies, writers' groups, and graphic artists' coalitions, on the one hand, and unions, 12-step programs, churches, and the PTA, on the other—they retain a dream of community that reaches far beyond what they manage to experience.

Maybe the dream they cherish is a romantic or utopian one. Its undeniable power may be a product of the isolation and estrangement they feel—a powerful wish that can't possibly be fulfilled. They may need to believe that such community exists, maybe in Paris, Berlin, or some locale they've heard rumors about. They may need to dream about moving to Taos or Bali. If they do spend their obligatory year in Paris, however, they're as likely as not to be disappointed, for the reality falls short of their expectations.

What, after all, are they seeking? What does this elusive community look like? What do we even mean by the word? The Association for Humanistic Psychology, addressing the issue of

We cannot bear connection. That is our malady. We must break away, and be isolate. We call that being freed, being individual. Beyond a certain point, which we have reached, it is suicide.

D. H. LAWRENCE

community at its 1991 annual conference, began its conference brochure with the following observation: "We know less about community than any other social form: is it an emotional state, a small group, a local place or a collection of widely shared values?"

M. Scott Peck, in *The Different Drum,* his book on community-building, provides one answer, describing community as a group where all are leaders, a group that operates by consensus realism, a place of inclusivity, commitment, and safety, and a natural laboratory. Artists would certainly want their definition of community to resemble Peck's, with the addition of the following conditions, which taken together do make for a utopian picture. An artists' community would be a place where artists experience a sense of shared values and ideals, collaborate, experience a general enthusiasm for art and share a general prosperity, see the aims of art regularly furthered, feel support for growth and maturation of each artist's work, and experience mutual respect and love.

If we try to envision a leaderless group of artists gathered in order to form community, we are struck by the fact that each artist will bring to the group his or her inability to relate. Each will bring a sense of estrangement, a need to maintain independence, a need not to be swayed by the opinions of the others, the artist's necessary arrogance, feelings of envy, art obsessions, and all the rest.

To take an extreme example, imagine for a moment spending two hours every Thursday night in a hypothetical 1880 men's group made up of Van Gogh, Wagner, Dostoevsky, Gauguin, Tchaikovsky, Hardy, and Tolstoy. Can anyone imagine such a group working to support its members? Wouldn't such a group be likely to provide two hours of utter mayhem, more a miracle to survive than a joy to attend?

Van Gogh, isolated and longing for community during his years in Arles, wrote to his brother Theo:

> The problem is simply this: If I looked about for someone to chum with, would it be a good thing, would it be to my brother's advantage and mine? Would the other lose by it or would he gain? My mind is running on these questions.

As Van Gogh's infamous episode with Gauguin attests, the artist is right to wonder how his personality may mesh with another

I am against a narrow nationalism, but I also do not think there is an art for the whole world, just as English cannot be the language for the whole world and Esperanto has not proved popular.

GU WENDA

I've never been able to collaborate with others. Another person with an idea is a problem for me.

JACKSON BROWNE

artist's personality. Several artists together multiply the effects. Any community formed by artists is more likely to look divisive and operatic than mutually supportive.

Many of the challenges discussed in this book contribute to the artist's inability to create and sustain community, but few artists will talk about their mood swings or about how they hunger for recognition or envy their fellow artists. Walls of strained silence and small talk stand between one artist and another. The artist remains a member of an orchestra, a ballet company, a writers' circle, an art school, but wears his public face. Around him he sees the public faces of his fellow artists. He feels the coldness, as they do, but concludes that his only course is to keep his distance.

When you look up at the sky, you have a feeling of unity which delights you and makes you giddy.

FERDINAND HODLER

Still, even if artists come to disparage the very idea of community effort and determine to measure their well-being in strictly personal terms, the desire for community remains strong. Even if they are discouraged from helping one another and disbelieve that help is available to them, artists retain the desire to give and receive help. Even if they grow tired of dreaming about fantastic community, their ears still prick up when they hear stories about the art colonies of Bolinas, California, or Sedona, Arizona. Even if they remain in isolation, tending their own gardens, and even if they believe that modern artists are doomed to have their desire for community thwarted, the desire does not die.

In an attempt to gain a measure of community, they rally around causes, give benefit concerts and readings, march against censorship, meet to play softball, give and attend classes, attend self-help support groups, spend one Saturday night a month at their local Mystery Writers' of America meeting. They make an effort to connect with their fellow actors during the run of a play. In these and a hundred other ways, they assert that they are trying to come together, trying to share their common humanity. But, despite these efforts, artists remain largely disappointed at the lack of community in their lives.

This analysis may not ring true for you. You may experience a strong sense of community in your church, among your friends, in your writing group, as a member of your culture, in your neighborhood. You may not hunger for any special community of artists or you may already experience that community.

On the other hand, you may be among the many artists I've known who do identify with the picture drawn here. If so, you're challenged to determine whether and in what ways you might seek out the community of other artists. Do you want to exert yourself in that direction and transform yourself and the world a little in the process? In so doing you might serve as a role model for the new-look community artist, in contrast to the more usual models of the artist as eccentric, outsider, or prima donna.

I feel strongly that it's more important to be a person than to be a dancer. One has to be a person first.

REBECCA WRIGHT

STRATEGIES

In order to serve both yourself and others in your social interactions, you need a clear understanding of the issues addressed in this chapter. To have a fair chance at acquiring better relationships and richer community, your first step is self-assessment, followed by personal transformation. The artist who is too envious, arrogant, estranged, or obsessed, who badly lacks self-esteem or who too quickly dismisses other people, must recognize the nature and extent of the problem, create a plan for personal transformation, and practice it in public. Make use of the following strategies to begin to accomplish these goals.

Engage in guided writing work. Many different issues have been raised in this chapter. In order to help you narrow your focus, the guided writing questions for this chapter have been divided into 8 sections. On general personality issues:

1. What features of my personality most hamper me in social situations?

2. What features of my personality best serve me in social situations?

3. What social situations best fit my personality?

4. What social situations bring out the worst in me?

5. What qualities are characteristic of a person who finds it easy to be in the world? Are any of those qualities attractive to me?

6. If I wanted to make over my personality so that I could function better in the world, where would I start? What would I change first?

On outsider issues:

Without the practice of the healing within ourselves, our art would not have a healing nature.

THICH NHAT HANH

1. How much do I feel like an alien from another planet?

2. Do I feel that people regularly misunderstand me?

3. Do I feel that people regularly fail to truly see or hear me?

4. Do I find it difficult to enter into the general enthusiasm of the moment?

5. Do I disagree with or find reprehensible or shallow the values and concerns of most people?

6. If I do in fact experience life as an outsider, and if that issue greatly influences my interactions with others, how do I mean to address the issue? Do I mean to change? Will I try to come in from the cold?

On art obsession issues:

1. Am I always working? Do I seem incapable of letting go of my art thoughts and preoccupations?

2. Do I feel more obsessed at certain times? For example, with a book deadline or a major performance approaching? When I'm learning new material or puzzling over an especially riveting problem?

3. How do my art obsessions affect my interpersonal relationships? Are they more a block to intimacy or an impediment in casual relationships?

4. How can I release the obsession, even if only for a few hours? What strategies have worked in the past? What new ones might I try?

5. Do I allow myself a real break between projects, a time when I can be present for others and free from thoughts about my art?

6. What do I obsess about with respect to my art? That I haven't done enough of it and should get back to it? Does every sight I see make me want to paint, every conversation I overhear make me want to write a story? Can I sometimes quiet these impulses and learn to better relax in the world?

On dependency, authority, and control isssues:

1. Upon whom do I feel dependent? In what ways are my dependency feelings disempowering and destructive? Can I work to put any such relationship on a new footing—by, for instance, asserting myself more, disputing statements meant to diminish me, and demanding fair treatment?

2. How would I define a dependent relationship? A codependent relationship? An interdependent relationship? Can I generate some guidelines for myself so that I can distinguish one from another?

3. How do I handle being the one in authority?

4. How do I handle having someone exert authority over me? Do I act out? Do I regularly prefer to sabotage my chances rather than compromise or submit?

5. Would it be in my best interests to dispute authority figures more? Am I too meek, submissive, and ineffectual? Do I hurt my own chances by my lack of assertiveness?

6. Am I wise about knowing what I really can and cannot control? Do I understand how little other people's behavior is in my control? How little I can control their reactions to my work? How much or how little artistic control I can hope to retain in my particular art discipline?

On self-esteem issues:

1. Do I come to social interactions feeling small, vulnerable, or unworthy?

2. Do I look confident but not feel confident?

3. Do I have trouble asking for what I want or need because I feel I have nothing to give in return?

I found that as a director I was able to create something outside of myself. It was a way of being involved in the theater without subjecting myself to the ego-crushing business of trying to be an actress.

ANN JELLICO

4. What would most increase my self-esteem? A certain kind of success? A better acceptance of myself as I am?

5. Do I need to take certain risks so that, by proving to myself that I can handle them, my confidence will grow? Do I need to speak more directly, maintain greater visibility, or actively lobby for my interests with people who can help my career?

6. Do I know any self-confident people? What can I learn from the way they act and the way they carry themselves in the world?

It is impossible, I feel, in this time when communications are so open, to set out deliberately to make an art which is Mexican, or American, or Chinese, or Russian. I think in terms of universality.

RUFINO TAMAYO

On envy issues:

1. How often do I feel envious of other artists? Sometimes? Regularly? Almost all the time?

2. Is envy a significant problem in my life? Even a disabling problem?

3. How might I address the problem of envy? What options are available to me?

4. How much do my feelings of envy prevent me from enjoying other artists' work?

5. How much do my feelings of envy prevent me from forming friendships with other artists?

6. Do I experience other artists as being envious of me? How can I best handle their envy? Can it be addressed openly?

On specific relationships:

1. How would I characterize my relationship with my parents? What about that relationship would I like to change? How might I effect such a change?

2. How would I characterize my relationship with my siblings? Do they understand my artist's life? Is it important that they understand it?

3. Have I been troubled regularly by interactions with my teachers? Am I still troubled by such interactions?

There's a Chinese proverb that I think is true: You often find your destiny on the path you take to avoid it.

HECTOR ELIZONDO

4. Was I harmed by any one teacher? What are the present repercussions of that unfortunate relationship?

5. How do I generally react when I find myself in a student-teacher relationship? With wide-eyed enthusiasm? Uncritically? Submissively? Suspiciously? Combatively? Is there any aspect of the way I approach such relationships that I would like to change?

6. Am I able to speak my mind with my teachers? Do I ask for what I need? Do I protect myself from abuse?

7. Am I regularly successful or unsuccessful at maintaining an intimate relationship? If I'm unsuccessful, to what do I attribute the problem?

8. Am I interested in addressing the problems that arise in my intimate relationships?

9. Do I devote enough time, energy, and care to my intimate relationships? Or do I put them second to my art and generally treat them cavalierly?

10. How would I characterize the dynamics of my intimate relationships? Do I understand them? Is it important that I understand them?

11. Do I value my significant other? What about him or her do I value? Do I acknowledge and celebrate what my partner is giving me? Does he or she value me and acknowledge my contributions to the relationship?

12. What do I believe are the best ways to cope in social situations? By relaxing more? By ventilating feelings on the spot? By speaking directly? By becoming a more practiced listener? By better understanding my feelings and making informed decisions based on an understanding of my feelings?

On community issues:

1. How would I define community, both ideally and realistically?

2. Have I experienced a sense of community in my life? When? Under what circumstances?

3. Do I need to actively work on community-building?

4. What about myself do I need to change in order to have a better chance of joining meaningfully with others?

5. Is friendship, communal feeling, and/or a sense of shared purpose available to me in any of the following relationships?

   • With my immediate family?

   • With my extended family?

   • With one or a few close friends?

   • With other women? With other men?

   • In a fraternal organization or cultural club?

   • In my present church, the church into which I was born, a branch or offshoot of that church (one, say, that affirms my worth as a woman or as a gay man), or a different church or spiritual movement that I consciously select?

   • In a 12-step group or other self-help group?

   • In an activist organization?

   • In a political organization?

   • With people from my day job?

   • In a recreation group such as a skiing, hiking, bicycling, or gardening club?

The first time I turned something down, I was made to feel so bad, so guilty. It made me realize how much I needed to say no.

SHELLEY DUVALL

Use the following strategies to become a strong, independent person.

Affirm yourself. You'll experience less anxiety, act out less, and have less reason to repress or displace your feelings if you interact with others in ways that are respectful of your own principles and desires and that affirm your right to exist.

Hold yourself in high esteem. Someone may be more talented, better-connected, more powerful, or more authoritative than you, but that person is not more worthy than you. Do not bow, do not vanish.

Acquire new language habits that support your independence. To questions that have as their subtext a desire to master or control you, reply with "Let's talk about it" or "We'll see," rather than a meek yes or a defensive no.

Gain freedom from the disabling parts of your past. Such freedom is a necessary piece of a personal definition of independence. Engage in inner work or individual therapy to gain such freedom. Assert yourself, affirm yourself, and free yourself from the bondage of your own formed character.

And courage, always courage. For however lovingly done, the work must be tested in fire.
WILLIAM GALBREATH

Practice habits of independence. Take an all-day vacation. Detach from everyone. Speak clearly, directly, and powerfully in conversation. Take a one-hour sabbatical from your obsessions. Practice walking meditation and cross the city. Act the equal of a powerful figure. Talk face-to-face with a rival. Take it for granted that you will be heard and seen.

Remember that you aren't the equivalent of your sources of income. Engage in inner work to prevent yourself from feeling diminished by the fact that you receive a check each month from your parents or that your day job is unsatisfactory. If possible, achieve a measure of financial independence through your art; construct a strong business action plan and implement it. At the same time make peace with the psychological fallout that results from your real position in the world, as a laborer in an industry that monetarily rewards a few people well and most people not at all.

Manage your anxiety. The agoraphobic is one sort of unfree soul, hidden away at home, the obsessive-compulsive another, binding anxiety through endless, repetitive rituals. The more anxiety rules your life, the more like a slave you'll feel. Begin an anxiety-reduction program that really addresses the sources of fear in your life.

Clean up your act. Begin the process of recovering from your chemical dependencies, addictions, and compulsions. Consider such recovery a crucial piece of your personal definition of independence.

Don't agree unless you mean to agree. Have social skills but don't be "nice." Attune to your own needs before you volunteer. Think for yourself. Dispute arguments that rely on the logic of authority.

Watch out for your displays of independence. Check to see if they are really angry outbursts, displaced aggression, a lack of impulse control, coverups for sadness or envy, or self-sabotaging behaviors of one kind or another.

Honor the independent-spirited parts of your personality. Remain skeptical, thoughtful, nonconforming, curious, and passionate. Honor the idea that you are on an important personal journey that no one can dispute or deny you.

> *Who can ever give enough thanks to a great poet, the most precious jewel a nation can possess?*
> LUDWIG VAN BEETHOVEN

Use the following strategies to become a strong, interdependent person.

Affirm others. The aloof artist, prideful and busy with his personal pursuits, gains his independence at the expense of his humanity. Practice the art of contact. Collaborate. Make friends. Join the world.

Honor the interdependent-spirited parts of your personality. Your ability to empathize with others, your love of art, and your need for an audience are among the many important aspects of your personality that draw you to people and require you to interact socially. To deny the reality of your desire to be with others is self-delusion. You may serve this part of your nature by entering into a single strong intimate relationship, by having a few close friends, or by joining with several others in a worthwhile project. Go out of your way to honor the part of you that is not satisfied with a life of estrangement and isolation.

Learn interpersonal skills and practice them. Holed away writing, painting, or practicing your instrument, you have probably missed many opportunities to practice interpersonal skills. It's also likely that you never much cared for small talk and the other conventions of social interaction. Improving your interpersonal skills—learning how to actively listen, how to negotiate and compromise, how to network— will be of great value to you with respect to both your business and personal relationships.

Engage in conscious community-building with other artists. Enlist other artists in a common cause—in a tea ceremony, for example, or in painting a mural. Evolve meaningful rituals and ceremonies for your time together. As Francine du Plessix Gray wrote, rituals are "structured sequences of actions that bring us a heightened sense of our own identity and meaningfulness." The dimming of the lights before the play begins is part of the ritual that makes the stage a sacred space. In the same way, gather artists for a sacred event that you co-create together.

Don't idealize independence or interdependence. They must coexist. Affirm your independence in small and large ways but also affirm your interdependence. Revel in the mystery that both must be affirmed. Identify yourself both as an independent artist and a community artist. Identify yourself both as an iconoclast and as a community member. Bow to the orchestra's will in the afternoon, but play your own music in the evening. Write to make your mark and secure your reputation in the morning, but at lunchtime write letters in a campaign to free political prisoners. Master *and* serve.

In each painting is found the beginning of the next, and the finished painting is a beginning, not an end.

VALERIO ADAMI

PART THREE EXERCISES

The Artist's World

No matter how solitary or introspective you may be, no matter how hard you try to keep the world at a distance, you remain always in the world—there is no escaping it. The world is your ground and context, if for no other reason than because out in the world is where your audience is located.

What, then, is your place as an artist in the world? What is the place of art in the world? What, indeed, is the nature of the world? These are enormous questions with which all artists wrestle. The following exercises offer you the chance to wrestle with these questions as part of your guided writing program.

Exercise 1. Audience

Virginia Woolf wrote, "No audience. No echo. That's part of one's death." How will you bridge the gap that exists between you and your potential audience?

Insofar as art-making is a meditation or the process of self-actualization, the artist needs no audience. She can practice her instrument and love the music she makes in that solitary practice room, learn about a character and learn about herself as she rehearses with a cast, meditate as she throws a pot on the wheel, or realize her potential as she paints or writes. All of this she does happily in the absence of an audience.

But art-making is more than a meditation or act of self-realization. It is also one of the most important ways we have of communicating what's on our mind and what's in our heart. It is as much a potent means of making contact with others as it is a personal meditation.

You therefore want and need an audience. As the pianist Eugene Istomin put it, "In order to function, I need a public. We all need it. And there is none of us who is free of that anxiety." Given that reality, how will you successfully bridge the gap to that audience? Develop strategies for overcoming any of the following obstacles that stand between you and your audience.

The best book is a collaboration between author and reader.

BARBARA TUCHMAN

It is difficult to obtain an audience because:

1. There are too many artists.

2. Most people are not really interested in art.

3. The main requirement is that you pander and compromise.

4. What I have to offer is not easily understood.

5. I have high standards.

6. I am not properly connected in the marketplace.

7. I have trouble communicating why someone should be interested in my work.

8. I don't play games.

9. I haven't the personality of a seller.

10. Nothing much in my genre is currently wanted.

11. The audience for the work I do is simply very small.

12. I put people off.

13. Something in my personality balks at making connections.

14. Nobody hears or sees me.

Exercise 2. Dynamics with Audience

The dynamics between artist and audience are often exceedingly complex. Some of these dynamics may encourage you to seek out an audience and some may encourage you to avoid or flee from an audience.

You may, for instance, find it strange and alienating that your audience knows you while you know nothing about them. Or you may doubt that your audience really understands you and sneer at their applause.

Is something in the artist-audience dynamic preventing you from seeking out an audience? Comment on any of the following that apply to you, and outline how you might meet these challenges.

I may be avoiding acquiring an audience because:

1. I suffer from performance anxiety.

2. I'm shy.

3. I refuse to be criticized or judged.

4. I am waiting to perfect my work.

5. I doubt that I'll be understood.

6. I doubt my talent.

7. I don't know what to say to people when they congratulate me or want to talk about my work.

8. I don't much like people.

9. I hate to appear as if I'm hawking my work.

10. I'm uncomfortable in the spotlight.

The union between the performer and the spectator is invisible and breathtaking at best; and when that union fails, the betrayal is overwhelmingly sad.

JOANN GREEN

It takes two to know one.

GREGORY BATESON

Exercise 3. Art Buddy

A popular concept among ground-breaking visual artists at the turn of the twentieth century was the idea of acquiring "an audience of one." By this they meant that, insofar as their art was too new, different, and disturbing to be liked by the masses, and insofar as they could not therefore hope to obtain a mass audience, they would at least try to find one person— literally a single person—who understood their work, one person who would echo and mirror them.

I've elsewhere called this one person an "art buddy." Whether "art buddy" or "audience of one," he or she can be of enormous value to an artist. What are the qualities you would want your ideal "audience of one" to manifest?

My art buddy should:

1. Respect my work.

2. Speak truly, but in a context of respect and love.

3. Have an eye for both the commercial and the artistic.

4. Share my world view.

5. Extoll my virtues to others.

6. Simply and genuinely suppose that I will succeed.

7. Offer me detailed analysis and concrete suggestions.

8. Call me great.

9. Respect me, even when my work fizzles.

10. Ask for something in return.

Is it important that you acquire an art buddy? If so, what will you do to make the idea a reality?

Exercise 4. This Time, This Place

Artists can be romantic daydreamers and ardent lovers of the art of other times and places. But the potential dangers of this disorientation are many. Artists so oriented may grow unnecessarily alienated from their own time and place. They may miss connecting with their own families, with their intimate others, with their children. They may fail to understand their own time and place and fail to contribute or receive what they otherwise might from the world in which they live.

There are many reasons why novelists write—but they all have one thing in common: a need to create an alternative world.

JOHN FOWLES

Comment on any of the following statements that ring true for you.

1. I understand what it means to be an artist today.

2. The times are changing so rapidly that it's impossible to keep up.

3. It is better to be rooted in tradition than to be wedded to the present moment.

4. I am less interested in the here-and-now than in perennial matters.

5. These are desperate times and I prefer to ignore them.

6. I understand what is required of today's avant-garde artist.

7. I prefer to live in my mind, where I am independent of this time and place.

8. I am unaffected by the goings-on of the world.

9. I would like to comment on or connect with the world I find myself in, if only I understood it.

10. Something in my past or personality prevents me from fully living in the present.

11. Neither my art nor my art business requires that I understand my time and place.

12. Great work was done in the past, but great work is not permitted in today's cultural climate.

13. People who are fully informed about current matters are faddish and superficial people.

14. I respect no one working in my art discipline today.

15. I do not really identify myself as a late-twentieth-century American.

16. My artistic and cultural roots run far back into distant times and other places.

17. I am alienated from this time and place.

18. I am well oriented in time and place.

19. It is to my advantage to become better oriented in this specific time and place.

I have forced myself to begin writing when I've been utterly exhausted, when I've felt my soul thin as a playing card, when nothing has seemed worth enduring for another five minutes.

JOYCE CAROL OATES

Exercise 5. The Artist's Ten Commandments

This last exercise is a recapitulation of important themes presented in this book. Reflect on these commandments as you courageously go about living your life in the arts.

The Artist's Ten Commandments

1. Look in the Mirror	6. Become a Master Juggler
2. Look out the Window	7. Practice Existential Magic
3. Do the Work	8. Relate
4. See the Synergies	9. Get a Life
5. Explore Your Anxieties	10. Artfully Adapt

1. Look in the Mirror. That is, reflect on the question, "Who am I?" The only person who can put the puzzling pieces of your personality together is you. The unexamined life may as a rule not be worth living, but for an artist not to examine her life is both foolhardy and dangerous. You are the one full of contradictory impulses and on a rollercoaster ride in the arts, and you are the one who must fathom your own being.

2. Look out the Window. You may be leading an isolated, introverted life, and this way of living may be a personality fit for you and your preferred mode of being. But there are both obvious and subtle negative consequences of this insularity. Therefore it is your job to look out the window: to see the world, to learn as much about it as you can, and ultimately to connect with it in meaningful ways.

3. Do the Work. It is your job as an artist to wrestle with issues of blockage and procrastination, to manifest your creativity and your talent, to maintain the necessary motivation to look for work and to do the work, to accomplish the work professionally when you obtain it, and to work both at your art and at the business of art. These are challenges that will confront you every single day for as long as you remain in the arts.

4. See the Synergies. The first three commandments involve your personality, the world you live in, and your work. These three aspects of your life are dynamically interconnected. When you audition, for instance, you bring your personality, your strengths and weaknesses, and your understanding or lack of understanding of the situation with you just as certainly as you bring your voice and your repertoire. Such moments, then, are your very best learning experiences, and it is your job to learn from them.

5. *Explore Your Anxieties.* Anxieties plague artists, and it is vital that you explore the role anxiety is playing in your life. Anxiety may be preventing you from learning difficult new repertoire, from trying your hand at painting in a new idiom, from entering competitions, from talking to agents, from doing your artwork or taking care of your art business. Assess your anxieties, become friendly and familiar with them, and begin to learn how to manage them.

The public and the private worlds are inseparably connected.

VIRGINIA WOOLF

6. *Become a Master Juggler.* It's the rare person in the arts who doesn't pursue many paths of employment simultaneously, who isn't pushed and pulled in a dozen different directions every day of the week. You may dream of quiet and simplicity, but you're more likely to find yourself confronted by noise and complexity. The ability to juggle—to manage time, to manage commitments, to be organized, to be able to move fluidly from task to task—is a vital skill for an artist to master.

7. *Practice Existential Magic.* Practice the art of creating new meaning in your life, of investing meaning in new ideas and projects and divesting meaning from ideas and projects that are no longer workable. Perhaps you've changed in the past decade or in the past year. Have you really looked at your beliefs, your principles, your career, your circumstances lately? Remember that meanings change over time, and it's crucial to assess current situations based on your most current thinking.

8. *Relate.* Busy mastering your craft and pursuing a career in art, working a day job, determined not to be sidetracked by the agenda of others, criticized and rejected in the marketplace, you may grow wary of people and put relationships on a back burner. But as difficult as it can be for an artist to form and maintain relationships, relating with your fellow human beings— with a single intimate other, with friends, with an art buddy, with other people in the arts—remains a vitally important component of your life.

9. *Get a Life.* While it's necessary that you work hard in order to have a career, and while it's true you may obsess and brood about your art or about that career to the extent that little else is allowed psychic attention, it's still crucially important that you maintain a rich life unrelated to art. This rich life might include relationships, a meaningful second career, social activism, creative work unrelated to the arts, or a spiritual practice, but should also include the ability to take time-outs, to relax, to enjoy, to visit with friends, to breathe. Whatever the specific ingredients, such a parallel life is necessary for mental health.

10. Artfully Adapt. What are workable decisions and an adaptive life-style for one artist may not be workable or adaptive at all for you. You will be faced by bewildering complexities with respect to the world you encounter, your own personality, and the difficulty of the work you undertake to do. No simple recipe or formula is available to you. Like any member of an unprotected and endangered species, you must artfully adapt, and that adaptation process is bound to present you with lifelong, never-ending challenges.

Transition Program:
Steps to a New Life in or out of Art

ONE ENORMOUS, LIFE-ALTERING transition some artists determine to make is the transition out of art. This does not imply that the challenges outlined in this book are so difficult and demoralizing that you have no hope of handling them. If that were true I would have defined staying sane in the arts as getting out of the arts. But virtually all creative and performing artists brood about this matter at least a little. For some, like dancers, the matter is thrust inexorably upon them with age. For a given number of others, for reasons of finances and personal fulfillment, leaving art may be the appropriate and even the life-saving thing to do.

The artist who believes that he or she must make the transition out of art can profitably employ the following 10-step program. It's also a model for understanding the transition process in general.

TEN-STEP TRANSITION PROGRAM

1. Reflect on the question.

2. Change your internal language.

3. Make your parallel life rich and valuable.

4. Plan to be recognized in new ways.

5. Take vacations.

6. Begin a process of inner career counseling.

7. Say it out loud.

8. Look before you leap.

9. Pay attention to your emotions.

10. Live your new life.

Reflect on the Question

Carefully let the question in: "Should I make the transition out of art?" A wall of denial may prevent you from asking that directly, even though you've whispered it to yourself many times. When you first ask yourself the question out loud, a wave of terror may engulf you. You may feel as if you're drowning. But take some comfort in the knowledge that your severe reactions to this line of self-questioning are absolutely natural.

Directly asking yourself this question is an event comparable to the alcoholic's hitting bottom. But it's just the beginning of the transition process. If you decide that it's wise to stop pursuing a career in art, expect to be buffeted by a host of contradictory and difficult thoughts and feelings. Begin, as best you can, to tolerate these thoughts and feelings.

Change Your Internal Language

Begin to let go of the charge attached to the phrases, "I am an artist," or "The only thing I want to do in life is be an artist." Doubt the truth of the threat, "I'll die if I give up my art-making." If it seems you have no other choices in life but to remain an artist, firmly dispute your thoughts. Inaugurate the following crucial cognitive change. Instead of saying "I am a musician," say "I am a person who loves music." A person is more than an artist, and when you understand that distinction you recognize that your life holds many more opportunities than you'd previously realized.

Make Your Parallel Life Rich and Valuable

Let more of the world in. Let nonartists into your life in new ways. Meet your relational needs in new ways, too, not according to whether you are admired as a singer, dancer, or actor but according to the rightness and soundness of the relationship. Parallel life work, after all, requires that you learn new things, acquire new friends, and practice new actions; it requires, in short, that you live creatively in brand-new ways.

Plan to Be Recognized in New Ways

Begin to dream up new ways of satisfying the recognition-seeking part of your ego. Might published articles about your life in dance satisfy some of your need to be known or to remain known? Would leading a workshop for actors, in which you teach the pre-audition centering technique that has worked for you, gratify your ego? Would gaining some recognition in a new career be fulfilling? It would be nice to imagine that, as part of leaving art-making, we might also leave behind what the writer William Thompson called "the trappings of the Wagnerian ego." Perhaps that is even part of the goal. But it may be wise to chart a course that allows for at least a little potential recognition, just in case our ego needs remain alive.

Take Vacations

Remove yourself from art-making and from the emotions that go with it. Take real vacations from striving, worrying, practicing, auditioning, brooding, creating, selling, performing, priming, rewriting, and all the rest. Say out loud, "I don't need to strive today." Say out loud, "I refuse to worry about the goodness or badness of my writing today." Say out loud, "I will not brood about being too old for all the good parts." Say out loud, "I am on vacation!" Go on vacation: take the afternoon off.

Begin a Process of Inner Career Counseling

Allow all that you are—your full identity, your different interests, your complicated personality—to enter into the process of choosing what you will do with your life after art. Imagine the job you would create for yourself if only the world permitted it. What new work could serve your introspective self or allow you to work in a nonconforming way? Can you begin a free-lance enterprise or home business that allows you the freedom to set your own hours and provides you with a measure of solitude? Can you make use of your empathy and curiosity in a new career as a psychotherapist?

Expect disappointments as you contemplate this matter. Few jobs may suit your personality as well as art-making does, and thinking about new work may remind you of that fact all over again. But it's a necessary part of the transition process to begin to face the world of new possibilities with your eyes open.

As you gauge how your personality might fit into the existing universe or into a universe of your own making, engage also in the process career counselors call *identification of transferable skills.* For example, Alan Pickman, a career counselor, names the following transferable skills that many dancers manifest: attention to detail, perseverance, intense concentration, determination, self-evaluative skills, ability to take direction and to improve performance. These are as much personality traits as transferable skills. The blurriness of the line between the two underscores the fact that, even as you look at yourself analytically through different lenses, you are in the end examining your indivisible self.

This inner career counseling involves you in making subtle identity alterations, as likely as not out of conscious awareness. You wear a new hat for a moment, an hour, an afternoon. As you practice in imagination running your small inn, seeing psychotherapy clients, inventing a better mousetrap, or (because you have the financial resources) volunteering your time in a worthy cause, you're also practicing letting go of the identity of artist.

Engage in an ongoing search for meaning as you choose your new life's work. At the same time divest meaning from your art-making. Determine that it isn't necessary to capture on canvas the powerful image that's just come to you. Determine that it isn't necesssary to audition for the part you hear about, even though it sounds just right for you. Determine that it isn't necessary to join the new band that's forming over at the club, even though the lead singer has her act together and has already lined up a series of gigs. Determine that you will not be seduced in all the old ways. Divest meaning and relax. If you can't relax, make use of your energy and throw yourself a party featuring dishes you've never before dreamed of cooking.

Say It Out Loud

The alcoholic engaged in the recovery process who makes use of Alcoholics Anonymous introduces himself at AA meetings by saying, "Hi, I'm Bill and I'm an alcoholic." Why this particular ritual? Because there is no more powerful way to reveal a secret or to combat lingering denial than to say a thing *out loud*.

Begin to say to friends: "I'm thinking about giving up art." "I might try my hand at writing plays but I don't think I'm going to audition any more." "I think I'm just about ready to stop writing short stories." "I need to think about my life after dance." "You know, Andy, I doubt I have more than a little time left with the band." "Hi, Mary, you're looking at a former poet!"

Maybe you'll have to whisper it at first. Maybe you'll have to practice it in front of a mirror. Maybe you'll have to spend a day recovering from the shock of having said it. Maybe you'll doubt your decision, change your mind, and suddenly want to audition or stretch canvas. These are all pieces of the transition puzzle.

Look Before You Leap

Look before you leap into a new career or profession. Try not to get overly excited about the first job or career opportunity that comes your way. While it's important that you invest meaning in the ideas you dream up, do so gingerly at first. While it's important that you accept meaning as you find it, accept it with all due caution. You don't want to adopt too quickly the identity of environmental lawyer, innkeeper, drama therapist, editor, teacher, beachcomber, theatrical agent, forest ranger, or anything else.

First peek behind many doors. Talk to people already doing the work you're contemplating. Visit their place of work, read their trade journals, try to discern what salary and conditions of employment you can realistically expect. Is there job security? Real possibilities of advancement? Is it work that will continue to be needed? Can you picture yourself doing the work? Assess the rewards and pitfalls associated with each possibility.

Pay Attention to Your Emotions

Getting out of art is at the very least a major change, and major changes bear a family resemblance to crises. There are real losses to grieve here, and grieving is a period of crisis. You experience a loss of identity, a loss of a pursuit that you once loved and may still love, the shattering of dreams, the loss of a world you knew, the loss of friends and fellow workers, the loss of excitement, the loss of a vessel that held so much meaning for you.

You'll find yourself wrestling with feelings of anger, sadness, frustration, and despair. Depression may set in. You may binge on food (no longer demanding a certain anorexic thinness of yourself) or on alcohol. You may find yourself seeking out prescriptions for tranquilizers or sleeping pills. These are natural and normal human reactions to profound and drastic change. The healing process must take time, perhaps a long time. On some days you'll have to deal with powerful emotions and full-blown crises. Between crises you'll still have to monitor the intricate transition process.

Live Your New Life

Accept the changes you initiate, make peace with the past, find renewal. Even if you remain with a hurt heart and struggle with thoughts about the past or about what might have been, you can still find renewal. You can still love art and life. But when you come back to loving art, after a short or long hiatus, it won't be as a full-time working artist with an investment in making a mark. You'll have made one of the most difficult transitions imaginable, a transition that nothing we were ever taught prepared us to make.

Resources

YOU ARE CHALLENGED TO BE resourceful as you go about the business of art. At a mundane level it's hard to find good, inexpensive framing or good, inexpensive head shots. It's much harder to keep abreast of the grants and fellowships available to you or to know who wants what in the marketplace. Still, as your own best friend and advocate, it's your business to learn.

Some of your business needs may be met by resources available through local, state, and federal organizations, and through the private and public institutions and organizations that exist to serve artists. Consider the following.

Legal Resources

Working artists are regularly confronted by personal and business matters for which they would seek legal advice if they could afford it. Legal advice is usually expensive. In the San Francisco Bay area, for instance, the leading authority on writers' contracts charges in the vicinity of $250 an hour.

Specialized books, for instance those published by Berkeley's Nolo Press (such as *The Writer's Legal Companion*, by Brad Bunnin and Peter Beren), offer the lowest-cost alternative to regular legal services.

Another low-cost alternative to full-fee legal representation is available in many areas through nonprofit organizations formed by lawyers to serve artists. Services offered often include lawyer referral, leading to a low-cost consultation; arbitration and mediation services, which help in resolving disputes outside of court; information on affordable residential housing and work space; educational services (such as copyright clinics, tax seminars, and workshops on songwriters' royalties rights, artist-gallery contracts, film and video contracts, publishing contracts, film distribution, and collaborative agreements); a library where sample contracts and research materials are available; and books for sale, with titles like *An Introduction to Contracts for Visual Artists; The Art of Deduction: Income Tax for Performing, Visual, and Literary Artists;* and *Independent Publishing: Contracts and Finance.* Check with your local arts council or professional organization for the name and telephone number of the volunteer lawyer organization nearest you.

Such lawyer referral groups include the following:

California Lawyers for the Arts, Fort Mason Center, Building C, Room 255, San Francisco, CA 94123.

Lawyers for the Creative Arts, 111 North Wabash Ave., Chicago, IL 60602.

Volunteer Lawyers for the Arts, 36 West 44th St., New York, NY 10036.

Resources for Visual Artists

The following organizations are among those that serve visual artists:

American Council for the Arts, 1285 Avenue of the Americas, New York, NY 10019 (books, resource materials, and legislative affairs).

American Craft Council, 40 West 53rd St., New York, NY 10019.

American Institute of Graphic Arts, 1059 Third Ave., New York, NY 10021.

American Society of Artists, Inc. 1297 Merchandise Mart Plaza, Chicago, IL 60654.

Art-in-Architecture Program, General Services Administration, 18th and F Streets NW, Washington, DC 20405.

Art-in-Architecture Program, Veterans Administration, Washington, DC 20420.

Art in Public Places, Visual Arts Program, National Endowment for the Arts, 1100 Pennsylvania Ave., Washington, DC 20506.

Artist-in-Residence Programs, Education Division, Federal Bureau of Prisons, 320 First Street NW, Washington, DC 20534.

Artists for Economic Action, 2557 Roscomare Road, Los Angeles, CA 90077.

The Artists Foundation, Inc., 110 Broad St., Boston, MA 02110 (accounting services).

Artists-in-Education Program, Office for Partnership, National Endowment for the Arts, 1100 Pennsylvania Ave. NW, Washington, DC 20506.

Arts Apprenticeship Program, New York City Department of Cultural Affairs, 2 Columbus Circle, New York, NY 10019.

Arts International, 1400 K St. NW, Suite 605, Washington, DC 20005 (international arts exchange programs).

Association for Resources and Technical Services, 1341 G St. NW, Suite 211, Washington, DC 20005 (for Hispanic artists).

Association of Artist-Run Galleries, 164 Mercer St., New York, NY 10012 (cooperative gallery information).

Association of Hispanic Arts, Inc., 200 East 87th St., New York, NY 10028.

Association of Professional Art Advisors, P.O. Box 2485, New York, NY 10163.

ATLATL, 402 West Roosevelt, Phoenix, AZ 85003 (for Native American arts and artists).

Business Committee for the Arts, 1775 Broadway, New York, NY 10019 (corporate art information).

Center for Occupational Hazards, 5 Beekman St., New York, NY 10038 (information on hazardous arts materials).

Coalition of Women's Art Organizations, Washington Women's Art Center, 1821 Q St. NW, Washington, DC 20009.

Deaf Artists of America, Inc., P.O. Box 2332, Westfield, NJ 07091.

Disabled Artists Network, P.O. Box 20781, New York, NY 10025.

Foundation for the Community of Artists, 280 Broadway, New York, NY 10007 (financial and other services).

Graphic Artists Guild, 30 East 20th St., New York, NY 10003.

International Sculpture Center, 1050 Potomac St. NW, P.O. Box 19709, Washington, DC 20007.

National Artists Equity Association, Inc., P.O. Box 28068, Central Station, Washington, DC 20038 (legislative issues).

National Association of Artists' Organizations, 1007 D St., Washington, DC 20002 (coordinates programs among arts organizations).

National Endowment for the Arts, 1100 Pennsylvania Ave. NW, Washington, DC 20506.

Opportunity Resources for the Arts, Inc., 1457 Broadway, New York, NY 10036.

Pro Arts, 1920 Union St., Oakland, CA 94607 (library, consultations, other services).

Social and Public Arts Resource Center, 685 Venice Blvd., Venice, CA 90291 (information on public art).

Third World Coalition of Minority Artists, 4911 Ames Ave., Omaha, NE 68104.

Western States Arts Foundation, Suite 200, 207 Shelby St., Santa Fe, NM 87501 (regional alliance of state arts agencies).

Women in the Arts Foundation, Inc., 325 Spring St., New York, NY 10013.

Women's Caucus for Art, Moore College of Art, 20th and Parkway, Philadelphia, PA 19103 (national organization).

Of special note:

American Council for the Arts Books, Department 90, 1285 Avenue of the Americas, Third Floor, New York, NY 10019. Sampling of books carried: *The Artist's Friendly Legal Guide; The Artist's Tax Workbook; The Artist's Complete Health and Safety Guide; Money for Artists; National Directory of Arts Internships.*

Resources for Dancers

A number of strong local service organizations are available to dancers, choreographers, dance teachers, and dance companies. Such organizations offer members the following sorts of services: group health insurance programs; dance resource centers, with information on jobs, auditions, touring, and nonprofit incorporation procedures; performance liability insurance; audition listings; fiscal agent programs and performance registries; a telephone referral service for dance studios, teachers, and choreographers. Some offer financial support for dance community members with AIDS and other life-threatening illnesses. One such service organization is Dance Bay Area, 2141 Mission St., Ste. 303, San Francisco, CA 94110.

Resources for Writers

American Society of Journalists and Authors, Inc., 1501 Broadway, Suite 1907, New York, NY 10036.

Asian American Journalists Association, 1765 Sutter St., Room 1000, San Francisco, CA 94115.

The Author's Guild, 234 West 44th St., New York, NY 10036.

California Writers' Club, 2214 Derby St., Berkeley, CA 94705.

Media Alliance, Fort Mason Center, San Francisco, CA 94123.

Mystery Writers of America, 236 West 27th St., Room 600, New York, NY 10001.

National League of American Pen Women, Pen Arts Building, 1300 17th St. NW, Washington, DC 20036-1973.

National Writers Union, 13 Astor Place, Seventh Floor, New York, NY 10003.

P.E.N. American Center, 156 Fifth Ave., New York, NY 10010.

Poets & Writers, Inc., 72 Spring St., New York, NY 10012.

Romance Writers of America, Inc., 5206 FM. 1960 West, Suite 208, Houston, TX 77069.

Science Fiction Writers of America, 333 Ramona Ave., El Cerrito, CA 94530.

Society of Children's Book Writers, P.O. Box 296, Mar Vista Station, Los Angeles, CA 90066.

Western Writers of America, 1753 Victoria, Sheridan, WY 82801.

Women in Communication, Inc., 2101 Wilson Blvd., Suite 417, Arlington, VA 22201.

Women in Film, 6464 Sunset Blvd., Suite 660, Los Angeles, CA 90028.

Writers Guild of America, East, 555 West 57th St., #1230, New York, NY 10019.

Writers Guild of America, West, 8955 Beverly Blvd., Los Angeles, CA 90048.

Resources for Actors, Directors,
Filmmakers, and Playwrights

In addition to familiarizing yourself with the unions in your industry (for example, Actors Equity Association, American Federation of Television and Radio Artists, American Guild of Musical Artists, Screen Actors Guild, Screen Extras Guild), you can learn much about your local theater community by joining your local actors' service organization. Such service organizations may provide information on local producers, publicists, and technical services; theater training; resources for playwrights; information on touring and theater space rental; agents and casting directors; and local branches of the performing arts unions. They may also provide members with access to group health insurance, photo and résumé talent files, a co-op credit union, a library with job listings, a hotline for late-breaking audition tips, public programs (in such areas as nontraditional casting), and money for critically ill theater workers. Some service organizations may provide specialized services such as support for female actors, playwrights, and directors, or full production and postproduction services for independent videomakers.

Service and union organizations include:

Actors' Equity Association, 165 West 46th St., New York, NY 10036, and 6430 Sunset Blvd., Los Angeles, CA 90028.

Actors' Fund of America, 1501 Broadway, New York, NY 10036.

Alliance of Motion Picture and Television Producers, 14144 Ventura Blvd., Sherman Oaks, CA 91423.

American Cinema Editors, Inc., 4416 ½ Finley Ave., Los Angeles, CA 90024.

American Federation of Television and Radio Artists, 260 Madison Ave., New York, NY 10016.

American Guild of Variety Artists, 4741 Laurel Canyon Road, North Hollywood, CA 91607, and 184 Fifth Ave., New York, NY 10017.

American Society of Cinematographers, 1782 North Orange Drive, Los Angeles, CA 90028.

Associated Actors and Artists of America, 165 West 46th St., New York, NY 10036.

Association of Independent Video and Filmmakers, Inc., 625 Broadway, New York, NY 10012.

Directors Guild of America, Inc., 7950 Sunset Blvd., Los Angeles, CA 90046, and 110 West 57th St., New York, NY 10019.

Dramatists Guild, 234 West 44th St., New York, NY 10036.

International Radio and Television Society, Inc., 420 Lexington Ave., New York, NY 10017.

Motion Picture Association of America, Inc., 1600 I St. NW, Washington, DC 20006.

National Conference of Personal Managers, 20411 Chapter Drive, Woodland Hills, CA 91364.

Screen Actors Guild, 7065 Hollywood Blvd., Hollywood, CA 90028-7594, and 1515 Broadway, New York, NY 10036.

Screen Extras Guild, 3629 Cahuenga Blvd., West Hollywood, CA 90068.

Resources for Musicians

American Composers Alliance, 170 West 74th St., New York, NY 10023.

American Federation of Musicians, 1501 Broadway, New York, NY 10036.

American Guild of Musical Artists, 12650 Riverside Drive, North Hollywood, CA 91607.

American Music Center, 250 West 57th St., New York, NY 10019.

American Society of Composers, Authors, and Publishers, One Lincoln Place, New York, NY 10023, and 6430 Sunset Blvd., Hollywood, CA 90028.

American Symphony Orchestra League, 633 E St. NW, Washington, DC 20004.

Black Music Association, 1500 Locust Ave., Philadelphia, PA 19002.

Broadcast Music, Inc., 10 Music Square E., Nashville, TN 37203, and 320 West 57th St., New York, NY 10019.

Country Music Association, 7 Music Circle N., Nashville, TN 37203.

Gospel Music Association, 38 Music Square N., Nashville, TN 37203.

National Association of Independent Record Distributors, 6935 Airport Highway Lane, Pennsauken, NJ 08109.

National Association of Recording Artists and Sciences, 303 N. Glenoaks Blvd., #140M, Burbank, CA 91502.

Society of European Stage Authors and Composers, 9000 Sunset Blvd., Los Angeles, CA 90069, and 10 Columbus Circle, New York, NY 10019.

Songwriters Guild of America, 276 Fifth Ave., Suite 306, New York, NY 10001.

Women in Music, P.O. Box 441, Radio City Station, New York, NY 10101.

Funding for Creative and Performing Artists

Tens of thousands of awards, fellowships, residencies, grants, and commissions are available to creative and performing artists each year. *Money for Artists,* edited by Laura Green, describes many of these.

Local, county, and state arts councils typically offer a variety of grant opportunities. The California Arts Council's Artists in Residence Program, for instance, provides funding for three programs: Artists in Schools, Artists in Communities, and Artists Serving Special Constituents.

Artists in several locations have available to them Foundation Center libraries (79 Fifth Ave., New York, NY 10003, (212) 620-4230; 312 Sutter St., Third Floor, San Francisco, CA 94108, (415) 397-0902; 1001 Connecticut Ave. NW, Suite 938, Washington, DC 20036, (202) 331-1400; 1442 Hanna Building, 1422 Euclid Ave., Cleveland, OH 44115, (216) 861-1933.

The Foundation Center provides orientations in the use of each center's extensive library and monthly Meet the Grantsmakers workshops, at which representatives of major foundations describe their groups' activities and answer questions. Center libraries contain a wealth of information, both general and specialized, including field of interest indexes, subject indexes, and specialized subject directories. Artists are well advised to attend a scheduled orientation and familiarize themselves with the grant process.

Miscellaneous Resources

Many of the resources available to creative and performing artists defy easy categorization or description. Some are designed to meet the needs of artists who share a spiritual, political, activist, or community vision or who want to make use of their art in therapeutic ways. Such resources are frequently listed in local alternative newspapers.

Recommended Reading

Introduction.

Adams, Kathleen. *Journal to the Self.* New York: Warner Books, 1990.

Cameron, Julia. *The Artist's Way.* Los Angeles: Jeremy P. Tarcher, 1992.

Foster, Carolyn. *The Family Patterns Workbook.* Los Angeles: Jeremy P. Tarcher, 1993.

Hagan, Kay. *Internal Affairs: A Journalkeeping Workbook for Self-Intimacy.* San Francisco: Harper & Row, 1990.

Mallon, Thomas. *A Book of One's Own.* New York: Ticknor & Fields, 1984.

Progoff, Ira. *At a Journal Workshop.* Los Angeles: Jeremy P. Tarcher, 1992.

Taylor, Cathryn. *The Inner Child Workbook.* Los Angeles: Jeremy P. Tarcher, 1991.

Note: Several additional books on journaling are listed as recommended reading for Chapter 2.

Chapter 1.

Briggs, John. *Fire in the Crucible.* Los Angeles: Jeremy P. Tarcher, 1990.

Edwards, Betty. *Drawing on the Artist Within.* New York: Simon & Schuster, 1986.

Edwards, Betty. *Drawing on the Right Side of the Brain.* Los Angeles: Jeremy P. Tarcher, 1979.

Fischl, Eric, and Jerry Saltz. *Sketchbook with Voices.* New York: Alfred van der Marck Editions, 1986.

Franck, Frederick. *The Zen of Seeing.* New York: Random House, 1973.

Hanks, K., and J. Parry. *Wake Up Your Creative Genius.* Los Altos, CA: William Kaufmann, 1983.

Harman, Willis. *Higher Creativity.* Los Angeles: Jeremy P. Tarcher, 1989.

Judy, Stephanie. *Making Music for the Joy of It.* Los Angeles: Jeremy P. Tarcher, 1991.

Leonard, Linda Schierse. *Witness to the Fire: Creativity and the Veil of Addiction.* Boston: Shambhala Press, 1990.

May, Rollo. *The Courage to Create.* New York: W. W. Norton, 1974.

Nachmanovitch, Stephen. *Free Play.* Los Angeles: Jeremy P. Tarcher, 1991.

Robbins, Lois. *Waking Up in the Age of Creativity.* Santa Fe, NM: Bear & Company, 1985.

Chapter 2.

Biffle, Christopher. *A Journey Through Your Childhood: A Write-in Guide for Reliving Your Past, Clarifying Your Present, and Charting Your Future.* Los Angeles: Jeremy P. Tarcher, 1990.

Farrell, Paula. *The Mystery of My Story: Autobiographical Writing for Personal and Spiritual Development.* New York: Paulist Press, 1991.

Furth, Greg. *The Secret World of Drawings: Healing Through Art.* Boston: Sigo Press, 1988.

Hughes-Calero, Heather. *Writing as a Tool for Self-Discovery.* Carmel, CA: Coastline, 1988.

Keen, Sam, and Anne Valley-Fox. *Your Mythic Journey: Finding Meaning in Your Life Through Writing and Story-Telling.* Los Angeles: Jeremy P. Tarcher, 1990.

McMurray, Madeline. *Illuminations: The Healing Image (Finding—and Learning from—the Inner Artist for Psychic Growth).* Berkeley, CA: Wingbow Press, 1990.

Rico, Gabriele. *Pain and Possibility: Writing Your Way Through Personal Crisis.* Los Angeles: Jeremy P. Tarcher, 1991.

Chapter 3.

ON DEPRESSION
Badal, Daniel W. *Treatment of Depression and Related Moods.* Northvale, NJ: Jason Aronson, 1988.

Flach, Frederic (editor). *Affective Disorders.* New York: W. W. Norton, 1988.

ON ANXIETY
Becker, Carol. *The Invisible Drama: Women and the Anxiety of Change.* New York: Macmillan, 1987.

Borne, Robert. *The Anxiety and Phobia Workbook.* Berkeley, CA: New Harbinger, 1990.

McCullough, Christopher, and Robert Mann. *Managing Your Anxiety.* Los Angeles: Jeremy P. Tarcher, 1988.

ON MEDITATION PRACTICE
Hanh, Thich Nhat. *The Miracle of Mindfulness: A Manual on Meditation.* Boston: Beacon Press, 1987.

LeShan, Lawrence. *How to Meditate.* New York: Bantam Books, 1988.

Ram Dass. *Journey to Awakening: A Meditator's Guidebook.* New York: Bantam Books, 1990.

ON MADNESS (PSYCHOSIS)
Bowers, Malcolm. *Retreat from Sanity: The Structure of Emerging Psychosis.* Baltimore: Penguin Books, 1974.

Fadiman, James, and Donald Kewman. *Exploring Madness.* Monterey, CA: Brooks/Cole, 1979.

Chapter 4.
Brebner, Ann. *Setting Free the Actor: Overcoming Creative Blocks.* San Francisco: Mercury House, 1990.

Field, Joanna. *On Not Being Able to Paint.* Los Angeles: Jeremy P. Tarcher, 1983.

Goldberg, Natalie. *Writing Down the Bones: Freeing the Writer Within.* Boston: Shambhala Books, 1986.

London, Peter. *No More Secondhand Art: Awakening the Artist Within.* Boston: Shambhala Books, 1989.

Nelson, Victoria. *Writer's Block and How to Use It.* Cincinnati: Writer's Digest Books, 1985.

Rico, Gabriele. *Writing the Natural Way.* Los Angeles: Jeremy P. Tarcher, 1983.

Ristad, Eloise. *A Soprano on Her Head.* Moab, UT: Real People Press, 1982.

Chapter 5.

Brouwer, Alexandra, and Thomas Lee Wright. *Working in Hollywood.* New York: Avon Books, 1991.

Caplin, Lee Evan. *The Business of Art.* Englewood Cliffs, NJ: Prentice-Hall, 1983.

Green, Laura (editor). *Money for Artists.* New York: American Council for the Arts, 1988.

Hoover, Deborah. *Supporting Yourself as an Artist.* New York: Oxford University Press, 1989.

Michels, Caroll. *How to Survive and Prosper as an Artist.* New York: Henry Holt & Company, 1988.

Weissman, Dick. *The Music Business: Career Opportunities and Self-Defense.* New York: Crown Publishers, 1990.

Chapter 6.

Chamberlain, Mary. *Writing Lives.* London: Virago Press, 1988.

Cummings, Paul. *Artists in Their Own Words.* New York: St. Martin's Press, 1979.

Gal, Hans. *The Musician's World: Great Composers in Their Letters.* New York: Arco Publishing, 1966.

Gam, Rita. *Actors: A Celebration.* New York: St. Martin's Press, 1988.

Gruen, John. *The Private World of Ballet.* New York: Penguin Books, 1976.

Herbst, Peter (editor). *The Rolling Stone Interviews.* New York: St. Martin's Press/Rolling Stone Press, 1981.

Johnson, Ellen H. *American Artists on Art from 1940 to 1980.* New York: Harper & Row, 1982.

Polak, Maralyn. *The Writer as Celebrity.* New York: M. Evans & Co., 1986.

Schickel, Richard. *Intimate Strangers: The Culture of Celebrity.* New York: Doubleday & Co., 1985.

Smith, Joe, and Mitchell Fink (editors). *Off the Record.* New York: Warner Books, 1988.

Chapter 7.

Kottler, Jeffrey. *Private Moments, Secret Selves: Enriching Our Time Alone.* Los Angeles: Jeremy P. Tarcher, 1990.

Storr, Anthony. *Solitude: A Return to the Self.* New York: The Free Press, 1988.

Wilson, Colin. *The Outsider.* Los Angeles: Jeremy P. Tarcher, 1982.

Woolf, Virginia. *A Room of One's Own.* New York: Harcourt Brace Jovanovich, 1989.

The following are a few classics in the literature of existentialism and provide valuable insights into the lives of social isolates, the issues of alienation and estrangement, and the problem of the outsider.

Camus, Albert. *The Fall.* New York: Random House, 1991.

Camus, Albert. *The Stranger.* New York: Alfred Knopf, 1988.

Dostoevsky, Fyodor. *Crime and Punishment.* New York: W. W. Norton, 1989.

Dostoevsky, Fyodor. *Notes from Underground.* New York: W. W. Norton, 1989.

Rilke, Rainer Maria. *The Notebooks of Malte Laurids Brigge.* New York: Random House, 1990.

Sartre, Jean-Paul. *Nausea.* Cambridge, MA: Robert Bentley, 1979.

Chapter 8.

Beattie, Melody. *Codependent No More: How to Stop Controlling Others and Start Caring for Yourself.* San Francisco: Harper & Row, 1987.

Bradshaw, John. *Bradshaw on: The Family.* Deerfield Beach, FL: Health Communications, 1988.

Ferguson, Marilyn. *The Aquarian Conspiracy: Personal and Social Transformation in Our Time.* Los Angeles: Jeremy P. Tarcher, 1980.

Kipnis, Aaron. *Knights Without Armor: A Practical Guide for Men in Quest of Masculine Soul.* Los Angeles: Jeremy P. Tarcher, 1991.

McCullough, Christopher. *Always at Ease: Overcoming Anxiety and Shyness in Every Situation.* Los Angeles: Jeremy P. Tarcher, 1991.

McKay, Matthew, Martha Davis, and Patrick Fanning. *Messages: The Communication Skills Book.* Oakland, CA: New Harbinger, 1983.

Mellody, Pia, and Andrea Miller. *Breaking Free: A Recovery Workbook for Facing Codependence.* San Francisco: Harper & Row, 1989.

Oldham, John, and Lois Morris. *Personality Self-Portrait: Why You Think, Work, Love, and Act the Way You Do.* New York: Bantam Books, 1990.

Ornstein, Robert, and Paul Ehrlich. *New World, New Mind.* New York: Simon & Schuster, 1989.

Peck, M. Scott. *The Different Drum: Community Making and Peace.* New York: Simon & Schuster, 1987.

Robinson, Bryan. *Heal Your Self-Esteem.* Deerfield Beach, FL: Health Communications, 1991.

Robinson, Bryan. *Work Addictions.* Deerfield Beach, FL: Health Communications, 1989.

Sanford, Linda, and Mary Donovan. *Women and Self-Esteem: Understanding and Improving the Way We Think and Feel about Ourselves.* New York: Penguin Books, 1985.

Subby, Robert. *Healing the Family Within.* Deerfield Beach, FL: Health Communications, 1990.

Tannen, Deborah. *You Just Don't Understand: Women and Men in Conversation.* New York: Ballantine Books, 1990.

Appendix 1.

Bolles, Richard Nelson. *What Color Is Your Parachute? A Practical Manual for Job-hunters and Career Changers.* Berkeley, CA: Ten Speed Press, 1990.

Hample, Henry. *Jobs in the Arts and Arts Administration: A Guide to Placement/Referral Services, Career Counseling, and Employment.* New York: Center for Arts Information, 1984.

Jackson, Tom. *Guerrilla Tactics in the New Job Market.* New York: Bantam, 1991.

Krannich, Ronald, and Caryl Krannich. *The Complete Guide to International Jobs and Careers.* Woodbridge, VA: Impact, 1990.

Langley, Stephen, and James Abruzzo. *Jobs in Art and Media Management: What They Are and How to Get One.* New York: Drama Book Publishers, 1986.

Sinetar, Marsha. *Do What You Love, the Money Will Follow: Discovering Your Right Livelihood.* New York: Dell, 1989.

Appendix 2.

Applebaum, Judith, and Nancy Evans. *How to Get Happily Published.* New York: New American Library, 1982.

Chamberlain, Betty. *The Artist's Guide to the Art Market.* New York: Watson-Guptill, 1983.

Directory of Artists' Organizations. Washington, DC: National Association of Artists' Organizations, 1989.

Directory of Hispanic Artists and Organizations. New York: Association of Hispanic Artists, 1984.

Frischer, Patricia, and James Adams. *The Artist in the Marketplace.* New York: M. Evans, 1980.

Gorton, Tonda, and Lin Lepore. *Resources for Artists and Writers: An Annotated Bibliography.* Phoenix: Arizona Commission on the Arts, 1982.

Huston, Carol (editor). *Directory of Minority Arts Organizations.* Washington, DC: National Endowment for the Arts, 1982.

Klayman, Toby Judith, and Cobbett Steinberg. *The Artist's Survival Manual: A Complete Guide to Marketing Your Work.* New York: Charles Scribner's Sons, 1987.

Meyer, Carol. *The Writer's Survival Manual: The Complete Guide to Getting Published Right.* New York: Crown Publishers, 1982.

Navaretta, Cynthia. *Guide to Women's Art Organizations: Groups/Activities/Networks/Publications.* New York: Women Artist News, 1982.

Persky, Robert. *The Artist's Guide to Getting and Having a Successful Exhibition.* New York: The Consultant Press, 1985.

Shagan, Rena. *The Road Show: A Handbook for Successful Booking and Touring in the Performing Arts.* New York: American Council for the Arts, 1985.

Shurtleff, Michael. *Audition.* New York: Walker & Company, 1978.

White, Virginia. *Grants for the Arts.* New York: Plenum Press, 1980.

Afterword

Because of space limitations, several important issues could not be addressed at length in this book. I hope to focus on them in future books, and I'd appreciate your thoughts on them. These issues include:

- the experience of women artists
- the experience of minority artists
- alcohol and drug use and recovery
- special issues in the different art disciplines
- the childhood of artists
- artists in intimate relationships
- artistic anxiety (sources of anxiety for artists)
- lifespan issues (changing challenges as artists age)
- art and spirit
- the evolution of the artist (the artist of the future)

I'd greatly appreciate hearing about any of your experiences as a creative or performing artist with regard to these issues or to any of the challenges described in this book. If you live, work, or interact with artists, I'd love to hear from you, too.

Please also let me know if I can quote you, use your name, and

possibly interview you. Include a little autobiographical information: your name and mailing address, your birth date (if you
don't mind), and a few details about your career. Please send your
correspondence to: Dr. Eric Maisel, P.O. Box 613, Concord, CA
94522-0613.

Thanks very much!

Index

Stravinsky, Igor, 99, 137
Streep, Meryl, 144
Stress, psychological
and creative blockage, 84
psychosis and, 55–56
Stress management, 67, 99, 124, 125
Stuart, Gilbert, 103
Stuart, Muriel, 127
Styron, William, 45, 46, 47
Success. *See also* Recognition
bursting balloons syndrome and, 141–143
challenges presented by, 135–148
defining and redefining, 150
as energy field, 151
"freeze frame" reaction to, 136–137
guilt over, 140
and intolerance of failure, 146
lack of preparation for, 135–136
mood disorders and, 142
personality and, 110–111, 113
possibility of, 5–6
pressure of, 139–143
redefining, 150
strategies for dealing with, 150–153
synergistic moment and, 110, 111
tyranny of, 143–146
Suicide, 46, 68, 173
Sullivan, Harry Stack, 59
Support groups, 69, 70
Support system, 34, 99–100, 152
Switzer, Margaret, 173–174
Syndromes, clinical, 52–53
Synergies, 208–209

Talents, of artists, 6, 13–19
defining, 13, 14
strategies for reflecting on, 20–21
Tamayo, Rufino, 199
Tan, Amy, 139
T'ao Ch'ien, 168
Tapies, Antoni, 153

Tavenner, Patricia, 49
Taylor, Elizabeth, 130
Taylor, James, 145
Tchaikovsky, Peter Ilich, 6, 133
Telemann, Georg Philipp, 126
Themes, grand, 21-22
Thompson, William, 213
Time management, 209
Time-outs, strategic, 180–181
Tolstoy, Leo, 25, 93
Topping oneself, 139–140, 153
Tranquilizers, use of, 51, 124
Transformation, personal, 77
Transition out of art, ten-step program for, 211–216
Tuchman, Barbara, 205
Tudor, Anthony, 147
Tunguely, Jean, 54
Turner, Kathleen, 142

Unconscious mind, incubation of work in, 22
Unproductive periods, 95–96

Vacations, in transition out of art, 213
Values, 4–5
Van Gogh, Vincent, 8, 9, 14–15, 38, 92, 171, 173, 194
Verdi, Guiseppe, 185
Verdy, Violette, 67
Vickers, Tom, 114
Victimization, sense of, 56
Virshup, Evelyn, 42
Visconti, Luchino, 104
Visser, Carel, 92
Visual artists, resources for, 218–220
Visualization, 124
to break through blocks, 99
of commitment to guided writing, xvii–xviii
self-exploration through, 42–44
using, in guided writing, xvi–xix

Walker, John, 153
Walker, Sandy, 49

Walk with Love and Death, A (Huston), 86
Wallman, Gerry, 65
Warhol, Andy, 16, 140
Watts, Alan, xiv
Wayne, June, 13
Way of Zen, The (Watts), xiv
Wenda, Gu, 194
Whistler, James McNeill, 188
Whitehead, Alfred North, 4
Wilbur, Richard, 49
Wilde, Oscar, 128
Williams, Tennessee, 143–144, 169
Williams, William Carlos, 63
Wilson, Colin, 184
Wilson, Sallie, 147
Winnicott, Donald, 165
Witt, Howard, 113
Woolf, Virginia, 8, 204, 209
Wordsworth, William, 149
Workaholism, 170–171
Work conditions, effective, creating, 23–24
Work methods, new, 23–24
Work paradoxes and contradictions, 155–156
Workshop environment, creating in, 33–34
World-criticism, 85–86
World-wariness, and creative blockage, 86
Wright, Rebecca, 196
Writers
career paths of, 114–120
mechanics and metaphysics in career paths of, 111–112
resources for, 221
Writer's Legal Companion, The (Bunnin and Beren), 217
Writing bubble, xviii–xix

Young, Robert, 93

Zen Buddhist maxims, xxi
Zimbardo, Philip, xxiv–xxv
Zinker, Joseph, 77
Zorina, Vera, 33
Zucker, E. M., 61–62

Discover more of yourself with Inner Work Books.

The following Inner Work Books are part of a series that explores psyche and spirit through writing, visualization, ritual, and imagination.

The Artist's Way: A Spiritual Path to Higher Creativity   BY JULIA CAMERON

The Artist's Way Morning Pages Journal: A Companion Volume to The Artist's Way   BY JULIA CAMERON

At a Journal Workshop (revised edition): *Writing to Access the Power of the Unconscious and Evoke Creative Ability*   BY IRA PROGOFF, PH.D.

Fearless Creating: A Step-by-Step Guide to Starting and Completing Your Work of Art   BY ERIC MAISEL, PH.D.

Finding What You Didn't Lose: Expressing Your Truth and Creativity Through Poem-Making   BY JOHN FOX

Following Your Path: Using Myths, Symbols, and Images to Explore Your Inner Life   BY ALEXANDRA COLLINS DICKERMAN

The Inner Child Workbook: What to Do with Your Past When It Just Won't Go Away   BY CATHRYN L. TAYLOR, M.A.M.F.C.C.

A Journey Through Your Childhood: A Write-in Guide for Reliving Your Past, Clarifying Your Present, and Charting Your Future   BY CHRISTOPHER BIFFLE

A Life in the Arts: Practical Guidance and Inspiration for Creative and Performing Artists   BY ERIC MAISEL, PH.D.

The Life We Are Given: A Long-Term Program for Realizing the Potential of Body, Mind, Heart, and Soul   BY GEORGE LEONARD AND MICHAEL MURPHY

Pain and Possibility: Writing Your Way Through Personal Crisis   BY GABRIELE LUSSER RICO

The Path of the Everyday Hero: Drawing on the Power of Myth to Meet Life's Most Important Challenges   BY LORNA CATFORD, PH.D., AND MICHAEL RAY, PH.D.

Personal Mythology: Using Ritual, Dreams, and Imagination to Discover Your Inner Story   BY DAVID FEINSTEIN, PH.D., AND STANLEY KRIPPNER, PH.D.

The Possible Human: A Course in Extending Your Physical, Mental, and Creative Abilities   BY JEAN HOUSTON

The Search for the Beloved: Journeys in Mythology and Sacred Psychology   BY JEAN HOUSTON

Smart Love: A Codependence Recovery Program Based on Relationship Addiction Support Groups   BY JODY HAYES

A Time to Heal Workbook: Stepping-stones to Recovery for Adult Children of Alcoholics   BY TIMMEN L. CERMAK, M.D., AND JACQUES RUTZKY, M.F.C.C.

True Partners: A Workbook for Building a Lasting Intimate Relationship   BY TINA B. TESSINA, PH.D., AND RILEY K. SMITH, M.A.

Your Mythic Journey: Finding Meaning in Your Life Through Writing and Storytelling   BY SAM KEEN AND ANNE VALLEY-FOX

To order call 1-800-788-6262 or send your order to:

Jeremy P. Tarcher, Inc.
Mail Order Department
The Putnam Berkley Group, Inc.
P.O. Box 12289
Newark, NJ 07101-5289

For Canadian orders:
P.O. Box 25000
Postal Station "A"
Toronto, Ontario M5W 2X8

_____	The Artist's Way	0-87477-694-5	$14.95
_____	The Artist's Way Hardcover Deluxe Edition	0-87477-821-2	$24.95
_____	The Artist's Way Morning Pages Journal	0-87477-820-4	$20.00
_____	At a Journal Workshop	0-87477-638-4	$15.95
_____	Ending the Struggle Against Yourself	0-87477-763-1	$14.95
_____	Fearless Creating	0-87477-805-0	$15.95
_____	Finding What You Didn't Lose	0-87477-809-3	$14.95
_____	Following Your Path	0-87477-687-2	$15.95
_____	The Inner Child Workbook	0-87477-635-X	$14.95
_____	A Journey Through Your Childhood	0-87477-499-3	$10.95
_____	A Life in the Arts	0-87477-766-6	$15.95
_____	The Life We Are Given	0-87477-792-5	$14.95
_____	Pain and Possibility	0-87477-571-X	$14.95
_____	The Path of the Everyday Hero	0-87477-630-9	$14.95
_____	Personal Mythology	0-87477-484-5	$12.95
_____	The Possible Human	0-87477-218-4	$14.95
_____	The Search for the Beloved	0-87477-476-4	$14.95
_____	Smart Love	0-87477-472-1	$10.95
_____	A Time to Heal Workbook	0-87477-745-3	$14.95
_____	True Partners	0-87477-727-5	$13.95
_____	Your Mythic Journey	0-87477-543-4	$ 9.95

Subtotal $ _____

Shipping and handling* $ _____

Sales tax (CA, NJ, NY, PA, VA) $ _____

Total amount due $ _____

Payable in U.S. funds (no cash orders accepted). $15.00 minimum for credit card orders.
*Shipping and handling: $3.50 for one book, $1.00 for each additional book, not to exceed $8.50.

Enclosed is my ☐ check ☐ money order

Please charge my ☐ Visa ☐ MasterCard ☐ American Express

Card # _____ Expiration date _____

Signature as on credit card _____

Daytime phone number _____

Name _____

Address _____

City _____ State _____ Zip _____

Please allow six weeks for delivery. Prices subject to change without notice.

Source key IWB